AN ETHICA

GUIDEBOO

THE ZOMBIE

APOCALYPSE

AN ETHICAL GUIDEBOOK TO THE ZOMBIE APOCALYPSE

How to Keep Your Brain without Losing Your Heart

Bryan Hall

BLOOMSBURY ACADEMIC
LONDON • NEW YORK • OXFORD • NEW DELHI • SYDNEY

BLOOMSBURY ACADEMIC
Bloomsbury Publishing Plc
50 Bedford Square, London, WC1B 3DP, UK
1385 Broadway, New York, NY 10018, USA

BLOOMSBURY, BLOOMSBURY ACADEMIC and the Diana logo are
trademarks of Bloomsbury Publishing Plc

First published in Great Britain 2020

A catalogue record for this book is available from the British Library.

A catalog record for this book is available from the Library of Congress.

ISBN: HB: 978-1-3500-8361-5
         PB: 978-1-3500-8362-2
       ePDF: 978-1-3500-8363-9
      eBook: 978-1-3500-8364-6

Typeset by Integra Software Services Pvt. Ltd.

To find out more about our authors and books visit www.bloomsbury.com
and sign up for our newsletters.

CONTENTS

LIST OF FIGURES

READ FIRST: A MESSAGE FROM THE ARCHIVIST TO THE READER

The manuscript after which this collection is named was found at the epicenter of one of the largest viral burnouts in North America where enormous hordes of the undead converged for final death. It offers a sometimes-reliable firsthand account of the pandemic. Items found at the scene either support or challenge certain aspects of this account.

The manuscript was found on a desk in the basement of a restaurant in Mexico. The restaurant was in a small town located in the former border region between Mexico and the United States. Vast numbers of dismembered late-stage undead were found at the same location, which was otherwise abandoned. Besides the account provided in the manuscript, the identity of the author is unknown.

The title and content of the manuscript suggest that the author thought it could be used as to teach Ethics in a post-apocalyptic world. The manuscript also cites much of the philosophical literature written during this time period, literature which is highly derivative of pre-apocalyptic sources. The author's work is no exception and consistently echoes three pre-apocalyptic Ethics primers: (1) Louis Pojman and James Fieser, *Ethics: Discovering Right and Wrong* (Boston: Cengage, 2011), (2) James and Stuart Rachels, *The Elements of Moral Philosophy* (New York: McGraw-Hill, 2015), and (3) Russ Shafer-Landau, *The Fundamentals of Ethics* (New York: Oxford University Press, 2018).

This account—the collected "field exercises"—serves as a confession of sorts, though a confession the author fails to acknowledge as their own. Given other items found at the scene that are part of this collection, it is clear that the author of the manuscript is the protagonist in the field exercises told from the first-person perspective and was at least present in the stories told from other perspectives.

To aid the reader unfamiliar with the pre-apocalyptic philosophical and zombie-cultural background of the manuscript, the archivist has added "Further study" sections, bolded technical terms, and created a glossary for the typescript version.

Notes on the collection

The amount of dried bodily fluid found on the manuscript and the erratic handwriting on later leaves suggest, furthermore, that the author "cracked up" soon after completing the text. Forensic epidemiologists discovered these items while investigating the viral burnout and delivered them to the War on Infection Archive. Full details below.

Reference Number: 26.15.13.295
Name and Location of Repository: War on Infection Archive—Denver, CO
Title: *An Ethical Guidebook to the Zombie Apocalypse Collection*
Time(s) of Creation: Phase 4 through post-pandemic
Extent: Large box containing the following items:

- one robe (white, religious, unworn, folded neatly)
- two manuscripts (one handwritten, titled *An Ethical Guidebook to the Zombie Apocalypse: How to Keep Your Brain without Losing Your Heart*. One typescript of original with supplements)
- one map (commercially produced with handwritten notes)
- one photograph (well-worn, depicts two individuals, one middle-aged Caucasian male, other individual disfigured)
- two plush toys (one bunny and one teddy bear)
- one rope (handmade, tied into noose)
- two weapons (handmade spear, M1 Garand with single 30–06 bullet)

Name of Creator: Unknown
Arrangement: In addition to the other materials found at the scene, there seems to be a relationship between the map and the content of the manuscript. The archivist has put together the following concordance relating sections of the manuscript to locations on the map following the marked path north-to-south:

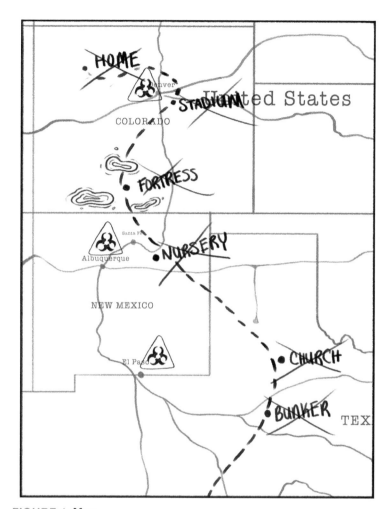

FIGURE 1 **Map**

Conditions Governing Access

OPEN—no restrictions. Instructors thinking about using the manuscript in a class (e.g., Philosophy, Outbreak History, or Zombie Studies), however, should be aware that it contains potentially offensive content and depictions of extreme violence.

INTRODUCTION: WELCOME TO THE END OF THE WORLD

There is but one truly serious philosophical problem and that is suicide. Judging whether life is worth living or undeath worth avoiding amounts to answering the fundamental question of philosophy.

—FROM *THE ZOMBIE SISYPHUS*

Some years ago I was struck by how many things I no longer valued that I had valued before the world fell. No longer an educator, a friend, or a spouse, I doubted those beliefs I had based on the values of my former self. I realized that it was necessary, once in the course of this apocalypse, to demolish all of my beliefs and start right from the foundation if I were to determine the value of anything—beginning with my own life. But the task looked to be an enormous one, and as the maelstrom of violence and death further separated me from my former self, it seemed impossible that I should ever tackle such an inquiry. This led me to put off the project for so long that I now no longer know whether anyone else might benefit from my answer.

Today, and for the foreseeable future, I find myself trapped with little hope of rescue, albeit well-provisioned and secure behind steel doors and barred windows. With the exception of the undead that shroud my refuge, I am quite alone. To distract my mind from the incessant scratching and ever-growing moans, I will devote myself sincerely and without reservation to the contemplation of the question I have neglected for so long.

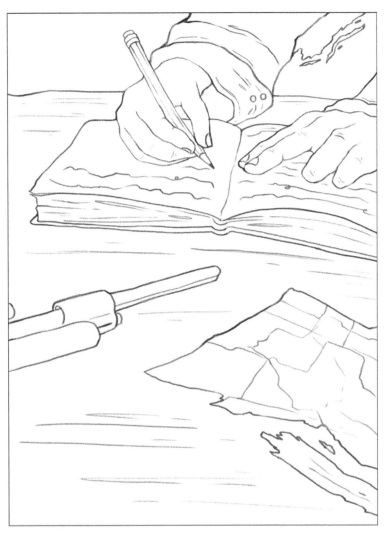

FIGURE 2 At work on this book.

In the years since the outbreak, I have lost everyone I have ever known, though surprisingly few to the ravenous hordes. Any survivors who have made it this long recognize that the greatest thing they have to fear from the apocalypse is not the zombies but themselves. When not murdered by others or robbed and left to die, we too often suffer complete psychological breakdowns and/or take our own lives. As the crisis for humanity deepened, humanity's perception of itself worsened to the point that most preferred to join the ranks of the undead than remain among the living. The purpose of this book, should I be fortunate enough to finish it, is to convince the reader—starting with myself—that life does have value.

If you are reading this book, you already know the tactics necessary to fight the undead, protect yourself from attack, and provide for your basic needs. You already know what is necessary to *survive*, but what many lack are the tools necessary to *flourish* among the undead. Without the possibility of human flourishing, however, it is difficult to see the value in remaining human. If what you do to survive undermines your capacity to flourish, it is unclear how you are different from the zombies who flourish wholly at your expense. If your existence is no better than the zombies you must constantly battle, why not give up the fight and join their ranks?

The answer to this question cannot be provided by a new martial arts move or zombie diversion tactic. It requires a special kind of reasoning, specifically *moral* reasoning. Although it seems almost absent from our fallen world, I will argue that it is absolutely necessary if we are to flourish within it. Before the dead rose to feast upon the brains of the living, I made my living as a Philosophy professor feeding the minds of my Ethics students. Over the course of the semester, the class would deal with questions of moral value, right action, and human flourishing. The relative comfort of our lives and the cocoon of the classroom, however, numbed us to the implications of our answers since we were rarely held to account after class was dismissed. Now that we—assuming there still is a "we"—have been stripped of all such luxuries, we must examine these questions anew since our answers may well determine whether we remain among the living or join the undead. I am not the first to take up this task and, during the many years it took society to decay, other philosophers grappled with the moral implications of the zombie pandemic. So that their words will not be lost to history, when relevant, I have inserted quotes from their most famous post-apocalyptic works throughout the manuscript. As perhaps the last philosopher, it seems I am now uniquely positioned to provide the final word on these questions—a task that would be the envy of any philosopher in another context.

Just as I do not want other philosophers to have written in vain, so too I do not want everyone I have ever known to have died in vain. When their lives (and deaths) embody important ethical lessons, I have woven them into the fabric of the book as a guide—though more often a warning—to those who remain. These stories are often told from the first-person point of view, so that you can better understand—and perhaps sympathize with—why they chose to do what they did. I have labeled their stories "field exercises" since they practically apply the ethical theories discussed in that chapter. When appropriate, I have also included drawings that illustrate key moments from these stories.

The structure of this book will generally follow the structure of one of my introduction to Ethics courses. In so doing, I hope to give the survivor the ethical tools necessary to flourish in a world overrun by flesh-devouring hordes of undead. The first two chapters examine a question that is even more fundamental than whether life is worth living. Before we can determine if *life* has value, we must first determine whether there are even *values* at all. There are two basic camps: moral realism and moral anti-realism. The moral realist holds that there are objective moral values—things that are valuable regardless of belief or opinion. In contrast, the moral anti-realist holds that there are no objective moral values. Either moral values are relative to belief or opinion, are expressions of an individual's emotions, or do not exist at all. After discussing various anti-realist and realist views, Chapter 2 defends a specific version of realism that will motivate what follows.

Assuming there is at least one objective moral value, Chapters 3 through 9 examine different views of what these values might be and what we ought to do in light of these values. Chapter 3 looks at the contractarian view, which holds that morality consists of a set of rules that rational people will accept on the condition that other rational people accept them as well. Humans flourish when they escape their solitary condition in a state of zombies and achieve the benefits of social living. Chapters 4 through 6 explore the Kantian (duty-based) approach to these same questions. According to this view, rational persons are intrinsically valuable and the moral value of one's actions is determined by the motive behind them, namely, were they done for the sake of duty or not? The Kantian view also offers us a rule-governed procedure for determining what our duties are. Chapters 7 through 8 investigate how the utilitarian approaches moral value as well as our obligations. According to the utilitarian, pleasure or happiness is the sole intrinsic value and we are morally obligated to maximize overall happiness. As we will see, the utilitarian has a much broader conception of what kinds of lives—as well as undeaths—are morally valuable as compared to the Kantian view. Chapter 9 considers a practical example that many survivors will have faced, namely, you control a stronghold that is protected from the ravenous hordes but is surrounded by a large group of living outside. The living are clamoring to get in and face the imminent danger of being devoured. What are your moral obligations to these people and how do you weigh these obligations against your obligations to those you are already protecting inside your stronghold? The chapter answers this question from a variety of ethical perspectives.

Chapter 10 examines issues of personal identity and moral responsibility within the context of a zombie outbreak. To what extent am I the same person after I turn as I was before I turned and is there some sense in which I am still morally considerable (even if I cannot be morally responsible)? Do the living still have some residual moral obligation to those that have turned, or to themselves if they have not yet turned but soon will? These questions are of paramount importance since survivors frequently hesitate to kill loved ones after they have turned (which often puts the survivors at risk), and they typically kill themselves when infected to avoid joining the undead.

The final chapter takes up certain themes in virtue ethics as they can be applied to the question of human flourishing within the context of a zombie apocalypse. Whereas most of the book has focused on what we ought to *do* as survivors, this chapter focuses on the kind of survivors we ought to *be*. According to virtue ethics, human flourishing consists in possessing the right kind of character—a virtuous character that only humans can have—and acting in accordance with that character. In addition to allowing you to flourish, such a character provides the practical wisdom for you to resolve conflicts between your moral obligations when they arise (e.g., in the stronghold case). Returning to the fundamental question, although a virtuous life is a life worth living, much better it is to be undead than to live a vicious life.

Further study

- Camus, Albert. *Myth of Sisyphus.* New York: Knopf, 1954
  - The first line inspires the opening quotation of this chapter.
- Mogk, Matt. *Everything You Ever Wanted to Know about Zombies.* New York: Gallery Books, 2011.

- See chapter 21, "Your Own Worst Enemy," for how survivors have much more to fear from themselves than from zombies during an outbreak.
- Robinson-Greene, Rachel. "Better Off Undead." In *The Walking Dead and Philosophy*, edited by Wayne Yuen, 119–128. Chicago: Open Court, 2012.
  - For further discussion of Camus's views within the context of *The Walking Dead*.

1 COPING WITH CHAOS THROUGH RELATIVISM

The small proportion of deviants choosing undeath is not a function of the fundamental sanity of our culture, but of the universal fact that, happily, the majority of the living quite readily take on any shape their culture values.

—FROM *ANTHROPOLOGY AND THE UNDEAD*

Can anything be of objective moral value—valuable regardless of belief or opinion—in a world gradually being overtaken by the licentious living if not the undead? For our purposes, let us define the **moral realist** as someone who believes there is at least one objective moral value, while the **moral anti-realist** holds that there are no objective moral values. Either moral values are relative to belief or opinion, are expressions of an individual's emotions, or do not exist at all.

Back before my university finally consumed itself in an orgy of bloodshed, I found that my students generally broke into one of two categories when asked the above question. One group thought that moral value depended simply on what one's culture endorsed while the other group thought that moral value depended simply on God's will. The students' views were nothing new, but reflected beliefs deeply rooted in the pre-apocalyptic world. These positions became even more popular, however, as the world fell apart. Since the groups viewed themselves as diametrically opposed to one another, they were surprised to learn that they actually endorsed similar forms of moral anti-realism. This chapter examines both these forms of anti-realism before turning, in the next chapter, to other forms of realism and anti-realism that may avoid the objections these positions face.

1. Field exercise: The fall

When they send their zombies, they're not sending their best. They're not sending you. They're sending people that have lots of problems, and they're bringing those problems to us. They're bringing infection. They're bringing undeath. They're bloodthirsty monsters. And some, I assume, are good people.

—PRESIDENT MENTEMURO

The outbreak started somewhere in the American Midwest. Some thought it had to do with the opioid crisis—perhaps one of the new synthetics the pharmaceutical industry created to keep people addicted ended up hooking more people than even they intended—but *nobody* knows for sure. The one thing *everyone* knew, however, was that lots of white people were dying. In fact, for a long while, those were the only infected faces you could see on television, staggering out of trailer parks and staring out from behind the closed fences of gated communities. The paler the skin, the easier it was to see the dark cracks that indicated accelerating infection.

That great bugaboo of American culture—race—drove the coverage in ways that were at once familiar and unexpected. That race was used to compromise our ability to understand the fundamental problem was familiar, but that the discussion centered on the potential danger of "whiteness" was unexpected. The infected white faces frightened the white pundits who amplified their own fear to terrify the white folks on the other side of the screen.

* * *

The video segment was from a local affiliate in Kansas. The grainy footage showed a man training a shotgun on an infected woman—maybe his wife—whom he could not bring himself to shoot. When she jumped on him and tore out his throat, releasing a geyser of blood, the segment broke off and coverage returned to studio.

"The rate of violence has spiked dramatically in the past six months." Chip was speaking with a concern bordering on sincerity to his counterpart, Claire. The two hosts sat perfectly coifed and resplendent on the couches of the morning set, a 1950s American fantasy brought to life in the savage present.

Claire was outraged. "Why are *we* doing this to one another, Chip? We're not used to seeing this kind of violence in the *real* America."

"What we know," Chip responded comfortingly, "is that *these* people aren't responsible for what they do. Your skin color isn't up to you, right Claire?"

"Besides the tan, of course, not!" the female host exclaimed, lightly tapping Chip on his wrist. Her tone had changed from horror to playfulness on cue. "You're saying that being *white* makes *us* more susceptible to infection."

He nodded. "That's right, Claire. Just like the sun, we're more *sensitive* than those *other* folks. But rest assured—with the nation's unflagging support—the government is putting every available resource toward the War on Infection."

Turning to the camera, he said sternly, "Immediately turn over to authorities those who have died or show signs of infection."

Claire chimed in on a more positive note, "The American Shield Act is entering its 10th year. Remember, you receive a healthy tax credit for each loved one."

"Use it, but don't abuse it," Chip scolded. "Penalties are severe for false reporting … Think of it as your patriotic duty," he counseled. "Your loved ones are fallen soldiers in the War on Infection. Although always tragic, it is a proud day when an Army officer visits your home and hands you your urn."

Claire held up a small porcelain box shaped like an American flag for the camera. "This one is mine!" A moment of emotion snuck through her protective layer of affected detachment.

Claire turned back to the camera, her placid mask restored. "It's time to remember our fallen heroes." The screen scrolled beaming white faces and names as "America the Beautiful" played in the background.

"Who more than self their country loved, and mercy more than life …"
SCREACH! SCREACH! SCREACH!

The faces stopped scrolling, replaced momentarily by a test screen. This screen was then replaced by a map of the United States with a number of highlighted dots. A disembodied voice—stern but encouraging—the kind you heard in old military recruitment commercials, narrated:

"Fifty of the largest stadiums, across the country, have been set up as safe zones. If you can get to one of these, authorities have a treatment that will prevent you from showing signs of infection, what is commonly called 'cracking up.' If a loved one has darkened veins spreading across their body, you must isolate them immediately. Although still alive, the virus now controls their minds and they are a danger to you and others.

Unfortunately, being cracked up is not the end of the threat. The virus is more virulent than the Centers for Disease Control and Prevention scientists previously thought. Even after a loved one has died, unless the brain is *destroyed*, they will resurrect in as dangerous a form as before. They are no longer living, but you can recognize them by their *moans*. Although the infected are commonly referred to as 'zombies,' it is important that you recognize the differences between the cracked up but living and the equally threatening undead."

The picture changed to a split screen showing video of a cracked up zombie sprinting down a street on one side with an undead moaner shambling aimlessly through a field on the other side. This split screen was replaced with a cartoon graphic of a brain with a big red X flashing across it. Finally, the crossed-out brain was again replaced by the original map.

"In closing, you—the American people—deserve to know one more thing ... a terrible truth. *All* of us have the virus. The drug available in your local stadium prevents the virus from replicating but cannot cure the virus itself. Since we have limited quantities of the drug, you must come to one of these safe zones *immediately*. Regretfully, the treatment does not work on those who have already started to crack up. If you show signs of infection, you will be thanked for your sacrifice and given an honorable death ... Everyone else is welcome. The American Shield Act is suspended until further notice. The government can no longer guarantee your safety at home. Please make your way to your closest stadium as soon as possible. Remember: community, stability, survival. America strong!"

* * *

Although the population had declined precipitously over the past ten years, these stadiums did not have enough room for everyone. Rumors spread through social media that the government was bringing people to these facilities to exterminate them. Rather than being a vaccine against it, the promised drug actually *accelerated* infection. Once online, the scattered facts combined with fantasy and fear to generate an alternate reality that made people even less informed than if they had been wholly ignorant. Religious sects cropped up that offered alternatives, some of which appeared preferable to a government crematorium. Enough people stopped cooperating with authorities for the outbreak to worsen and for the authorities to lose control. Once the stadiums started to fall, those that remained panicked and started to make a run for the border—the southern border—there being too much to fear in the great white north. As the mass migration was starting, Mexican media outlets picked up the American media coverage and projected the racialized terror through their own cultural prism to a receptive domestic audience. Public opinion quickly turned against the northern influx and the media, now reflecting popular sentiment, called the invaders an existential threat to Mexican identity and culture. Even though people with other racial backgrounds were being infected and turned on both sides of the border, Mexican popular opinion, bolstered explicitly by the media and implicitly by the government, continued to act as if the problem were uniquely American. Infected Mexicans were portrayed as the victims of a threat that originated north of the border. Although you could be infected by your brown-skinned neighbor just as easily as a "gringo"—which became a catch-all term for anyone considered too light-skinned—only gringos were rounded up by the authorities, warehoused in cages, and then deported back to the post-apocalyptic wasteland that America had quickly become.

This did nothing to stem the tide of refugees, however, and so the Mexican authorities started to separate children from their parents with the thought that this would dissuade the gringo families from trying to cross. Of course, for these families, nothing was worse than the violence that awaited them back home, which meant they were willing to risk *everything* in the hopes of crossing undetected. Even after the border was closed to Americans, people still managed to sneak across the open desert while others were smuggled in trucking containers. If those crossing the desert were already infected, they would turn in the wilderness, creating a deadly gauntlet for those that followed—a virtual "wall" of the undead. By contrast, if even a single person were infected in a trucking container, by the time it reached a major Mexican city, the now undead cargo had become a biological dirty bomb.

The media branded the gringos a terrorist threat and the slogan "Mexico for Mexicans" soon became a cultural touchstone. Both the gringos and anyone trying to help them were met with swift vigilante "justice." When not turning a blind eye to the violence, authorities would often stop the deportation buses just short of the border so that the gangs could ensure that the gringos did not cross it again. Entire families were routinely hung, their pale converted corpses hanging—kicking and swinging—from bridges near the border. These strange fruits—differing only in ripeness—served as a macabre warning to dissuade those still considering the dangerous journey.

Finding a convenient scapegoat to the north, the Mexican government, headed by President Mentemuro, continued to blame the gringos not only for the infection but also for all the socioeconomic ills that plagued his country. He insisted that Mexican law did not protect them and that every patriotic Mexican had an obligation to eliminate the northern threat. Although his myopic focus on the gringos boosted his domestic popular support, it also undermined his country's ability to face the real threat. Infection embraces you regardless of race, ethnicity, or culture. Egalitarian to the last, it does not discriminate as we do.

* * *

FIGURE 3 President Mentemuro.

"And some, I assume, are good people."

The crowd exploded in derisive laughter and started a chant—common at Mentemuro rallies—that grew to a deafening roar: "Hang them high! Hang Them High! HANG THEM HIGH!"

The president flashed a sardonic grin across his sagging face and stuck two thumbs-up to the crowd of supporters. The tricolor was everywhere. There were dozens on stage and everyone in the crowd had wrapped themselves in the flag in one way or another. Even the two young women the aged Mentemuro had flanking him on stage were wearing what could be charitably called "cocktail dresses," fashioned from modest amounts of green, white, and red. As the crowd had died down, someone stepped forward near the front.

He yelled, in Spanish, "I'm a good person!" and pulled a tricolor bandana from his face revealing brown skin cracked like porcelain with dozens of thin black lines—the tell-tale signs of someone about to turn.

Visibly shaken, Mentemuro bellowed into the microphone, "Get him the hell out of here!"

As the crowd descended on the man, he jumped lithely on stage, turned his cracked face to the lights and yelled:

"See! We're all the same!"

The crowd got a hold of him and was pulling him back. On his way down, he bit into the ankle of one of the young women flanking Mentemuro. She turned almost immediately—although egalitarian, the virus nonetheless affects each of us differently—and pinned her scantily clad compatriot to the floor. She tore out the other woman's throat and the subsequent spray hit Mentemuro in the face and soaked the floor surrounding him. Turning to escape, his slick leather soles slid in the pool of blood, and he tumbled heavily to the floor. Struggling to raise his corpulence from the gore, the last thing he saw was the second woman, covered in blood, mauling his groin. Only one color remained on the flag covering her chest, a symbolic elegy to the culture he had hastened to its demise.

2. Cultural relativism

A popular view before the outbreak—and perhaps even more so after it—is that morality depends on the culture that you live within. This is a form of moral anti-realism since it holds that there are no *objective* moral values, i.e., things that are valuable regardless of belief or opinion.

For **cultural relativism**, moral values are always *relative* to the beliefs or opinions of individual cultures. Morality is a matter of opinion and these opinions vary from culture to culture. Admittedly, we do not have "cultures" in the way that we had them before the outbreak, but we still have groups who have come together under certain shared beliefs and who approximate the cultures of the civilization we once had.

Let's start, however, by examining the civilizations we once had. During the outbreak, America and Mexico had different ways of stemming infection. As we saw above, Americans turned their infected and dead over to government disposal before welcoming them home as cremated heroes. The thought was to control infection by controlling those who had become infected or who were dead but could harbor the virus. By contrast, Mexicans tried to stem infection by eliminating those that were considered most likely to spread it: the gringos. Whereas the lives of gringos were morally valuable in America, they were of no value south of the border. Each group would likely think the practices of the other to be morally abhorrent. Clearly, white America would view the Mexican practice as barbaric. Conversely, many Mexicans would view America's practice as leaving everyone else in danger of coming in contact with potentially fatal *whiteness*. Although the distinction between "American" and "Mexican" is foundationally a political one having to do with national identity, it also came to be viewed as a cultural distinction, one that became infused with racial and nativist overtones as the outbreak worsened. It is this distinction that the cultural relativist would seize upon. Since these different cultures believe different things about morality—for example, the moral value of gringo lives—perhaps there is no moral fact of the matter. The cultural relativist would conclude that morality is just a matter of opinion which varies from culture to culture.

Turning to the post-apocalyptic present, the cultural relativist believes that different groups of survivors have different moral codes and that the moral code of a particular group determines what is right/wrong for the members of that group. There is no objective moral standard that can be used to determine that one of these codes is better than another. Just because your group has a certain moral code does not entail that it is better than the moral code of another group, and it would be arrogant to claim otherwise. Instead of criticizing the moral codes of other groups, you should tolerate them.

Does the cultural relativist have good reason for concluding that there is no objective truth in morality? In order to answer this question, we need to ask what the **philosophical argument** is supposed to be for cultural relativism. A philosophical argument has two main components: the *premises* provide reasons for accepting a particular statement. This statement is the *conclusion* which should follow logically from the premises. What this means is that *if* the premises are true, *then* the conclusion will be true as well. When this happens, an argument is **valid**. If the premises can be true and the conclusion false, however, then the argument is invalid. Assuming that an argument is valid, the only remaining question is whether it is **sound**. This means that the premises are, *in fact*, true. When it comes to philosophical arguments, our aim should always be *soundness* (validity + true premises). The argument for cultural relativism is actually quite simple. It consists of only one premise and a conclusion:

(1) Different cultures believe different things about moral value.

(2) Therefore, there are no objective facts about moral value. Moral values are just a matter of cultural opinion and these opinions vary from culture to culture.

The main reason for accepting the conclusion seems to be that different cultures believe different things about morality. For example, American and Mexican cultures have different views on the value of gringo lives. It certainly seems like the premise is true. Does that mean that the argument is sound? Not so fast. What we need to know is whether the premise could be true and the conclusion false. If it could be, then the argument is invalid and hence unsound.

Here's the problem: the premise has to do with what cultures *believe* while the conclusion has to do with *fact*—what really is the case. Just because different groups of survivors have different beliefs does not entail, on its own, that there is no fact of the matter with respect to their point of difference. The argument is *invalid* since the conclusion would not follow from the premise. Consequently, the argument will also be unsound since validity is required for soundness.

To illustrate the problem, consider another example. Think of all of the different "cures" to infection that have come and gone. Some religious groups even relied on "reconversion camps" where they promised to "pray the infection" right out of your son or daughter. According to these groups, people were infected by sin and so prayer was the appropriate remedy. These camps were often isolated, so that when they were overrun from within, the undead could wander for miles in every direction spreading the infection before authorities were able to fight their way to the unholy source. By contrast, you had what remained of the scientific community telling people that a virus was the underlying cause of undeath and destroying the brain was the only sure way to end it. Consider how one might approach this disagreement using the cultural relativist's reasoning:

(1) Different groups believe different things about the cause of undeath.

(2) Therefore, there are no objective facts about the cause of undeath. The cause of undeath is just a matter of a group's opinion and these opinions vary from group to group.

Since different groups (the religious and the scientific) believe different things about the ultimate cause of undeath, there must be no *fact* of the matter. In other words, there is *no* actual cause of undeath at all. This is crazy talk. Even though we do not know how to cure the virus that causes undeath, we do know that there is such a virus. Just because some people do not believe in the virus does not, unfortunately, usher the virus out of existence. That there are no *facts* does not follow from a difference of *belief* about them.

Even if the cultural relativist lacks a good reason for believing what she does, this does not entail that cultural relativism is false. In other words, invalid arguments can still have true conclusions. I could simply have really bad reasons for believing something that happens to be true. For example, for a long while I thought a cricket bat would be a fantastic zombie fighting weapon *because* it featured prominently in my favorite, pre-outbreak, zombie film. I had much better reason, of course, when I started using one to fight zombies myself. I also discovered that other weapons that I favored for similar cinematic reasons—e.g., shotguns and chainsaws—were of limited utility in an actual outbreak. A broken clock is right twice a day and cultural relativism could still be true in the absence of a good reason to accept it. There are, however, some fairly compelling reasons for thinking that cultural relativism is false.

To begin, there are some distasteful—pun semi-intended— consequences to accepting cultural relativism. First, you would never have grounds for criticizing your own group's moral code. If your group were to discriminate against some members on the basis of arbitrary features, like skin color, you would have no basis to criticize this practice since the group's moral code would be the only standard for what is right or wrong. For example, if you lived in Mexico and thought there was something morally suspect about summarily executing gringos, you would just be wrong according to cultural relativism. The *only* thing you need to know in order to know whether a practice, like racial discrimination, is morally permissible is to consult the moral code of your own society. Second, there would be no basis for criticizing the practices of other groups. For example, it would be moral hubris for Americans to criticize Mexicans for summarily executing gringos if they tried to cross the border to escape the violence to the north. Finally, there would be no such thing as moral progress if cultural relativism were true. Consider again, discriminating against gringos was based on the color of their skin. If Mexicans were to eliminate this practice, one could not say that the society had become better from the moral point of view since the only standard of morality would be the moral code the society accepts at a particular time. This moral code can *change* but it can never get morally *better* or *worse* on pain of assuming a standard of morality that is external to the culture and its beliefs.

Of course, a cultural relativist could simply bite the bullet with regard to these three consequences. There are objections, however, that the cultural relativist simply cannot accept. The first is that although groups may have different *practices*, the moral *values* that underlie these practices are often shared. Although Americans and Mexicans had very different ways of trying to stem the outbreak, they were driven to do what they did because they both fundamentally value the lives of the living. This may seem ridiculous. How can the Mexicans be said to value the lives of the living if they exterminate so many? If the fundamental rule, however, is to preserve human life, both the Americans and the Mexicans have adopted it. They only differ in what they consider to be *exceptions* to the rule. Whereas the Americans view everyone who is cracked up but not yet undead as an exception, the Mexicans view everyone who is a gringo as an exception. Even so, these exceptions are carved out with the goal of saving as many lives as possible. If they didn't share this value, if they didn't value human life as a rule, both cultures would quickly die out. As a matter of fact, both did die out, but it wasn't because they didn't value human life. Rather, they died out because they mischaracterized the fundamental threat to human life.

Even if one assumes, as the cultural relativist does, that there are moral differences among cultures, the cultural relativist faces a dilemma. On the one hand, if moral claims are taken literally, as saying certain things are morally right or wrong, then the view generates contradictions. Americans believe killing unturned gringos is morally wrong. Mexicans believe it is morally obligatory. One and the same act—killing gringos—is both morally right and morally wrong. This problem grows even more pressing when one considers that the immigrant gringos are a *subculture* within Mexican society. The ethical code of the gringos (that killing gringos is morally wrong) conflicts with the ethical code of Mexican culture (that killing gringos is morally right). One and the same action is both moral and immoral from the perspective of the subculture which is contradictory.

The only way to avoid this problem is to say that the Americans and the Mexicans are not—contrary to their intentions—saying anything about the morality of *killing gringos*, but rather simply about their *attitudes* concerning the morality of killing gringos. If one were to take this other option, then the contradictions would disappear. There is no contradiction, after all, with Mexicans *approving* of killing gringos while Americans *disapprove* of killing gringos. A subculture could, furthermore, disapprove of the same thing that the larger culture approves. Even so, there is a cost to taking this route, namely, there can no longer be cross-cultural moral disagreement (something the cultural relativist insists upon). Presumably, this would take both the Americans and the Mexicans by surprise.

The biggest worry for cultural relativism, however, is that there are some values that cultures need to have in common if they are to survive. General prohibitions on lying, murder, stealing, and so on are necessary for cultures to function effectively. Most fundamentally, a culture must value life over undeath if the culture is to survive. For example, imagine the internet trolls were right and the American government was trying intentionally to turn all of its citizens. The society would simply cease to exist—or rather, it would become a zombie horde. The necessity of valuing life over undeath is a fact more fundamental than just what a culture might happen to believe. Contrary to the conclusion of the cultural relativist's argument, there are some values that cultures *must* share if those cultures are to continue to exist and—since they do not depend on cultural belief or opinion—they would be objective moral values.

Although this seems to be a decisive objection to cultural relativism, it does not show that valuing life over undeath is an objective moral value since one might still think that *survival* is not of objective moral value. In fact, in the next section, we will look at a group that holds this view. This book started with the question of why we should choose life over undeath, and one cannot simply beg the question against those who would make the opposite choice. What it seems we can say, at this point, is that *if* there are objective moral values, then survival has to be one of them since survival is a necessary condition for anything else to be of moral value. In a world filled only with the undead, there would no longer be any room for Ethics and with it moral value. It is only because some of *us* still survive that there may yet be room for Ethics and, with it, moral value. If survival is morally valuable, it has to be dependent on something else that is intrinsically valuable. What this something might be will be explored in later chapters.

3. Field exercise: Congregation of the Living Dead

Bless and approve our offering; make it acceptable to you, an offering in living flesh and blood. Let it become for us the resurrected body and blood of Jesus Christ, your only Son, our undead Lord.

— "EUCHARISTIC PRAYER," CONGREGATION OF
THE LIVING DEAD

"Congregants, we are gathered here today to celebrate that most holy right of our Church, the sacrifice of the living to our undead Lord, fulfilling his command by transforming ourselves into his likeness," the preacher solemnly intoned.

As he spoke, an orderly line of the living, in white confirmation gowns, entered the fortified chancel, singing a version of "I Come, O Savior, To Thy Table." Their jubilant voices were met by cheers from the gallery high above the nave on the opposite side of the church. It was full of true believers hoping one day to join those on the chancel stage.

The chancel screen was made of wrought iron with a single vertical sliding door, so narrow that only one person could pass through at a time, and so heavy that it took two men to winch it into its open position. In the nave, a few feet below the chancel screen, a writhing mass of zombies had gathered in eager expectation of their communion feast.

Visibly elated, the preacher continued, "On the third day after his crucifixion, Christ rose from the dead and promised his disciples he would return again. Our apocalypse is not the end, my brothers and sisters, but rather the beginning." His words were again met by the gallery's full-throated approval.

Reaching the climax, he gestured with open hands at the undead horde gathered in the nave below the chancel, "He has risen from the dead again, my brothers and sisters, though this time through the bodies of our undead brethren. They are a sign of God's infinite mercy which conveys a divine command. We are to recreate ourselves in *his* image. Apotheosis through zombification!"

"Apotheosis through zombification!" the gallery returned in unison.

The door on the chancel screen shot up and the first to be confirmed passed through. Once the door had crashed back down to the floor, she dove cruciform into the cold embrace of the waiting horde. Her white gown quickly sprouted red blooms before disappearing into an orgy of broken limbs and entrails. After her screams had subsided, those still in the chancel kept singing, though their volume was noticeably reduced. Whether this was due to the loss of her voice or the loss of their nerve was unclear. Regardless of whatever misgivings each may have had, they continued one by one through the door—the screech of metal followed by the whoosh of a falling weight—a gurgling scream followed by a harmony gradually reduced to a solo. Finally, the soloist stood in front of the open door, desiccated hands grasping blindly at his ankles. His arms out to either side, in a tremulous voice he cried:

"Lord, may my body and my blood ... Be for my soul the highest good!"

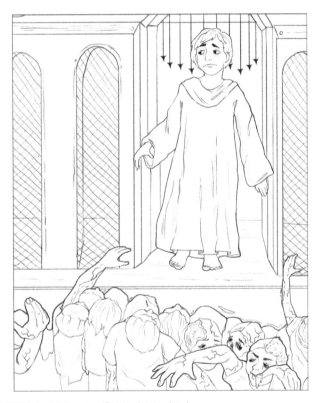

FIGURE 4 A living sacrifice to the undead.

As the door came crashing down, his last note was replaced by the dissonance of the horde. The gallery again let forth its own cacophonous roar.

Wearing a broad smile, the preacher took up his sermon again. He pointed to the gallery, "Like the twelve original apostles, you too are disciples charged with spreading God's word. Each of you has taken a solemn vow not to undergo apotheosis until you bring twelve more like yourselves. Once you have fulfilled your obligation to the Lord, you may join him in undeath. Go forth and tell those that still live of God's infinite mercy as well as the punishment for ignoring his command!"

With that, he grabbed a pistol from the altar, strode to the adjoining sacristy, and dragged back a man wearing tattered black clothing and what remained of clerical collar. As he straightened himself, one could see that he had been beaten but he stood defiantly as the preacher walked around him. The preacher put the pistol to the man's swollen face.

"In the spirit of Christ's forgiveness, I give you one last chance to comply with his divine command. Find redemption in his undead embrace or face final death." The preacher gestured toward the door in the chancel screen. Instead of moving, the priest mustered the strength for one last homily.

Looking with fierce indignation at the gallery, he shouted, "How can *you* claim to decipher God's will in this maelstrom of violence and death? Although the undead *exist*, this does not mean God wishes that we *ought* to become them. Above all, morality does not depend simply on God's *command*, but rather on the *nature* of what God has created."

"God created *undeath*!" one voice rang out from the gallery. Others started hooting and whistling in scornful agreement.

The preacher, still smiling, put his finger to his lips.

"My children ..." The crowd settled into rippling murmurs. "Let him confess his ignorance to his creator," he said in a patronizing tone.

The priest held his nerve and started again, "No doubt he has *allowed* undeath, but he *created* you with inherent dignity, freedom, and responsibility to your fellow man. God cannot command you to be a zombie without frustrating his purpose in creating humanity. If you choose to become one of those things, what was created in God's image will cease to be. Although a shambling husk remains, God will hold you responsible for your spiritual suicide ..." He trailed off as the catcalls from the gallery started to drown him out.

As the preacher circled behind him, the catcalls thinned out, and the priest started to recite "The Lord's Prayer." Just like the soloist, his solitary prayer was likewise silenced by a loud bang, and the hushed pause that followed was quickly replaced by the bloodthirsty cheers of the gallery.

4. Divine command theory

As the field exercise in Chapter 1.1 noted, when traditional societies started to falter, religious sects often stepped in to fill the void. Many of them subscribed to **divine command theory** (DCT) which holds that something is morally right (wrong) simply because God commands (forbids) it. Although this was already a popular view before the outbreak, it gained even greater support after civilization fell. DCT is a form of moral anti-realism though, at first blush, it might seem strange to classify it as such. Wouldn't morality be objective if it depended only upon divine will? Remember, moral realism requires that at least one value is *not* relative to belief or opinion. Whereas cultural relativism makes morality relative to the beliefs or opinions of different cultures, DCT makes morality relative to the beliefs or opinions of only one individual, God. DCT is a form of moral anti-realism insofar as morality depends—albeit exclusively—on God's will.

DCT is a very old view, and one of the earliest Western philosophers, Plato, posed a famous dilemma for it. Using the above terms, the dilemma would ask whether something is morally right because God commands it or if God commands something because it is morally right. DCT clearly has to take the first option—something is morally right simply because God commands it—since to take the other option would make morality *independent* of God's command. If God commands something because it is morally right, then it would already have to be morally right apart from God's command. To give a parallel example, if I cut off my hand because a zombie bit it, the bite has to have already happened. The bite provides the reason why I cut off my hand. Likewise, according to the second horn above, the moral rightness of something provides the reason why God commands it. In contrast, DCT must subscribe to the first option since it holds that moral rightness depends entirely on God's command. This option, however, faces a number of objections.

According to the first option, "moral rightness" is *identical* to being "commanded by God." Plato's main concern was that this does not really help us to understand what moral rightness is. Consider the field exercise above, what if one was to define "undeath" as what God commands? Although it is true of undeath—according to the Congregation of the Living Dead (or CoLD, for short)—that God commands undeath, isn't there more to being undead than this: moaning, shuffling, a constant hunger for living human flesh, etc.? Knowing that God commands undeath does not really help you to understand what undeath is. By extension, knowing that God commands (forbids) something does not really give you a better grasp of moral rightness (wrongness). A related worry is that this option makes morality mysterious. After all, what would it mean for God to *make* something—like feeding ourselves to the undead—morally right? It cannot be in the same way as CoLD made its undead nave. God is not fencing off a section of a church and filling it with moaning zombies. According to DCT, God does not fashion moral rightness by rearranging the physical environment, and it is not as if God is making the act of being devoured by the undead less painful: a gentle tickle rather than (literally) gut-wrenching pain followed by conversion. DCT holds, in contrast, that being fed to the undead—the same undead that survivors know and fear—would itself be morally right if God were to command it.

This leads directly into the next problem. DCT makes God's commands arbitrary. Nothing is morally right or morally wrong prior to God's command. God's command is what makes something morally right. Consequently, God could have just as easily chosen to command us to feed ourselves to the undead rather than to forbid it (or vice versa). There is nothing about being fed to the undead, in itself, that makes it morally right/wrong, since only God's command makes it morally right/wrong. This problem also helps to underscore why DCT is not, contrary to initial appearance, defending a form of moral realism. There is nothing *objective* about morality if all moral claims are wholly *arbitrary*.

DCT cannot respond by saying that God would never command us to feed ourselves to the undead because he is all-good and he knows that such an act is morally wrong. Again, all moral value is reducible to God's command, according to DCT, and so to say that "God is all-good" is only to say that "God does not forbid himself from doing anything that he in fact does." Moral claims about God are empty and trivial if DCT is true. Also, from the perspective of DCT, it makes no sense to say that God *knows* that feeding ourselves to the undead is morally wrong as if there were some moral fact of the matter about random violence that God could come to know. For God to know that feeding ourselves to the undead is wrong is only for God to know his own will.

The final problem with taking the option that says something is morally right simply because God commands it is that it provides the wrong reasons for moral principles. There seem to be all kinds of reasons why feeding the living to the undead is morally wrong. It causes intense suffering, destroys the victim's sense of self, removes a moral agent from the world, and adds to the legion of undead that threatens other survivors. For DCT, however, all of these reasons are morally irrelevant. The *only* thing that matters, according to DCT, is whether God commands or forbids feeding ourselves to the undead.

The good news for theists—those who maintain their faith despite this post-apocalyptic nightmare—is that one does not have to subscribe to DCT in order to be a theist. Quite to the contrary, many features of DCT should strike the theist as sacrilegious, e.g., that moral claims about God are empty. Fortunately, the theist can simply choose the other horn of the dilemma: God commands certain things because they are morally right. Although this option is incompatible with DCT, it is compatible with a standard theistic conception of God as all-knowing, all-powerful, and all-good. Since God is all-knowing, he knows *all* the facts, including the moral facts. Since God is all-powerful, God can command whatever he likes. Since God is all-good, however, God would only command that which he knows to be morally right. Taking this option, however, entails abandoning the moral argument for God's existence, since you can no longer argue from morality to the existence of God. Also, you would need to find some way of explaining what it means for there to be independent moral facts.

It should be noted that the priest, in the field exercise above, offers a theistic alternative to DCT in his final homily. Catholicism subscribes to **natural law theory**. This view holds that values and purposes are built right into the fabric of nature. Everything in the natural world has a certain purpose, and something is good insofar as it serves its purpose well. The natural purpose of a human being, according to this view, is to be *rational*. Through our reasoning, we discover the laws of nature which describe not only how things *are*, but also how they *ought* to be. God created us with the capacity to reason and through reason to discover what we ought to do. When we use reason appropriately, we fulfill our purpose as human beings, and live as we ought to live. This is why the priest is so horrified by what CoLD is doing. According to natural law theory, the congregation is doing the very opposite of what they ought to do. When they sacrifice themselves to the undead, they are destroying themselves as rational beings and so frustrating God's purpose for humanity. Unlike DCT, according to natural law theory, God cannot arbitrarily decide to make undeath morally obligatory. God could not do this without changing the essence of what it is to be human. Undeath is contrary to our natural purpose—reason—and so is morally impermissible according to natural law theory.

Since we are *all* infected, however, does this mean that humanity has a *new* natural purpose? As CoLD would likely argue, perhaps we *ought* to be undead. This exposes a fundamental problem with natural law theory, though it is not a problem unique to natural law theory. We will see it arise in a number of different ethical contexts. Just because we naturally *are* a certain way—e.g., rational, cracking up, or undead—does not entail that we *ought* to be that way. Unfortunately, knowing that we cannot infer the *ought* from the *is* leaves us no closer to understanding what we ought to do or the kind of people that we ought to be.

Summary

This chapter examined the two most popular views on moral value inherited from the pre-apocalyptic world. Both cultural relativism and DCT are forms of moral anti-realism that claim moral value is relative to belief or opinion. For cultural relativism, moral value is relative to the belief or opinion of individual cultures. For DCT, moral value is relative to the will of only one individual—God. Both views have significant flaws that the zombie apocalypse has brought into stark relief.

Further study

- Benedict, Ruth. "Anthropology and the Abnormal." *The Journal of General Psychology* 10 (1934): 59–80.
  - This article makes one of the strongest cases in favor of cultural relativism and the quote that opens this chapter is adapted from the last line of this article.
- Cowan, Steven. "Maybe Jenner Was Right." In *The Ultimate Walking Dead and Philosophy: Hungry for More*, edited by Wayne Yuen, 19–30. Chicago: Open Court, 2016.
  - Discusses how some characters invoke God to provide meaning within the context of *The Walking Dead*.
- Grant, Mira. *Feed*. London: Orbit, 2010.
  - Presents a world where civilization has struggled on for years despite the outbreak. Although everyone is infected, zombie conversion occurs when you are bitten by someone who has already converted, when you die, or when the virus amplifies spontaneously. For the most part, the rules of her post-apocalyptic world apply in this world as well.
- Hawkes, Gordon. "Lie or Die." In *The Ultimate Walking Dead and Philosophy*, edited by Wayne Yuen, 49–61. Chicago: Open Court, 2016.
  - Uses examples from *The Walking Dead* to illustrate how moral anti-realists can use moral dilemmas to argue that there are no objective moral values.
- Plato. "Euthyphro." In *Five Dialogues: Euthyphro, Apology, Crito, Meno, Phaedo*, translated by G.M.A Grube, 1–20. Indianapolis: Hackett, 2002.
  - Contains the classic presentation of DCT (something is holy simply because the gods love it) as well as Socrates's objections to the view.
- Rachels, James. "The Challenge of Cultural Relativism." In *The Elements of Moral Philosophy*, edited by Stuart Rachels, 15–32. New York: McGraw-Hill, 2015.
  - Presents the argument for cultural relativism before discussing why the argument is both invalid and the conclusion is likely false. The two cultures he highlights are the Callatians and the Greeks who had different practices for disposing of the dead (eating and burning them, respectively).

- *The Walking Dead* (2010–et present), [TV Program] AMC.
  - Although based on the comic book series, references in this book will be to the television series. One character in the television series who is not in the comic books is Lizzie. She is a child who makes offerings to the dead and even intentionally converts the living in season 4.14 "The Grove."
  - Herschel talks about God's providence in connection with the outbreak at several points in season two, starting with the first episode, "Bloodletting."
  - The cannibals of Terminus provide a good illustration of some of the distasteful consequences of accepting cultural relativism. In particular, see season 5.1 "No Sanctuary."

2 HOW TO FIND MORAL VALUE IN THE APOCALYPSE

The problem is one of finding room for ethics, or placing ethics within the disenchanted, zombie infested world which we inhabit, and of which we are a part.

—FROM *RULING INFECTION: A THEORY OF PANDEMIC REASONING*

Although the forms of relativism discussed in the previous chapter found roots in a world without infection, the problems inherent to these views were laid bare by the outbreak. Even so, there may be other positions on the nature of moral value that are able to avoid these problems. This chapter briefly examines the other anti-realist options before digging into the different forms of moral realism. All of these views face challenges, but in the end I will recommend a particular form of moral realism that I believe survivors should endorse in this post-apocalyptic world.

1. Field exercise: The hunter

The man who does not value himself is essentially undead since he cannot value anything or anyone.

—from *Selfishness: The Virtue of Avoiding Undeath*

The voice was already lecturing him when he came to, but his head was still reeling from the shock of whatever trauma he had endured but thankfully forgotten. He couldn't move, but the voice came into focus periodically through the cycle of his heartbeat, pounding painfully in his head, reminding him he was still alive.

"I need you to understand the reasons why …" POW, POW, POW … "Being the best hunter makes me happy …" Pow, Pow, Pow … "Good hunters don't spare the prey …" pow, pow, pow …

His heartbeat began to subside as the rhythmic cadence of the lecture soothed his head into a steadily aching torpor.

Along with his hearing, his vision came into focus. He saw a figure looming in the darkness, bars slicing through the inches that separated them. The figure was carrying a long stick that waved menacingly in cadence with the voice.

FIGURE 5 Man in cage.

"Therefore, you must become meat," the voice concluded matter-of-factly.

A wave of fear cleared whatever fog still clouded his senses. Struggling to maintain his composure, he blurted out the first thing that came to mind.

"What about me? I want to be happy!"

"Good! I'm glad you've decided to participate," the voice replied with enthusiasm. "But when we can't both be happy, guess who gets to be happy?" The figure seemed to shrug before giving him a quick poke in the kidney.

"You just happen to be on the wrong end of the stick."

He rolled over in agony. Before saying anything else, he decided to take stock of his predicament. The cage was definitely handmade. The basic construction was two rows of wooden slats that formed a three-sided cage about four feet wide and two feet deep. The slats were stacked two high—about six feet—and tied together with bailing wire. He inferred that his hands and feet were likely bound behind him in much the same way, which would account for the sharp slicing sensation anytime he tried to separate them. There was a closed door on the side without slats, bolted from his side, but with a slide that extended beyond the slats.

None of it made much sense. If he wasn't tied up and in so much pain, he could probably break the whole thing down in a couple of minutes. Hell, he could open the door from his own side with a bit of dexterity. The wooden slats had a nice finish on them which allowed him to see all the tooth marks. He concluded that other poor bastards had probably tried to gnaw their way out before the hunter had turned them into dinner. When the zombies didn't get you, the cannibals often did. With rueful irony, he reflected that so many folks were surviving by turning into what they tried so hard to avoid becoming. He resolved to do everything he could to open that door, but was pulled from his plans by the resumption of the lecture.

"It's your fault you're in here you know. You'd still be out there," the figure waved the stick, "if you hadn't taken the bait."

The hunter was right, he thought to himself. He didn't know anyone was watching the shipping container, but he shouldn't have ventured into it on his own. The supplies—canned food, antibiotics, sealed water bottles strewn outside the cracked door—were the perfect lure for any survivor. His people were desperate though and he needed to gather as much as he could. The last thing he remembered was trying to open the door to the shipping container. As soon as he put his shoulder into the opening to get some leverage, something—probably the stick now swinging like a metronome as the hunter spoke—smashed into his temple. Next thing he knew, he was in this cage and on the menu.

He had to stall for time. If he could scoot his body over next to the door, he could probably get on his knees and open the latch with his teeth. Since he only had his mouth to work with, he decided to give talking another chance.

"So you think I ought to do what makes me happy and you ought to do the same, right?"

"Yeah … so sacrificing my happiness"—the stick pointed at the darkened figure—"just so someone else can be happy"—the stick pointed again at him—"is always going to be the wrong call."

"O.K.," he said, "but what if making other people happy is what makes me happy?" Before the hunter could interject, he continued, "You're a *hunter*, but I'm a *gatherer*. My happiness doesn't come from the number of people I kill, but the number I save. I entered that shipping container not for *me*, but for all the *people* that I can keep alive with what's inside."

The figure turned away from him. He allowed himself to entertain the thought that perhaps he had struck a nerve. While they had been talking, he had slid closer to the door. As he neared it, he could hear muffled noises on the other side. His heart jumped at the possibility of another survivor. Perhaps, if he could open it, both of them together could turn the table—so to speak—on their would-be diner. Sliding his back up the door, he resolved to push the hunter's conscience in this moment of indecision.

"You said that your happiness matters more than mine, but why is that? What makes you so damned special? There are racists and sexists, but you're a *selfist*—you think that only your happiness matters. You're full of crap though, just like those other bigots. My happiness matters just as much as yours and I shouldn't have to die just so you can have a full belly."

Still facing away from him, the hunter spoke in a hushed tone, "Yes, you're right. The happiness of others can matter as much as my own … more than that … I would have been willing to sacrifice myself."

"So you're not going to eat me after all?" His voice feigned relief, but he wasn't going to wait for an answer. He clenched his teeth around the slide and pulled with all the leverage he could muster.

The door swung immediately inward and cracked his teeth as the force toppled him over. He rolled to face the opening.

"*I* never said *I* would … again, you're the author of your own punishment," the hunter replied with sorrow mixed with gratitude. "I can't bring them with me, but I can't bear to leave them alone … thank you for sacrificing yourself in my stead." Two small forms pushed through the darkness. Their ashen faces were covered in cracks, like life-sized porcelain dolls. When they saw him through their lifeless eyes, they smiled revealing tiny teeth, happy drool replaced by streams of gore. One was an ankle biter while the other went straight for his wrists. Clearly, the bailing wire served a secondary purpose, cutting up their food as a parent would have when they were alive. As the throb of his rushing heartbeat again overwhelmed his thoughts, he felt the bailing wire being cut and heard the sound of a door gently closing. Once turned, he would become their undead guardian—releasing them from the macabre menagerie their cribs had become—creating a new horde that would hunt its own living prey.

2. From subjectivism to egoism

Beyond cultural relativism and DCT, other forms of moral anti-realism have also increased in popularity since the outbreak. Some survivors even challenge the idea that moral claims could, in principle, be true. For example, **emotivism** holds that moral claims are neither true nor false but are rather just expressions of emotion—"Cannibalism is morally *wrong!*" = "Cannibalism *boo!*" (rather than hooray)—where the degree to which one approves is typically proportional to how hungry one is. Even more extreme, the **nihilist** believes that *all* moral claims are false since there are no moral facts that would make a moral judgment true. Even so, the nihilist recognizes that individuals (falsely) *believe* they are saying something informative when they make a moral claim.

More common among survivors, however, is a form of moral **subjectivism** whereby folks believe morality is relative to an individual's belief or opinion. Moral claims are true, but what makes the moral claim true is simply that the individual *believes* the moral claim. According to this view, cannibalism would be wrong just in case I believe that cannibalism is wrong. Of course, for someone with different beliefs, for example, the *cannibal*, the situation would be quite different. DCT is really just a special case of moral subjectivism. Whereas the moral subjectivist holds that moral value is relative to the will of the *individual*,

DCT goes a step further in claiming that *God's* will is the only individual will that matters from the moral standpoint.

What determines whether a survivor *believes* something is morally right or wrong? A common explanation is that these beliefs are driven by what the individual perceives to be in his/her individual self-interest. I only care about what is best for *me*, what gets *me* out of the latest undead attack unscathed, and surviving for another day. This is called "egoism," and it breaks down into two different varieties. The **psychological egoist** claims that an individual's voluntary actions always *are* in his/her individual self-interest. The **ethical egoist**, in contrast, claims that an individual's voluntary actions always *ought* to be in his/her individual self-interest. It is important to note that although subjectivism is a form of moral anti-realism—what is morally valuable depends upon individual belief—ethical egoism is actually a form of moral realism. The ethical egoist holds that something is morally valuable regardless of belief or opinion, namely, whatever happens to be in your self-interest. If my subjective beliefs fail to correspond with what really is in my self-interest—for example, the man in the field exercise above who opens the door to his demise—then I fail to do what I ought to do according to the ethical egoist. Put simply, the subjectivist who subscribes to ethical egoism really isn't a subjectivist at all.

If psychological egoism is true, however, there is little point in reading the rest of this book. If people *are* always going to act selfishly, it does not make any sense to ask whether or not they *ought* to act differently. *Ought* implies *can*, so if survivors cannot do other than what they do (act from selfish motives), they cannot be obligated to do otherwise. Without a doubt, survivors often act from selfish motives. I have personally witnessed one man shoot another in the leg so that a pursuing horde would devour the wounded man rather than his former comrade. Even if survivors band together for greater security, when the group is under a threat of collapse, it is very often every person for themselves. I heard about one compound that was overrun by the undead in the dead of night. Although the survivors were able to take it back the next day, they discovered that the quartermaster—under cover of darkness and in the fog of war—had cleared out and taken all the food with her. This meant that most of the community starved, but would you have acted differently had you been the quartermaster? Here is the key question: even if it is very *common* for survivors to act in their own self-interest, must they *always* act in their own self-interest? This is the very strong claim that the psychological egoist is making.

The psychological egoist would argue that we are always motivated by our own individual desires. Even if this is true, however, do our desires always need to correspond to our individual self-interest? For example, as in the field exercise above, couldn't a hunter desire to give a juicy cut of human prey to a loved one even though the hunter does not individually benefit from acting on this desire? The psychological egoist might respond that the hunter shares not because of some altruistic motive, but rather because sharing with the loved one makes the *hunter* happy. After all, the hunter did not spare the victim even though doing so would have made the victim happy—one can only assume the victim did not desire to be turned into a human smorgasbord. Making the hunter's loved ones happy makes the hunter happy because they are the hunter's loved ones. That the hunter's loved ones are zombies, in the above field exercise, does not make the relationship any less genuine, at least from the hunter's perspective. Before the outbreak, many hunters loved their pets (e.g., their hunting dogs) just as much if not more than other human beings. Are these relationships less genuine because they are not relationships with other living human beings?

The real problem here is that the psychological egoist is trying to reinterpret motives in a way that is not convincing. Just because the hunter might have self-interested motives in feeding their loved ones does not entail that the hunter did not have other motives. It is plausible that the hunter is motivated by a genuine concern for the *loved ones* rather than just the hunter's own *self-interest*. In fact, it is not unreasonable to think the hunter wants to feed the children only because the hunter cares unselfishly about them. The psychological egoist often conflates the *intended* and *foreseen* consequences of actions. Although the hunter could surely foresee that the *hunter* would be happy if the loved ones were fed, what the hunter presumably intended was for the *loved ones* to be happy. Whether it is even possible for zombies to be happy and what this might mean will be dealt with in Chapter 10, "What Are Your Obligations to Undead Loved Ones?"

Consider how heavy the burden of proof is for psychological egoism: if we can identify even *one* instance of altruistically motivated action, then psychological egoism is false. Even though we have plenty of examples of actions that have clearly been motivated by self-interest during the apocalypse, we also have plenty of examples of actions that cannot easily be explained in terms of self-interest. For example, I have seen a mother sacrifice herself to an oncoming horde in order to save her fleeing children. Although it is true that she loved her children and this was the only way of saving them, how can we reinterpret the action as being motivated by self-interest? Yes, she was plausibly motivated by what was in her *children's* self-interest, but it is hard to pull *her* self-interest from the jaws of the undead.

Even if we do not *in fact* only act in our own self-interest, perhaps we *ought* to only act in our own self-interest. As mentioned above, ethical egoism is not itself, strictly speaking, a form of moral subjectivism since it would be immoral to act on individual beliefs that are contrary to one's own self-interest. This is not a problem for those survivors whose beliefs as to what they ought to do perfectly coincide with what is in their own self-interest. Among those who remain, this may be the most common outlook, and ethical egoism offers a convenient moral justification for their selfishness.

There are a number of reasons why a survivor might be tempted to adopt this view. First, who knows your interests better than yourself? When you try to help others, you might well get it wrong and end up not helping them at all. According to this view, perhaps everyone would be better off if they dedicated themselves solely to acting in their own individual self-interest.

Within the context of a zombie apocalypse, when people are just struggling to survive, is it reasonable to assume that you really cannot know what others need? What if your comrades are locked in a desperate battle against the undead? Can you justify fleeing to safety, or shooting your comrades to slow down the horde, by saying that you could not really be sure that helping them in their battle would have served their interests? Also, notwithstanding all of the difficulties that living within a group of survivors brings with it (e.g., danger of theft, murder, rape, etc.), it is much better to be in a group than trying to survive on one's own. This is the central theme of the next chapter.

Another reason to favor ethical egoism is that altruism might not seem to value the individual *enough*. If I am required to endanger myself in order to save others, for example, by offering my sturdy staff in support of the common cause, how do my interests matter at all? By requiring me to fight and perhaps die—or worse—have I not been turned into a sacrificial lamb thrown onto the altar of the infected?

Selfishness may be the only way of ensuring that I am sufficiently valued as an individual, that my interests are properly considered. Consider the same argument in terms of happiness. Assume that human beings *ought* to be happy. This is not so strange. We often tell loved ones that we "just want you to be happy," and some of the philosophers that we discuss later go so far as to make happiness the *only* thing that is valuable for its own sake. If I have an obligation to be happy, but altruism (in contrast to egoism) requires me to sacrifice my own happiness for the happiness of others, does it not frustrate this fundamental moral obligation?

The problem with this defense of ethical egoism is that it mischaracterizes the opposing view. Altruism, as we will see in later chapters, requires that you weigh your own interests *equally* with the interests of others, not that you ignore your own interests entirely in favor of the interests of others. In fact, using the above example, ethical egoism would require that you ignore the interests of others entirely as long as promoting those interests do not somehow promote your own.

One final reason one might be tempted to endorse ethical egoism is that it provides a single principle from which the obligations of common sense morality can be derived. One ought not to rape, murder, or pillage other survivors since this would make it more likely that these same calamities would be revisited upon you. As one might suspect, nothing makes another survivor more apt to kill you than killing someone that survivor cares about. This generates a version of the "Golden Rule": do unto others as you would have them do unto you. If ethical egoism generates the Golden Rule, it can't be that bad, right?

Alas, there are problems with this defense of ethical egoism as well. The Golden Rule is not really a *rule* from the ethical egoist's perspective, since it ought to be broken whenever doing so is necessary to pursue one's self-interest. For example, if your loved one has something I need to survive (food, weapons, etc.) and I can kill your loved one and get away with it—perhaps by killing you as well—it would clearly be in my self-interest to do so. In fact, ethical egoism would require that I ignore the commands of common sense morality, or any other morality for that matter, if doing so is necessary to pursue my self-interest.

Even if we reject all of the reasons for accepting ethical egoism, the view could nonetheless still be true. To give a parallel example, even though all the various cures for the infection have failed that does not entail that the infection cannot be cured. There are good objections, however, to ethical egoism as a normative moral theory. An initial worry, already suggested above, is that ethical egoism violates our common sense moral beliefs. Not only is nothing wrong in itself with murdering, raping, or pillaging, but these actions may well be *obligatory* if doing them are necessary for you to satisfy your own self-interest. There are no moral rights, for example, life, liberty, property, if ethical egoism is true. Of course, the ethical egoist might well be happy to bite this bullet as long as no one else knows they are biting it! This is a point worth emphasizing: If you are convinced of ethical egoism, you will want to keep these convictions secret, since others will not help you if they are likewise convinced that you will stab them in the back as soon as doing so would serve your self-interest.

An even more serious worry with ethical egoism is that it is paradoxical. Assume that human happiness requires, at least in part, genuine loving relationships with others—friends, family, etc. As I will argue below and in later chapters, these relationships are necessary for human flourishing which is what makes surviving the apocalypse worthwhile. Since the fall of civilization, these relationships have become as valuable as they are rare. Even so, survivors have consistently sought out others to try to form these kinds of bonds again. One might say that the motivation for these relationships is self-interest. I am happier with others than I am alone. Consider what maintaining these relationships—especially in this violent hellscape—requires. Must we not at least sometimes promote the self-interest of others over our own in order to maintain these relationships? Diving into a ravenous mob with only a staff to protect me is never in my individual self-interest, though it might well be necessary to protect those that I care about and whose happiness is integral to my own.

A final reason to reject ethical egoism is that it arbitrarily makes my own interests all-important. Why are my own interests intrinsically more important than your interests or the interests of anyone else? As the victim notes in the field exercise above, just like racism, sexism, or any number of other "isms," the *selfism* of ethical egoism makes arbitrary moral distinctions between people. Just as it is unclear how the color of my skin or my gender could imbue me with a special moral status, it is likewise unclear how being *me* gives me a special moral status. Not only are we not motivated solely by our own self-interest (contrary to psychological egoism), the ethical egoist has given us no reason to think that we ought to be so motivated.

3. Field exercise: Safe zone

COMMUNITY, STABILITY, SURVIVAL

—MILE HIGH SAFE ZONE MOTTO

The stadium was completely full, but people were chill—a refugee camp turned *Burning Man*. Although there were *way* too many of us, we did our best not to get in one another's way. The stadium sound system did its best as well. The Zombie Nation jock rock had thankfully—given the circumstances—been replaced by a rock-steady Reggae soundtrack. A guy in fatigues was attempting to squeeze a garbage can up a stairway packed with people. He recognized me.

"What's up? Looking good!" he said. I must have been swaying to the music.

"Hey, McDermott, where's your gun?" I yelled over the din of Bob Marley's "Concrete Jungle."

"Oh, that thing just gets in the way." He was smiling cheerfully as he continued his Sisyphean task.

The soldiers had started off as crowd control, but as the days had stretched into weeks, they had turned more into stadium workers. Cleaning up garbage, cooking food, keeping the water running … that last bit was the most important part.

I decided to give McDermott a hand and pushed the garbage can from behind as we climbed the stairs that led to the upper deck. Once we made it to the top, we dumped our load over the side into a mass of the undead—as crowded together as the living within—but a mass that reached from the mountains to the stadium and then on to the city. There must have been millions of them. Although the stadium was massive, it felt like an ark floating on a sea of undeath.

I looked back down the stands to where the field had once been. The authorities had turned it into an amusement park of sorts. Fountains, pools, and water slides sat between the hash marks. When you were down there, you felt great. It was like being a kid on summer vacation. At times, it was easy to forget that an apocalypse was on. The music, the water, the sunlight—they all conspired to create a happy illusion. It wasn't just a matter of keeping clean, hydrated, and distracted. The *water* was itself the prophylactic. Like sunscreen, it had to be applied constantly to

FIGURE 6 Stadium surrounded by zombies.

ensure that none of us would start to turn from the latent virus that we all carried within.

Before the stadium was surrounded, the soldiers would sometimes go out looking for survivors, mainly to keep those inside the stadium from trying find loved ones on their own. That's how McDermott found me … or rather, I found him. Although I *looked* like I had turned, he was *acting* like it. He was huddled in the street, convulsing with chills and nausea. I didn't see any dark lines on his skin, however, so I dragged him back to the stadium. The only reason the soldiers didn't shoot me is because they saw him hanging from my side. They took us straight to the water where both our conditions washed away as soon as we slid back into it. Eventually, no one even wanted to leave, though this choice was made for us once enough of the undead arrived at our gates.

McDermott turned to me, "Hey, didn't there used to be more people up here?"

I looked around. The only people I saw were alone, hunched over, rocking back and forth. Almost everyone was crowded into the lower bowl and the field. It was like Spring Break at Daytona Beach. The field was absolutely packed—a single glistening mass of undulating human happiness—as "Jamming" played on the PA system.

More people kept pouring onto the field which pushed those already there, slowly but surely, into the ground-level concourse. McDermott and I ran over to the edge of the upper deck to see what was happening. People were getting pushed closer and closer to the metal gates that held back the army of the undead. Some people noticed their proximity, but then just turned around and kept on dancing.

"Jesus, Mary, and Joseph … What the hell are they doing?" McDermott asked, suddenly quite serious.

"What does it matter?" I replied, swaying to the music myself—"We're protected from whatever the undead have."

As if to prove the point, one guy started dancing with the ghouls on the other side of the gate. He would grab one zombie's decaying hands extending through the grates and sway for a moment in its embrace before spinning away to his next undead partner.

The next time he tried to spin, however, several hands grabbed him from behind and pulled him against the gate. Sensing the living flesh that was within its collective grasp, the undead mass surged, breaking through the gate and tearing him limb from limb.

As the undead rushed in, they found a buffet of compliant dining options. People were convinced of their immunity and physically numb to what was happening. As the mass of the undead mingled with and started to consume the mass of the living, the PA switched over to UB40 singing "Red Red Wine."

McDermott was screaming into his radio. "Breach! Breach! We need an airlift immediately! We are on the upper-deck—section 542."

"What's the rush, man?" said a relaxed voice on the other end. The radio crackled followed by some incoherent yelling and a couple of rifle shots that we didn't need the radio to hear.

Both of us looked in horror at the orgy of violence below. It was like a Hieronymus Bosch painting brought to life—or rather undeath—on the canvas of the former football field. Everything was painted in a crimson palate. The fountains and pools were filled with gore and dismembered bodies, the still living and undead, writhing in a collective mixture of agony and ecstasy.

McDermott grabbed me and started yelling in my face. "There is no protection. They were lying to you … lying to all of us. It's just synthetic opiates … trying to keep people happy and calm … When the undead get you … there's no stopping the virus … you become one of them!"

Although the upper deck remained largely empty, we could see those the next level down working their way up—either fleeing the chaos below or seeking the fresh flesh that the field no longer offered. As the crowd ran up the stairs, the living were caught, one by one, from behind and replaced by cracked up versions of themselves or their undead pursuers.

McDermott and I backed up slowly until we reached the last row of seats on the upper deck. I looked at him with steely resolve, "Better to be dead … than the alternative."

I stepped onto the final guardrail at the top of the stadium. At that moment, I heard a deafening roar behind me. The cacophony combined with a gush of wind that made me lose my balance.

As I started to fall, I felt a tight embrace from above and felt another from below. McDermott was hanging from my legs. We were in the air, but weren't falling. We were going up and away from the undead—now tumbling over the edge of the upper deck we had just escaped. I looked up to see my rescuer and the Army chopper to which he was connected by a cable.

The man was screaming. "We can't winch this weight!"

I felt McDermott's grip loosening. "NO!" I screamed and grabbed for his hand. But by the time I reached down, he had let go.

I'll never understand why. Maybe he thought he was paying me back. As he floated down to the awaiting horde, I saw him smile. There was no cure, but he gave me the most precious gift that remained—time.

As the cable winched me up, and the chopper turned, I noticed the sun setting over the mountains. Their long shadows obscured the endless horde of undead that still pursued us below. It could have been mistaken for one of those massive buffalo herds of the nineteenth century. Perhaps, I thought to myself, the world was returning to a semblance of what it once was and was destined to be again after we were gone.

4. Moral naturalism and intuitionism

Our current task is to make room for moral value within a landscape overrun by armies of the undead. We began by considering a number of moral anti-realist views—cultural relativism, DCT, subjectivism—before turning to ethical egoism, which is itself a form of moral realism. All of these views, however, seem to face intractable problems. This section will explore some other forms of moral realism in the hopes of finding a view on moral value that avoids the problems that the other positions we have considered face. The goal is to find at least one objective moral value, that is, something that is valuable regardless of belief or opinion.

One form of moral realism is **moral naturalism**. The moral naturalist believes that there are objective moral values, and these values can be explained in terms of natural properties. Although ethical egoism is a form of moral naturalism—what is in the self-interest of an individual is a natural feature of that individual—another common form of moral naturalism is **hedonism**, which claims that pleasure or happiness is the sole intrinsic value, the only thing valuable for its own sake. The value of almost anything can be explained in terms of either it causing happiness itself or its being a means toward something else that causes happiness. Why do you destroy the zombie that is attacking you? Why do you forage for food? Why do you reinforce the walls of your stronghold? You do these things because you want to survive. Why do you want to survive? If you do want to survive, you almost certainly are doing it because you think things can get better than they are now. What does it mean for things to get "better"? More food, more comfort, more security—all things that will ultimately make you *happier* than you are now. Alternatively, if you are putting a gun to your head, your reasons for doing so probably boil down to avoiding *unhappiness*. You think your situation will only get worse, ending in being devoured by the undead, provided you do not deprive them of the opportunity. In either case, the thing that you ultimately value is happiness.

The hedonist can also grant that there are many paths to a good life and that what makes individuals happy will differ from person to person. The hedonist insists neither on one single conception of happiness nor on a single means of achieving it. Although the hedonist tolerates different conceptions of happiness, she does not tolerate different conceptions of the good. Again, for the hedonist, happiness or pleasure is the *sole* intrinsic good. There are good reasons, however, for thinking that other things are valuable besides happiness.

Even before civilization fell apart, we had already devised very sophisticated ways of escaping it. Virtual reality technology has reached a point such that you could enter a gaming environment that felt just like the real world. You even had the option of blocking your memory while in the game so that you would believe that you were in the real world as you played.

Imagine you were to find one of those machines today, in a well-protected space constantly supplied by solar power. What if you could reprogram it so that all you experienced was "happiness"? Let this term denote whatever would stand—for you—in starkest contrast to the rotting world you actually inhabit. Let's assume that there are IVs available and you could plug yourself into this machine indefinitely without suffering physical harm. Would you do it? I can only assume that given how *painful* the actual world is for most of us, many would prefer the indefinite *pleasure* of this virtual one. Even so, there would be sacrifices involved and getting clear on what these are can help us to understand what else might be valuable besides pleasure.

Although you might have the *experience* of doing things in this virtual world, you are not *actually* doing them. You may have the experience of relationships with others within the game you create, but those relationships are not genuine and the character you cultivate through your actions is counterfeit as well. Even if you chose to plug yourself into the machine to escape the horrors of one's actual existence, giving up on reality requires sacrificing things that also seem to be valuable regardless of their impact on the pleasure or pain you feel.

Likewise, consider the situation described in the field exercise above. In order to minimize the number of people at risk of being turned, the government created giant safe zones—usually in stadiums that could be easily fortified—where large numbers of the uninfected were brought. Since the conditions were crowded and there was a fear that people would leave and try to come back (increasing the risk of infection) these safe zones intentionally addicted everyone to an opiate placed into the water supply. The water was carefully controlled by the authorities, and people were told that the water was treated with a special chemical that would keep them protected from infection as long as they continued to drink it. Not only did the drug make people happy and compliant, but also their desire for the drug eventually ensured that they would stay in the safe zone. When the zombies finally broke through the defenses—as they always do when they reach sufficient numbers—they found themselves in the middle of an intoxicated smorgasbord of the living. Because of both the drug and the false belief that they were immune from infection, people did not feel the need to fight back. Like the virtual reality machine, these safe zones—now turned into hot zones—illustrate that something other than happiness or pleasure is valuable. In this case, it would seem that *autonomy* is important. Even though the people in the safe zones were happier without their autonomy, their lives were impoverished without it. One might argue that the only reason we judge them this way is because they were *unhappy* in the end, for example, as they felt themselves turning while the zombies gnawed away at their numbed bodies. Even if the zombies had never broken through, however, it still seems that we would feel the same way. There is something important missing from a life of happiness without freedom.

The important thing to note about these counterexamples is that they do not show that happiness is *not* intrinsically valuable, only that it is not the *only* thing that is intrinsically valuable. Someone who is a moral naturalist can make this concession even though it does require giving up on hedonism as providing a complete definition of the good.

Depending on what else is considered intrinsically valuable, one may also have to give up on moral naturalism. Perhaps, there are objective moral values that cannot be explained in terms of natural properties. The natural features of our world could always have been different than what they are. In a completely undead world, for example, there may be no such thing as pleasure and pain, since there would be no creature that could experience these sensations. In a world without pleasure, is pleasure intrinsically valuable? There are certain facts, however, that could not be different than what they are, for example, $2 + 2 = 4$. Although this truth can be illustrated in the natural world—two zombies and two zombies make a horde of four zombies—the truths of math and logic do not *depend* on the natural world. Likewise, there may be moral truths that are similar to mathematical and logical truths. The **moral intuitionist** argues for this position, holding that there are objective moral values but these values cannot be defined in terms of natural properties. Moral intuitionism is a form of moral realism, one that often compares objective moral truths to mathematical and logical truths. The intrinsic value of human freedom might be a good example. Autonomy could be intrinsically valuable without being reducible to any natural feature of human beings insofar as all these natural features are governed by natural laws. We will return to this theme again in Chapter 4 when discussing Kant's moral theory.

In what follows, we will assume that moral realism is true. Some things are of objective moral value, even in a zombie apocalypse. Instead of focusing myopically on *pleasure*, however, I would suggest that we broaden our conception of objective moral value to include all things that contribute to human *flourishing*. I will argue that this is a type of rational activity, in accordance with a certain kind of character, which allows you to achieve your individual goals while also cultivating meaningful relationships with other survivors. It is hard to think of any value—feeling pleasure, having true beliefs, being free, etc.—that does not connect back to human flourishing in some way. As mentioned above, it is flourishing, broadly construed, that makes surviving valuable. Without the possibility of human flourishing, it is unclear why one would choose to survive rather than join the ranks of the undead since this possibility is what sets us apart from our undead counterparts. The theories that we will turn to in subsequent chapters all try to determine what we ought to *do* or the kind of survivors that we ought to *be* assuming that there are objective moral values. Although they disagree on what the "oughts" are, as well as what is necessary for human flourishing, they all value flourishing nonetheless. Examining and deciding between these different theories will help us to determine how to go beyond surviving and begin flourishing in this undead world.

Summary

Like cultural relativism and DCT, subjectivism is also a form of relativism, one that makes moral value dependent on the belief of the individual. Although ethical egoism might seem closely aligned with subjectivism, it is actually a form of moral realism, but it likewise faces serious problems as the story about the hunter illustrates. After discussing the different forms of moral realism—both intuitionist and naturalist—I argued that survivors should agree that human flourishing (rather than simply pleasure) is an objective moral value since it provides the reason why we should still struggle to survive the apocalypse.

Further study

- Ayer, Alfred Jules. *Language, Truth, and Logic.* Harmondsworth: Penguin Books, 1936.
  - See chapter 6 "A Critique of Ethics and Theology" for a philosophical

defense of emotivism, that is, the view that moral claims are neither true nor false, but are rather the expression of emotions.

- Blackburn, Simon. *Ruling Passions: A Theory of Practical Reasoning*. Oxford: Oxford University Press, 1998.
  - See p. 49 for the passage that inspires the quote that starts this chapter, one which poses a significant concern for moral naturalism.
- Hobbes, Thomas. *Leviathan*. 1668. Edited with introduction. Indianapolis: Hackett, 1994.
  - See chapter 14 "Of the First and Second Natural Laws and of Contracts" for a philosophical defense of a position that approaches psychological egoism. Hobbes argues that everything we desire must contain *some* good for ourselves, but not that everything we desire must contain *only* good for ourselves.
- Huxley, Aldus. *Brave New World*. London: Chatto and Windus, 1932.
  - Although there is no zombie threat, the society depicted in this novel uses a drug called "soma" to keep the population placid and compliant. The stadium described in Chapter 2.3 used a similar approach.
- Mackie, John Leslie. *Ethics: Inventing Right and Wrong*. London: Penguin, 1977.
  - See chapter 1 "The Subjectivity of Values" for a defense of moral nihilism/ skepticism. This is the view that moral properties would be required to make moral judgments true, but since there are no moral properties, all moral judgments are false.
- Mill, John Stuart. *Utlitarianism*. 1863. With related remarks from Mill's other writings. Indianapolis: Hackett, 2017.
  - See chapter 2 "What Utilitarianism Is" and chapter 4 "Of What Sort of Proof the Principle of Utility Is Susceptible" for some compelling reasons to accept hedonism—a form of moral naturalism—and one of the three central tenets of utilitarianism.
- Mogk, Matt. *Everything You Ever Wanted to Know about Zombies*. New York: Gallery Books, 2011.
  - See chapter 19 "The Human Threat" for how humans, driven by their own self-interest, can be a greater threat than the zombies themselves.
- Moore, George Edward. *Principia Ethica*. Cambridge: Cambridge University Press, 1903.
  - See chapter 1 "The Subject-Matter of Ethics" for an argument against moral naturalism and in favor of intuitionism. This is the view that moral values cannot be defined in terms of natural properties though they are still objective and meaningful.
- Nozick, Robert. *Anarchy, State, and Utopia*. New York: Basic Books, 1974.

- His Experience Machine (pp. 42–44) serves as the inspiration for the virtual reality machine discussed in this chapter. Although Nozick intends for it to be a counterexample to hedonism, when one must choose between a painful post-apocalyptic actuality and thoroughly pleasurable virtual reality, the right decision is less clear.
- Rand, Ayn. *The Virtue of Selfishness*. New York: New American Library, 1964.
  - In addition to containing the inspiration for the quote that begins Chapter 2.1, this book contains a number of essays arguing against altruism and for ethical egoism.
- *The Walking Dead*, [TV Program].
  - Although he justifies it in terms of saving others, Shane shoots Otis in the leg in order to save himself from an oncoming horde in season 2.3 "Save the Last One."

3 CREATING AN ESCAPE FROM THE STATE OF ZOMBIES

Whatsoever therefore is consequent to a time of war, where every man is enemy to every man; the same is consequent to the time, wherein men live without other security against zombies, than what their own strength, and their own invention shall furnish them withal. In such condition, there is no account of time; no arts; no letters; no society; and which is worst of all, continual fear, and danger of violent undeath; and the life of man, solitary, poor, nasty, brutish, and, for the lucky, short.

—THE MATTER, FORM, AND POWER OF SURVIVOR COMMUNITIES

Before the outbreak, all of us lived in societies of one form or another. Life was a lot easier. I had the cushy job—even more so in retrospect—of a philosophy professor. This was a highly specialized field for which I went to college for far too many years. All of life's wants and needs were at my fingertips. If I was hungry, I could order food and someone would bring it to my door. If I was concerned for my safety, I could call the police and they would come to my home. If I was in medical distress, an ambulance would whisk me to the hospital. Things are now, of course, quite different. Each of us must provide for ourselves. If I am hungry, I must hunt, gather, forage, or steal. If I am threatened by another survivor or the undead, I must rely on my own strength and ingenuity to save me. If I am injured, I must tend to my wounds or resign myself to turning.

The mere thought of going to college—a life of arts and letters—is increasingly unimaginable. Although we can all agree that life was a lot better when we had societies, the **contractarian** position in Ethics goes a step further claiming that morality is itself a set of rules that individuals agree upon in order to reap the benefits of social living.

1. Field exercise: Prisoner's dilemma

The sun was already starting to dip toward the horizon, but I had yet to find a place to hole-up. I had been cycling all day trying to escape my memories of the previous night. We thought we could keep them caged up, using them for our own needs, but their needs proved greater. Overrun from within, their moans quickly replaced our screams in the darkness.

Although I could spot them at a distance and avoid them by day, by night I could peddle right into a horde without knowing it. They don't start moaning until they *sense* your living flesh; I have no idea how. What I do know is that the erupting chorus of moans would be the last thing I would hear. Cresting the next hill, I spotted a small town in the valley below. Seeing neither obvious evidence of survivors nor the undead, I decided to investigate.

My curiosity was almost immediately rewarded: three yellow triangles against a faded black background promised safety for the night. These Cold War relics were rarely maintained and even more rarely marked, but they had thick concrete walls and strong steel doors that would offer more than adequate protection against the undead. If these structures could protect their inhabitants from a nuclear explosion, what would they have to fear from the rotting limbs of some shambling corpses? Like the trademark of a luxury hotel, the signs for these fallout shelters represented the gold-standard for overnight survivor accommodation.

On the door was a schematic of the shelter. There were two entrances on either side of the building, "Harry S. Truman Elementary" in this case, with a 20 x 20 foot shelter in the middle. The shelter itself likewise had two doors with a hallway that surrounded it and led to the two entrances. Following best practices for blast protection, the doors opened outward into the hallway so that they could not be collapsed into the shelter. In addition, the doors could be latched to the opposing wall to block the hallway, creating clear paths for ingress/egress from the two entrances.

I tried the door to the entrance and my heart skipped a beat when it yielded. After peering through the wired glass window to make sure nothing was waiting on the other side, I swung it open and walked down the darkening hallway. The door to the shelter itself was closed. I opened it and looked with horror across a writhing orgy of gore to see another survivor, framed like a mirror image, in the doorway opposite my own. Save for her dark hair, she could have been my sibling in another life. The gore appeared to rise from the floor as a single organism. The ghouls, bathed uniformly in the blood of their former feast, turned outward to face the doorways and moaned as one. As the carrion mass spread outward toward the open doors, both of us slammed them shut simultaneously.

FIGURE 7 Zombies contained inside room.

Sitting down, I put my back against the door just as the moaning mass slammed into it, pushing me into the hallway. Putting my feet against the wall, I pushed back with all my might, locking my knees so that the door would stay closed. Although the collective force on the other side quickly grew and almost overwhelmed me, the pounding pressure soon stabilized into a throbbing though manageable agony. These zombies were fresh—mostly cracked up—with a strength that an older generation would not possess. The pounding was rhythmic, as if the heart of the massive infected organism were pushing up against the door struggling to break free. As long as this beating infected heart was divided between me and my counterpart, however, I knew I could hold out.

At the same time, I had to wonder what I was holding out for. It's likely that there was a schematic at the other entrance too, which means that she would know the layout as well. I examined the wall opposite the groaning door. There were concrete stops built into it. If I let the door go, it could open no further than 90°. The hallway would be blocked, providing me with an easy escape, but dooming her to almost certain (un)death. Before she would feel the pressure letting up on the door, the ravenous horde would have already turned the corner, blocking her direct route of escape. She could try to open her own door, but the zombies would already be tearing into her flesh, pushing the door closed from the outside.

A rush of fear washed over me. Her thoughts must be racing in the same direction as my own! I felt an almost uncontrollable urge to run toward the entrance as fast as I could—to hell with the other person. She might resemble me, but she isn't me! As my legs started to buckle, another thought popped into my mind replacing the flood of fear with an icy dread. If both of us released our doors at the same time, both of us would be caught by the now divided horde rounding the corners before either of us could escape. I looked right, fully expecting to see the ravenous creatures descending upon me. All I saw, however, was the fading daylight trickling through the window at the entrance.

For the moment, dread had won the battle for my will, leaving me frozen, my feet firmly planted against the opposing wall. The pounding behind me drew my thoughts from my present predicament to the fates of those who now aimed to devour me. How did so many undead get into the bunker? Perhaps the survivors had unwittingly admitted someone in the early stages of infection only to find themselves later attacked from within. It seemed impossible that the undead could have opened the door from the outside. Even if they had sensed the living flesh, they would have just piled up against the door, allowing the survivors to escape through the opposite door.

Shaking my head to focus again on the present, I decided to try to communicate with my would-be sister. Shouting with all the force I could muster, I yelled:

"Hey! You hear me? Just hang in there and keep your door closed! I'll do the same! Someone's bound to find this place!"

I struggled to hear myself over the din of moans and fleshy thumping behind me. If I couldn't even hear myself, what reason was there to think she could hear me? Even if she could hear me, what reason would she have to believe what I was saying? Isn't that just the kind of thing that someone would say before they let go of their door and made a run for the exit? Ruefully, I acknowledged that I wouldn't have believed me were I in her shoes.

I looked again toward the window. The light reflecting off the concrete had turned from a straw yellow to a burnished orange. Soon the light would darken into nothing at all. If my fate is already sealed, I thought to myself, perhaps it is better not to see it coming in the inky blackness. I pulled myself out of this deepening sense of melancholy by remembering that both of us had been drawn to this location by the signs outside the building, signs that any survivor would be searching for at this time of day. Perhaps, it was just a matter of time before help arrived on the scene. Surely, with a few more weapons at hand, we could turn the advantage on our undead attackers. Even so, any survivor who had made it this long would never wander by choice at night and as the light faded so did my hopes for rescue.

Notwithstanding the fear and dread that stabbed at my consciousness, the growing darkness and rhythmic pulsing on my back were lulling me to sleep. The pounding was having the effect of a Swedish massage and the din of moans served the function of a white noise machine. It had been a long day after all, and I had an even longer night to look forward to, assuming I could make it through the night. As I started to slip into unconsciousness, the massage suddenly stopped, and the moans switched direction.

I felt the sharp pain of betrayal. Although we had never *explicitly* agreed—how could we?—to hold our respective doors shut until rescue, since we had made it this long, I felt like there was an *implicit* agreement, one she had now violated. My fate was sealed. I needed to resign myself to be eaten alive. I looked blindly in the darkness toward the exit, praying to see through the window that flash of light the bunker had originally been designed to protect its occupants from ever having to see. Instead I heard a shout:

"Get down!"

The imagined flash of light was replaced by the reality of periodic flashes framing the exploding heads of the undead—momentarily frozen in time—just a few feet from where I now cowered prone on the floor. The report of the rifle was deafening in the concrete hallway. The eighth "POP" was followed by the distinctive "PING" of an M1 Garand. My sister—now savior—switched on a headlamp to inspect her handiwork. Although it seemed like she had been firing blindly, all of the zombies—thankfully only eight—had been shot in the head.

"Sorry I waited this long, but I needed to make sure you were worth it. No way was I going to hole up with somebody who might unleash the undead on me in the middle of the night."

My better self—the resemblance really was striking—paused before continuing, "Some folks are vicious by nature while others are vicious by choice."

Opening the door, she flashed the light inside revealing several crates of ammunition in a now otherwise empty room. "The last guy couldn't help it. Even though he didn't tell us he was infected, he didn't want to hurt us. He just didn't want to die alone."

Once both of us were inside, she turned to close the doors. Slowly turning back, she said, "The ones you have to worry about are those that choose to be this way."

She never finished the turn, but instead fell to the ground, a knife protruding from a body that under different circumstances could have been my own. An M1 had always been more reliable than friendship and, in the present context, far more valuable. As the life was passing out of my rescuer turned victim, I confessed:

"I don't know what 'vice' or 'virtue' could possibly mean anymore. There is just survival. It's not personal. I just need your gun."

With that, I started laying out the crates to form a makeshift bed. Before settling down, however, I made sure to stab her through the temple so that I would not awake to a similar surprise as my better self. Although I would have preferred a world in which I was not alone, in this worst of all possible worlds, I would have to settle for a good night's sleep.

2. The state of zombies is a state of war

Living without society—in a state of zombies—is arguably the worst possible place that one could be. The philosopher Thomas Hobbes would certainly agree. He argues that the **state of nature**—people living on their own without the protection of civil government—is a state of war. His argument is straightforward. People are more or less equal in strength and intelligence. In the state of nature, there is a scarcity of the resources that people need to survive. Since there is a scarcity of resources and people are more or less equal, they are going to compete over those resources. Just as in the above story, if you are competing against someone for something that both of you need to survive, you aren't going to trust the other person and you will do everything—up to and including killing the other person—to survive. Even if you are not *actually* at war with another survivor, the specter of violent death is *always* there, and that's why the state of nature is a state of war according to Hobbes.

For example, whereas I could get almost any kind of food delivered to me before the outbreak, the vast agricultural, communication, and transportation infrastructure that conspired to bring that piping hot pizza to my door ceased to exist with the end of civil society. Without its protections—police, military, etc.—people stopped farming. Why would you farm if your crops could be stolen in the middle of the night? Without the farmers, there were no ingredients for my pizza. The electrical grid did not last long and without that there was no cellular service and so no way to order my pizza. Without gas stations being refilled, roads being maintained, and with the constant fear of carjacking, there was no one to bring me my pizza. As any survivor knows, in our post-apocalyptic hellscape, people routinely kill one another *over* food and, as we have seen, even *for* food. Even if no one—or thing—is trying to turn you into a human slice right now, the threat is always there. The state of zombies is a state of war.

3. Cooperation and community

For Hobbes, even though people's actions in the state of nature might seem horrific, there actually isn't anything morally *wrong* with what people are doing. As a contractarian, Hobbes believes that there is no moral right or wrong in the absence of civil society. In the state of zombies, moral rules are what rational survivors would accept on the condition that all other survivors accept them as well. Without an *agreement* (contract) that specifies what is morally right and wrong, as well as the mechanisms that society has to *enforce* this contract—police, courts, etc.—survivors have license to do whatever they perceive to be in their own self-interest.

To see the problem, consider the **prisoner's dilemma**. The illustration and field exercise at the beginning of this chapter examine their plight. Two survivors imprisoned by a ravenous zombie horde have managed to contain it in a room behind two opposing doors that is surrounded by a hallway. When these doors are open, they block the hallway. If one of the survivors blocks the hallway with their door, this survivor can escape, but the other survivor will be devoured (and vice versa). They have the choice of either releasing their door to escape, or holding the door closed with the knowledge that they would eventually be rescued. If both release their respective doors, both will be devoured. The best outcome *overall* would be achieved by both holding their doors and waiting, at least until morning, for eventual rescue. The best outcome for each *individually*, however, is to release their door and run off while the other survivor dutifully holds their own door closed until devoured by the horde. Of course, if they both reason this way, focusing on individual self-interest, they will both end up undead! In the field exercise, the prisoner's dilemma is initially resolved through firepower. One of the survivors saves the other. Ultimately, however, the power of self-interest proves too strong for the other survivor. This survivor kills the savior in order to claim the gun for themselves. I say "kill" and not "murder" since from Hobbes perspective—a perspective shared by the killer—there is nothing morally wrong with the killer's action. The survivor is simply pursuing their own self-interest which is neither right nor wrong in the absence of civil society and its coercive power.

This helps to illustrate why enforcement is vital for contractarianism. Enforcement is what ensures that people do what is best for them *collectively* rather than simply as *individuals*. Since the best outcome for *me* is for everyone else to follow the moral rules except for me, there must be some mechanism that ensures I follow the moral rules producing the best outcome *overall*. Consider the small survivor communities that came into being after all the major governments fell to the zombie hordes. Even though these communities provided a degree of security, basic necessities were almost always in short supply. If I happened to be the trusted quartermaster of the community, the best thing from my perspective would be for everyone else to respect the rules of rationing while I took a little extra for myself—stealing—which would break one of those rules that we all ostensibly agreed to live by. As long as I didn't get caught—unlikely since I was the quartermaster—I would be a lot better off than if I had followed the rules like everyone else.

This problem of **free-riders**—people who enjoy the benefits of social living without the sacrifices associated with it—is what enforcement mechanisms are supposed to solve. The reason the quartermaster should not consider stealing goods from the community stores is because the punishment for being caught is so severe—e.g., being handed over to the undead and then shot when turned—that the quartermaster does not view it as being in their interest to take the risk, even if the risk is relatively low. If the protagonist in the field exercise had a similar fear, it is far less likely that they would have chosen to kill their former savior. In fact, for the contractarian, the existence of a community that has the power to punish this individual is what would make it a case of (moral) murder rather than (amoral) killing.

There are a number of advantages to the contractarian theory of Ethics. First, we are only bound to follow those rules that are of mutual benefit, for example a prohibition on theft or murder, but are not bound to follow rules that do not benefit everyone equally or do not benefit anyone at all. For example, when some rules are discriminatory, those who are the targets of discrimination are not bound to follow these rules. Second, the contractarian theory explains why it is rational for us to follow the moral rules, namely, because we benefit from following the rules and will be punished if we do not. This would have been the fate of the killer in the field exercise, were the killer to live in a society of rules that were enforced. Third, it explains why we are not bound to follow the rules if someone else has broken them. When someone has exempted themselves from the rules that everyone else is bound by, we are not obligated to follow the rules, for example the rule that prohibits murder, when dealing with the rule-breaker. Although it would be wrong to kill an individual under normal circumstances, it would be acceptable if someone, for example, the protagonist in the field exercise, has violated the moral rules everyone else abides by. Finally, you cannot be expected to accept rules that you cannot expect others to follow. For example, a rule that requires a member of the community to sacrifice themselves to the undead in order to save the community as a whole is not one you could reasonably expect a member of the community to follow. You cannot reasonably expect people to throw themselves to a hungry horde for the sake of others. The visceral fear of being eaten alive would be sufficient motivation for most not to comply.

4. Objections to contractarianism

One classic objection to contractarianism is that the *original* contract is a mere heuristic device, a historical fiction, which cannot obligate anyone today. Before society was torn apart by the outbreak, with the exception of naturalized citizens and the like, few of us *explicitly* agreed to the social contract. That is to say, few of us signed a piece of paper or made a verbal oath to support and defend our country's constitution and laws. Even if you had always lived in your society, it is hard to say that you even *implicitly* agreed to live by the social contract that governed your society. Although most of us remained in the countries we were born into, the fact that we did not leave does not entail that we actually agreed with the country's constitution and laws. Most people did not have the opportunity—economic, political, etc.—to leave the societies within which they are born. Put simply, just because you find yourself playing a certain game, does not entail that you ever wanted to play it. The most one could say, before society fell, was that the moral rules are those that rational people *would* accept under the condition that others accept them as well. Rational people would accept these rules because they mutually benefit those that live under them. Although this is still the case, most of us have been compelled by the communities that have adopted us to explicitly agree through some kind of community oath to the rules of the community. Unless you are coerced at the muzzle of a gun, in which case it really isn't "agreement," the main reason you agree is that you think that you will be better off following the rules of the community than you would be without its protections, fending for yourself against the hungry legions of undead. Put in terms of the previous chapter, when everyone is following the rules, it is more likely that you—and they—will attain the individual and social goods that constitute human flourishing.

Even when we have not been required to explicitly agree, the *implicit* agreement is pretty clear. If you don't like the rules of the community, you are free to try and survive beyond its walls. Good luck! It still is rather strange, however, to think that you are *only* obligated to do what you have agreed to do either explicitly or implicitly. Is it morally permissible for me to kill whomever I would like as long as I never agreed not to kill anyone? Again, just as it was in society before the outbreak, the contractarian could say that you are bound to whatever rules that free and rational beings *would* agree to for mutual benefit. Even so, as the field exercise that starts this chapter illustrates, any agreement—either explicit or implicit—is non-binding in the absence of enforcement. The community has to enforce its rules in order for you to be bound by them.

Here is another worry with contractarianism: What if there is *disagreement* on what rules everyone should *agree* to follow? When deciding on the rules, should we consider a perfectly free and rational agent who is unaware of anything that makes their lives uniquely their own? Put differently, should we only agree to those rules that individuals would agree to follow if they were ignorant of their personal situation in this zombie-infested world? It would be much easier to figure out what these rules would be if we did not have to take into account all of the features that make us the particular survivors that we are. For example, I am relatively weak, often hungry, and until recently generally terrified of being devoured by the undead. Someone strong, well fed, and with a more sanguine disposition in the face of violent undeath might choose different rules than me. The contractarian does not provide clear guidance on how we should decide such disputes and only seems to avoid these disputes by distancing potential contractors from the *actual* individuals they are. Although a fine strategy for daydreaming oneself out of the apocalypse, it is of little use once one awakes firmly back within it.

Even assuming that we could come to a consensus on what the rules are supposed to be, there could be situations when the rules come into conflict with one another. One could imagine rational beings agreeing, for mutual benefit, to a rule that prohibits stealing as well as a rule that requires helping others. In many communities, however, these two rules could come into conflict with one another, especially when resources run low. If the only way I can provide for the neediest in the community is to steal from those that are best-off, what should I do? As we will see, this problem of conflicting moral obligation is one faced by nearly every ethical theory we will discuss.

A final worry for contractarianism is that *only* contractors are subject to and so protected by the rules of the contract. We agree on these rules, furthermore, because of their *mutual* benefit. Individuals that cannot *benefit* us if we abide by the rules and, importantly, cannot *harm* us if we fail to abide by these rules, have no moral claim on us. We have moral obligations only to those whose cooperation is necessary in order for the rest of us to benefit. Some examples of those left unprotected might strike you, at least at this point, as morally unproblematic. For example, zombies are not contractors. They do not refrain from infecting you because you follow the rules, and the reason they bite you is not because you broke a rule. There is no sense in which zombies could give their consent to the contract or cooperate with its terms, so there is no sense in which they are protected by the terms of the contract.

There are, however, more problematic cases. For the contractarian, *might* does seem to make *right* in an important sense. If a group of contractors has the power to subjugate another group and extract benefits from them without any realistic threat of retaliation, it is morally permissible for them to do so, since the subjugated are reduced to the level of *moral* zombies. Although some communities use zombies as labor, for example yoking dozens to plows with a single child walking ahead to keep them on track, it would be perfectly permissible to enslave other human beings as long as they were powerless to harm you for doing so. We see this kind of situation in many survivor communities where some members of the community benefit without the consent of those that are exploited. Although capturing and enslaving other communities is common, is it morally permissible? The contractarian would suggest that it is. The theories that we will examine in the next few chapters come to a very different conclusion.

Summary

Many survivor communities have embraced a contractarian conception of morality in order to escape from the state of zombies. Given the savage anarchy that lies outside our strongholds, it is tempting to view morality simply as a set of rules that survivors agree to for mutual benefit. Even so, there are a number of problems that contractarianism faces. The view does not preclude a community from enslaving or killing those that do not belong to it. Even though the view may reduce violence within communities, it does nothing to reduce violence between communities or against those who belong to no community at all.

Further study

- Brooks, Max. *The Zombie Survival Guide*. New York: Three Rivers, 2003.
  - See pp. 46–47 where the author recommends the M1 Garand as one of the very best firearms to have in a zombie apocalypse. On pp. 108–109, he argues for the bicycle as the best form of transportation in an undead world.

- Da Silva, Michael and Marty McKendry. "Anarchy, State, and Apocalypse." In *The Ultimate Walking Dead and Philosophy*, edited by Wayne Yuen, 123–134. Chicago: Open Court, 2016.
  - Uses *The Walking Dead* to discuss social contract theory, different forms of consent, and the conditions under which it might make more sense to stay in the state of zombies rather than enter a survivor community.

- *Dead Set* (2008), [TV Program] Endemol UK.
  - This series dealt with the problem of cooperation for mutual benefit by examining how contestants on the reality show *Big Brother* would behave during a zombie outbreak.

- Drezner, Daniel. *Theories of International Politics and Zombies*. Princeton, NJ: Princeton University Press, 2011.
  - Covers many of the same themes of this chapter, but from the perspective of nation states rather than individuals, for example asking whether nations could cooperate with one another in the face of a global zombie pandemic.

- Gauthier, David. "Why Contractarianism?" In *Contractarianism and Rational Choice*, edited by Peter Vallentyne, 15–30. Cambridge: Cambridge University Press, 1991.
  - Offers a more contemporary account of contractarianism that attempts to avoid some of the problems that the classical (Hobbesian) account faces. In particular, it tries to show that the contract does not require coercion in order to ensure stable compliance as long as it offers equally favorable terms to everyone.

- Hobbes, Thomas. *Leviathan*. 1668. Edited with introduction. Indianapolis: Hackett, 1994.
  - The subtitle of the book is "The Matter, Form, and Power of a Commonwealth Ecclesiastical and Civil" which inspired the title of the work quoted at the beginning of this chapter. The quotation itself is adapted from part one, chapter 13 which contains Hobbes's description of the state of nature as well as his explanation for why Ethics requires a "common power" that can enforce the moral law.

- Murray, Leah. "When They Aren't Eating Us, They Bring Us Together: Zombies and the American Social Contract." In *Zombies, Vampires, and Philosophy: New Life for the Undead*, edited by Richard Greene and K. Silem Mohammad, 211–220. Chicago, IL: Open Court, 2010.
  - Discusses different social contract theories—including Hobbes's view—within the context of George Romero's *Dead* films.
- Rawls, John. *A Theory of Justice*. Cambridge, MA: Harvard University Press, 1971.
  - See chapter 24, "The Veil of Ignorance" for Rawls's thought experiment involving perfectly free and rational individuals—ignorant of the contingent features that make them particular individuals in society—deciding on the rules that would govern society. Rawls's idea is that since these individuals would have no knowledge of their actual position within society, they will choose rules that are fair to all.
- Shepard, Si. "Realistically, Nice Guys Finish Last." In *The Walking Dead and Philosophy*, edited by Wayne Yuen, 129–140. Chicago: Open Court, 2012.
  - Mentions Drezner's book and argues for the superiority of a Hobbesian (Realist) order within the context of *The Walking Dead*.
- Walker, Jason. "What's Yours Still Isn't Mine." In *The Walking Dead and Philosophy*, edited by Wayne Yuen, 81–96. Chicago: Open Court, 2012.
  - Uses *The Walking Dead* to examine the differences between John Locke's version of contractarianism—with its focus on inalienable natural rights—and Thomas Hobbes's version of contractarianism which was discussed in this chapter.
- *The Walking Dead,* [TV Program].
  - In seasons three through four, the show examines the town of Woodbury ruled by "The Governor." This is a society where outsiders are treated very differently than citizens/contractors. Not only does the Governor brutally kill newcomers he views as potential threats to the town, but he also seeks out and attacks other communities he considers potential threats. Eventually, in 3.16 "Welcome to the Tombs," he breaks the contract with his own citizens, killing all those that survived the attack on Rick's prison community.
  - In seasons four through five, the series examines the Terminus society. It is, in some ways, the limiting case of exploiting those that are not party to the contract. The people of Terminus actively lure and then cannibalize survivors who refuse to become cannibals themselves. Their motto "Never Again. Never Trust. We First, Always" is revealed in 5.16 "Conquer. " It reflects the tragedy they have collectively suffered in the Hobbesian state of nature, a suffering that has led them to a very narrow conception of who is protected by the moral rules.

- In seasons seven through eight, the show looks at the Savior society which offers a good example of a community where there is *mutual* benefit though these benefits are grossly *unequal*. The Saviors' main base is "The Sanctuary" where there is a strict socioeconomic hierarchy. The Saviors protect the workers at the bottom from the undead and these workers survive through a point system which is really a form of perpetual subsistence. They receive only enough goods to keep them surviving (and laboring) into the next day. When the Saviors are no longer able to provide even this basic level of benefits, the workers briefly revolt in 8.5 "The Big Scary U."

4 UNDERSTANDING YOUR RIGHTS AND DUTIES DURING THE PANDEMIC

Two things fill the mind with ever new and increasing dread and reverence, the more often and more steadily one reflects on them: the ravenous hordes outside me and the moral law within me.

—THE CRITIQUE OF PANDEMIC REASONING

The previous chapter argued that morality depends upon an agreement that survivors make with one another as a group, and have a means of enforcing, to ensure mutual benefit. As we saw, there is a problem with this view from the perspective of someone who does not belong to the group. If you do not belong to their group, it is morally permissible for them to brutally torture and kill you. The reason this is permissible is because you were not party to their social contract. Just as you have no responsibilities under the contract, you are also not protected by it.

Another worry with the contractarian position is whether anything goes outside the domain of enforcement. Is it really morally permissible for me to do whatever I want to whomever I want provided that I and the object of my desire/wrath are beyond the reach of the law? What if one lives in a *lawless* condition, as almost all remaining survivors do? Even if the *civil* law has broken down or you are beyond the reach of that law, the philosopher Immanuel Kant argues that you are still subject to the *moral* law as long as you walk among the living and not the undead. Kant provides you with a step-by-step procedure for moral decision making that does not depend upon the existence of any group of the living to make or enforce the moral rules. As long as there is still one rational person in this wasteland of shambling corpses, the moral law still applies.

1. Field exercise: Infected liar

"Are you infected?" the voice squawked. The megaphone shielded its owner's face, and the blazing sun in the background made it impossible for him to make out anything more than a vague outline. He could see, however, that the building was heavily fortified with a high fence topped with razor wire.

It crossed his mind to be cheeky about it and answer in the affirmative. You can't lose your sense of humor just because the world has ended. In point of fact, *everyone* was infected. That's how his last camp was overrun. One of the elderly folks passed of natural causes overnight, resurrected, and turned the rest of the camp before daybreak. Both the old man and his wife were strong as mules and equally mean. The further they traveled with the group, the less the group considered the danger of their advancing age. It would have served us well to remember that infection just adds to time's advantage in a game we will never win.

From the tone of the squawk, he didn't think the gatekeeper would appreciate the existential joke. In any case, this isn't what they meant. What the person wanted to know was whether or not he had been bit … was his infection accelerating … would he soon be undead?

"What stupid questions!" he thought to himself. Regardless of whether or not you are infected, he wondered why anyone would ever answer "yes." If you are infected and you tell the truth, the best you can hope for is to be turned away at the door. More likely you'll get shot, though this is perhaps better than the alternative. No one wants to be stuck out here alone, infected, and languishing. At best, you will convert in desperate solitude. At worst, your only companions will be your soon to be brethren, devouring you as you are still yourself but too weak to escape their clutches. If you answer "no," there's at least a chance the gatekeeper will let you inside where you could live out your last hours—perhaps even days—in relative safety and comfort.

"No!" he yelled, with all the strength and confidence he could muster, to the shadowy figure atop the fortress.

He tried to maintain his focus on the gatekeeper, but his head was throbbing, whether from the sun beating down on him—or something else—he could not tell. The latter was more likely. In the deepening chaos of the previous night, the septuagenarian's equally aged wife had surprised him. Freed by conversion from her arthritic pain, he was unprepared for her lithe quickness. When she bit into his wrist, he was equally astonished. He had always thought she used dentures, but apparently her teeth were all her own.

"Are you alone?"

The squawked reply snapped him momentarily back to the present, but his mind soon wandered back to the campground in search of an answer. He had escaped by grabbing a bike and peddling into the inky darkness. That the moans were behind him indicated that he had escaped, but also that he was still being pursued. He had cycled through the night,

FIGURE 8 Infected liar.

mustering the courage to switch on his headlamp only when the moans had faded into silence.

The throbbing in his head started to match the throbbing in his wrist. "Why haven't I cracked up?" he thought to himself. He knew it was in the mail … Although it was crazy, he couldn't stop thinking that the pulsating only he could hear was a homing beacon for his now undead pursuers, drawing them inexorably to him. Was he *really* alone? Like the earlier question about infection, this isn't what the gatekeeper meant. What this person wanted to know was whether others were hiding in the rocks behind him … were they armed … did they intend to attack as soon as the gate opened?

"I'm alone!" he yelled, but his voice broke on the final vowel. The megaphone cracked static followed by an interminable pause. Feeling the opportunity might be slipping away, he stopped trying to rationalize his lies and let them flow out freely.

"C'mon, let me in! I'm totally fine. I haven't seen the undead much less the living in weeks … I've just been out in the field a bit too long … a bit weak … had trouble finding food or water."

His entreaties were met only by the pounding of his temples.

"Look, I've lost everyone I've ever known, and I'll do anything not to stay out here alone. I *promise*, give me a little something and I'll do right by you. My bike's good for trade, and I'll work hard … you'll see!"

He saw the gate open, and the rush of relief temporarily overwhelmed the throbbing. The megaphone squawked loudly before the voice returned.

"Proceed through the gate to the open cage inside the building." There was another pause. "We will give you food and water, but you have to stay in quarantine for 24 hours."

As he got closer to the building, a shadow was cast by the roof revealing a large shanty town just behind the fence. Blinded by the sun, this mass of humanity had been hidden from his view. There were armed guards on either side of the open gate. Passing through, he pulled his sleeve down as far as he could so that the aching carbuncle on his wrist would not betray him. Entering finally into the cool shade of the building, he handed his bike to the guard next to the cage and sat quietly on the bench within. The guard handed him a water bottle and a couple of energy bars before closing the door.

"Thank you," he said quietly. His voice trembled and tears streamed down his face creating narrow rivulets in the filth that covered it.

Whatever terrors the future held, at least he knew he would not face them alone.

"Looks like you're cracking up," the guard quipped. Once he got the joke, the icy fear of having been discovered melted into a warm afterglow. He responded with a thin smile. After all, you can't lose your sense of humor just because the world has ended.

2. Kant's ethical theory

Kant would hold that the protagonist in the field exercise violated the **moral law** by lying and so did something morally wrong. In order to clarify what he means by "moral law," Kant contrasts it with **natural law**. The natural law describes how things are (natural) while being both universal and necessary (law). Although the moral law necessarily applies to everyone that falls under it by virtue of being a law, it describes not how things *are* but rather the way they *ought* to be. Since the moral law concerns what ought to be the case, it only applies to those individuals capable of recognizing what they ought or ought not to do. These are rational moral agents, what Kant calls "persons," or more commonly, "people." To illustrate, it is a *natural* law that bitten humans convert into bloodthirsty fiends—"crack up"—before undeath. The law applies to all humans (universal) without exception (necessary). In contrast, Kant would hold that it is a *moral* law that one ought not to turn others intentionally so as to achieve your own ends (e.g., to overrun an enemy stronghold with a bloodthirsty legion of the undead). Whereas the natural law above applies to all humans, the moral law applies only to people since only they are capable of recognizing what they ought or ought not to do. Although all people are humans (as far as we know), not all humans are people (e.g., zombies). Even though zombies are still biologically human, they lack the rational capacities of people.

Kant would draw a firm moral distinction between people who are capable of recognizing what they ought to do and zombies whose powers of recognition are limited to fulfilling their desire for living human flesh. More important for present purposes, people are capable of recognizing what they ought to do and are able to do it even if there is no one there to force them to do what they ought to do (contrary to contractarianism). Since the moral law is necessary and universal, furthermore, this ethical theory will have a moral realist foundation. As we saw in Chapter 2, such a foundation has distinct advantages over moral anti-realism within the context of the zombie apocalypse.

Assuming that at least some things are still objectively right or wrong in a world of undeath, how do we figure out what these things are? According to Kant, we must start with a **maxim**. This is a rule for your actions that you personally endorse. For example, like the protagonist in the above story, I might endorse the rule that "if I am bitten and desire refuge, I will lie about my condition to gain access." What makes this a "maxim" is that it is action guiding for *me*, but perhaps not for *you*. For example, as a rule, you might choose to be truthful, or not to seek sanctuary if bitten. Even if I *do* endorse this rule, however, this does not entail that I *ought* to endorse it.

In order to figure out whether I ought to endorse the rule, Kant suggests that one consider whether the maxim can take on the form of the **categorical imperative** which he contrasts with the **hypothetical imperative**. As imperatives, both of them command us to do something. Whereas the categorical imperative commands *absolutely* regardless of what we might desire, the hypothetical imperative commands only *conditionally* since it depends upon us having some relevant desire. In the above example, the imperative that I "ought" to lie about the bite depends on me desiring asylum from the pursuing zombie hordes. If I do not desire refuge for some reason (e.g., I resign myself to being devoured and turned more quickly), then I am no longer obligated to lie since I no longer have the desire the lie was required to satisfy. For Kant, *moral* obligations must have categorical form. Below we will consider two ways of understanding the categorical imperative: the universal law formula and the humanity formula. Both formulations promise step-by-step procedures for moral judgment that can be deployed with speed and accuracy, valuable features in a world where one must often make life and (un)death decisions at a moment's notice.

3. Universal law formula

To ask whether my maxim can command absolutely (categorical imperative) is to ask whether it can consistently take on the form of the moral law (universal and necessary). To help us answer this question, Kant suggests that we return to his distinction between the moral law and the natural law. Notwithstanding the difference between the moral law and the natural law, in order to figure out whether my maxim could take on the form of the moral law, I need to consider what it would be like for it to take on the form of a natural law. Put differently, in order to figure out whether people *ought* to do something, I need to consider whether everyone could *in fact* do it. If people could not act upon my maxim when applied universally and necessarily to everyone (natural law), then they cannot have a universal and necessary obligation (moral law) to act upon it.

For example, imagine a world in which everyone lies about being bitten to gain shelter as long as they want this kind of protection. If someone came to the doors of your stronghold begging for protection and you asked them if they were bitten, would you believe them if they said they had not been? Wouldn't you be an idiot to trust them if you knew that *anyone* who was bitten would deny it if they wanted your protection? If you do not know who in your fortress has an active infection and who does not, you run the very real risk of being overrun from within. For Kant, this is the key problem with the maxim: When it is willed as a law (universal and necessary), you cannot act upon it. The maxim undermines itself. No one would believe you and so you would never be granted refuge, which was the whole purpose of acting on the maxim in the first place.

This leads to the first formulation of Kant's procedure for figuring out what is morally permissible or impermissible: if you can consistently will your maxim as a universal law, it is morally permissible to act upon it. If you cannot consistently will your maxim as a universal law, it is morally impermissible to act upon it. The lying bite maxim cannot be willed as a universal law and so you *ought not* to act upon it. In contrast, there is no contradiction in a maxim that demands that you tell the truth. Consider a world in which everyone who was bitten told the truth about their condition when seeking sanctuary. Although you might just get a bullet to the head, you could also be offered asylum if they have somewhere safe for you to live out the time that remains before you turn without threatening anyone else. The point is that there is no *contradiction* in such a maxim when willed as a universal law.

4. People and things

Although Chapter 8 ("Are All Zombies Equal?") will complicate our moral picture of zombies, for present purposes, suffice it to say that Kant would see a clear moral difference between us (rational) and zombies (non-rational). Whereas we are capable of recognizing what we *ought* to do, zombies simply lack this capacity. Zombies are slaves to their desire for human flesh, whereas we are at least capable of controlling our desires through reason. This is not to say that we always do control our desires. In fact, the atrocities survivors have so often perpetrated against one another during the outbreak attest to the fact that we rarely do what we ought to do. More often our behavior resembles that of zombies rather than our former selves. Kant himself recognizes the problem and even concedes that "out of the crooked timber of humanity no straight thing was ever made." Nonetheless, as the epigraph of this chapter notes, we can still recognize the moral law within ourselves even when surrounded by ravenous hordes that would reduce us to a state of irrational bloodlust. Returning to Chapter 2.4, this capacity is what allows for human flourishing from the Kantian perspective. If we are doomed to be wholly driven by our basest desires, then we are morally equivalent to zombies. The ability to act on the moral law even when it runs counter to what we desire is the mark of a moral person.

The distinction between zombies and us reflects Kant's distinction between **mere means** and **ends in themselves**. Whereas ends in themselves are *people*—rational autonomous agents capable of recognizing what they ought to do and setting their own goals, mere means are *things*—objects that lack freedom and are governed wholly by forces outside their control. Even though people rarely live up to their own rationality and often show as much bloodlust as the zombies that they fear becoming, they at least have the *capacity* to do other than what their baser instincts would dictate. Whereas people are subject to a moral law that tells them what they *ought* to do (even if they fail to do it), zombies are subject only to the natural law. They are driven by their need for human flesh just as surely as a bullet is driven by physical forces from the barrel of a gun. The zombie and the bullet that destroys it are mere things, objects that are governed wholly by natural forces beyond their control.

Kant's distinction between ends in themselves and mere means reflects not only a difference in moral *consideration* but also moral *responsibility*. Whereas people are morally considerable, that is, I must consider whether I ought or ought not to treat people in a certain way, zombies do not deserve this kind of consideration. For Kant, there is no moral difference between the virus and the zombies infected by it. From the moral standpoint, both are non-rational things that are equally worthless.

For much the same reason, both cannot be held morally responsible. You cannot hold a zombie morally responsible for biting you any more than you can hold the virus morally responsible for infecting you. They do only what natural law dictates. Moral responsibility requires rational agency, the ability to consider the moral law and whether or not you ought to do something in light of it. This is a capacity both the virus and the zombie lack. For Kant, if you cannot be held morally responsible, then you cannot be morally considerable and vice versa. Both moral consideration and responsibility require *reason* and applying these categories to anything *non-rational* would constitute a potentially deadly philosophical mistake.

Most of us that still remain have seen this mistake made far too many times: a parent, spouse, child, or friend is bitten and turns, but the person who remains cannot bring themselves to put an end to the zombie that resembles their loved one so strongly. Self-deception takes over—"maybe they're still in there," "maybe we'll find a cure," etc.—and they are unable to pull the trigger. Even though I have categorized this as a philosophical mistake, could there still be some sense in which we have moral obligations to the undead? Even if we do not have moral obligations to zombies, could we still have obligations to the people they once were even after they have turned? Put differently, do we have a duty to respect the wishes of the now undead?

Back before the world fell, we recognized obligations to the dead. For example, there were commonly recognized duties to discharge a person's last will and testament, distribute their property in the way they directed, and dispose of their remains in the way they wished. We recognized these duties even though the people we felt obligated to were no longer around to make these moral demands upon us.

What if an infected person made similar demands? Some cases might strike us as unproblematic. For example, someone might simply wish that their undead corpse be treated with respect and disposed of humanely. Other cases, however, complicate the view that our obligations to the undead parallel our previously recognized obligations to the dead. For example, what if someone directed that, upon their undeath, all of their ammunition is to be shot off in a salute and that their shambling corpse is to be set free in the countryside? All that noise will likely attract the undead to your location and the waste of ammunition will make you less prepared to defend yourselves against them. In addition, the decision to release your now undead comrade could quite literally come back to bite you. Are you really obligated to respect their wishes?

To push things a bit further, if we are required to respect the wishes we *know*, what about the hypothetical wishes we *don't* know? For example, is it wrong to use a zombie merely as a means to your own ends if the person that zombie once was would not have wished her undead corpse to be used merely as a means? For example, it is quite common to bait a booby trap with a moaning zombie on the well-established theory that the moans will attract more zombies to their demise. What if the person who is now a zombie would not have wished to prolong their undeath moaning endlessly in a pit of punji sticks? Although there is clearly some biological connection between the zombie and the person they once were and perhaps even some residual subjectivity (e.g., an inherited claustrophobia felt in the darkness of the pit), are we required to consider what a person would have wished for their undead counterpart before doing anything to that counterpart? If so, this could render Kant's ethical theory totally impractical within the context of a zombie apocalypse.

These questions touch on thorny issues of personal identity (Chapter 10) and moral considerability (Chapter 8) that will be dealt with at greater length below. Even so, Kant would likely be skeptical of obligations to the undead. From Kant's perspective, there is a clear moral difference between being a person (rational moral agent) and being (biologically) human. Although both your infected comrade and his soon to be undead counterpart are human, only the former is rightly considered a person. When the person ceases to exist after cracking up and then resurrecting as the undead, so too do our moral obligations to that person.

This is not to say that Kant thinks that we should feel free to do whatever we would like to zombies. Even though they are not morally considerable, we should nonetheless destroy them quickly and in the most humane manner possible. Kant's concern is not with any moral obligation we have to their once living counterparts or with any moral harm we would inflict upon the zombies were we to torture them. His concern is rather with the moral harm that such torture inflicts upon the torturer. For Kant, cruelty to things harms not the things (this is impossible) but rather the person who is cruel. Kant's particular worry is that this cruelty will erode the agent's moral judgment making it more likely that the agent will be cruel not only to things but eventually to other people as well. This provides a partial answer to a question raised at the outset of this book, namely, how can survivors avoid morally debasing themselves to the point that joining the undead seems a more attractive option than continuing the struggle to survive?

5. Humanity formula

The distinction between mere means (things) and ends in themselves (persons) can provide another way of figuring out whether or not I ought to act upon a maxim. Kant believes we are always obligated to treat humanity (more specifically, *people*) as an end in itself. Again, consider the maxim that "if I am bitten and desire refuge, I will lie about my condition to gain access." If I were to act upon this maxim, how would it treat the person I am lying to? Am I treating the gatekeeper as an end in themselves or merely as a means to achieve my goal of gaining access to the stronghold? I am certainly not giving the gatekeeper the opportunity to consent to what I have planned (i.e., admitting an infected person into their community) and, for Kant, this holds the key to what is wrong with what I am considering doing. Consent is a special ability. Although zombies bear a rotting resemblance to ourselves and we can do many of the same things as one another (walking, moaning, biting, etc.), zombies cannot consent to what is happening to them. Even though someone might consent to turning rather than being killed, that is the last thing to which they will consent. Once turned, a zombie can no longer consent. The crucial ability that we possess that zombies lack is the capacity for reason and, for Kant, this reflects the fundamental moral difference between ends in themselves (people) and mere means (things).

If you lie about your bite to the gatekeeper to gain access to the fortress, you are treating someone who is an end in themselves (rational agent) as if they were a mere means (irrational zombie). You are depriving the gatekeeper, who as a rational being is capable of consenting to your plan, as if they did not have that capacity. Even if you are not putting a bullet in their head, by treating them as if they could not consent, you are treating them no differently than you would treat the undead.

There is also a difference, according to Kant, between treating someone as a *means* and treating them as a *mere* means. Whereas the latter is impermissible, the former is perfectly fine. If you told the gatekeeper the truth about your stricken condition and they gave you access, you would be treating them as a *means* toward your own protection but not *merely* as a means. Providing them with the choice between shooting you and giving you asylum, with full knowledge of the stakes involved, constitutes the crucial moral difference. When you lie to the gatekeeper about your condition, you are treating them *merely* as a means to your own protection. When you tell them the truth about your condition, you are treating them as a *means* to your own protection, but are still respecting their status as an *end* in themselves (rational agent). You are treating the gatekeeper as a rational agent since you are allowing them to make an informed decision about whether to protect you or kill you.

This distinction between ends in themselves and mere means provides another formulation of Kant's step-by-step procedure for determining what is morally permissible and impermissible: if your maxim treats yourself or another person as an end in itself (rational agent), then it is morally permissible to act upon the maxim. If your maxim treats yourself or another person as a mere means (non-rational thing), then it is morally impermissible to act upon the maxim. It is morally impermissible for you to lie to the gatekeeper about your condition, since doing so would treat them merely as a means.

6. Duties, rights, and moral worth

If something is morally obligatory, I have a duty to do it. Conversely, if something is morally impermissible, then I have a duty not to do it. These duties serve as a guide to the kinds of rights that individuals possess. Generally, if you have a duty *to do something* for someone else, then they have a **positive right** to that good or service. For example, if someone is being attacked by a zombie, holding all else equal, you have a duty to help them which corresponds to their positive right to your aid. Conversely, if you have a duty *not to do something* to someone else, then they have a **negative right** not to be interfered with in that way. For example, if someone is among the living and still has their wits about them, you have a duty not to kill them which corresponds to their negative right to life. This distinction between negative and positive rights will prove to be very important when we discuss "hordeology" in Chapter 6.

The concept of duty lies at the heart of Kant's ethical theory and allows us to understand the different ways he evaluates the morality of actions. Actions that are performed in accordance with duty but not because of it are amoral. For example, if I save someone who is about to be devoured by the undead because I want him to reward me with some of his food, my action has no moral worth. I did the right thing (responding to a positive right), but I did it for my own selfish reasons. The same desire can also lead to an immoral action if it is contrary to duty. Consider another situation where you are so motivated by your desire for food that you kill and eat another person (cannibalism). Instead of saving a person from becoming food, in order to fulfill your desire for food, you instead turn a person into food in order to satisfy this desire. The desires are not different in kind, but killing a person to satisfy this desire is clearly contrary to your duty since your dinner had a right to life. In order for your action to have **moral worth**, you must not only do the right thing but you must also do it for the right reason. In the case of the person who is about to be devoured by a zombie, you must not only save them, but you must also save them *because* it is your duty to do so if your action is to be morally praiseworthy. Kant admits, however, that it may be impossible for us to know the true reasons for our actions and those that seem motivated by duty may ultimately have selfish motivations.

Even if it is impossible to know if my actions have moral worth, Kant's procedure still seems well suited to these treacherous times. As long as I do the right thing, does it matter if I know whether I should be praised for it? We all have rules of conduct that we personally endorse (either implicitly or explicitly). The question is whether or not we *ought* to endorse these first person rules (maxims). When a ravenous mob of the infected is descending upon you, you do not have much time to make a decision, and the facts of the situation (e.g., personal connections to those under attack or a lack thereof) as well as the possible consequences of your action (e.g., life, death, or something in between) might make that decision difficult. The two formulations of the categorical imperative above provide an easily implemented, step-by-step procedure for figuring out whether or not you should act upon your maxim. This procedure can be completed in very little time since it does not require you to consider the facts of the situation, or the possible consequences of your action, but only the content of the maxim itself. Can it be willed universally? Does it treat myself or others merely as a means? These are the only questions you need concern yourself with which should make your decision relatively straightforward. When it comes to your survival as a moral person, worry first about doing the right thing. Take care of this, and you will have plenty of time to worry about whether you did it for the right reason. As we will see in the next chapter, however, it can sometimes be hard to figure out what the right thing is when you are obligated to do two (or more) things but cannot do both.

Summary

For Kant, it is morally impermissible for you to rob, murder, or lie to another person even if society—and its mechanisms of enforcement—have broken down. By virtue of being a *person*, a rational autonomous agent, they are worthy of respect. This is what distinguishes survivors and zombies from Kant's perspective. When a survivor is considering a particular course of action, for example lying about being bitten, they need to consider whether the rule for action they are endorsing could be willed as a universal law and respects the other person. If the answer is "no," as it would be in this case, then it is morally impermissible for the bitten survivor to lie.

Further study

- *Dawn of the Dead* (2004), [Film] Dir. Zack Snyder, USA: Universal Pictures.
  - This remake of Romero's 1978 classic is strongly disliked by many fans, but he does manage to bring the lying bite maxim to life ... or rather undeath.
- Feinberg, Joel. *Harm to Others*. Oxford: Oxford University Press, 1984.
  - See chapter 2 for a defense of posthumous harm.
- Grant, Mira. *Feed*. London: Orbit, 2010.
  - For a description of a society where it is nearly impossible to lie about a bite successfully and where the civil and natural laws reflect the (moral and natural) laws discussed in this chapter.
- *Hi-Phi Nation* (2017–present), [Podcast] https://hiphination.org/episodes/episode-one-the-wishes-of-the-dead/.
  - "Wishes of the Dead," from season one, explores whether or not we have obligations to the dead.
- Kant, Immanuel. *Critique of Practical Reason*. 1788. Translated with introduction. Cambridge: Cambridge University Press, 2015.
  - For a rather challenging presentation of his ethical theory. The Conclusion contains the inspiration for this chapter's epigraph (5:161).
- Kant, Immanuel. *Groundwork of the Metaphysics of Morals*. 1785. Translated with introduction. Cambridge: Cambridge University Press, 2012.
  - For a (slightly) less challenging presentation of his ethical theory. See especially Section II for the universal law (4:421) and humanity

formulations (4:429) of the categorical imperative. For the difficulty in determining whether or not an action has moral worth, see 4:407.

- Kant, Immanuel. "Idea for a Universal History with a Cosmopolitan Aim." 1784. In *Kant: Political Writings*, edited by H.S. Reiss, 41–53. Cambridge: Cambridge University Press, 1991.

  ○ For the source of the "crooked timber" quote above, see the Sixth Proposition (8:23).

- Kant, Immanuel. *Lectures on Ethics*. Cambridge: Cambridge University Press, 1997.

  ○ See the section *Of Duties to Animals and Spirits* for Kant's explanation of why we should not be cruel to animals or (it would seem) zombies.

- McKendry, Marty and Michael Da Silva. "I'm Gonna Tell Them about Wayne." In *The Walking Dead and Philosophy*, edited by Wayne Yuen, 53–64. Chicago: Open Court, 2012.

  ○ For an argument that we do have Kantian obligations to the undead.

- Taylor, James Stacey. *Death, Posthumous Harm, and Bioethics*. London: Routledge, 2015.

  ○ For why the dead (and presumably undead) cannot be harmed.

- *The Walking Dead,* [TV Program].

  ○ Although there are many good examples of Kant's conception of "agent harm" in the show, "The Wolves" from seasons five through six, may be the best example of persons whose moral judgment is compromised through repeated acts of violence. As the name suggests, their agency has been reduced to that of a predatory pack of animals.

5 DO THE INFECTED HAVE A RIGHT TO SUICIDE FROM ALTRUISTIC MOTIVES?

If he destroys himself in order to escape undeath, he makes use of a person merely as a means *to maintain a tolerable condition until final death.*

—GROUNDWORK OF SURVIVOR ETHICS

Despite the distraction writing this guidebook has afforded me, the incessant scratching and constant moans draw me inevitably back to my predicament. Alone in this room, surrounded on all sides by the undead, I know that a terrible choice awaits me. Although I have sufficient food and water for some time, I am down to my last bullet. Eventually, I will starve or the zombie horde gathering on the other side of my door will manage to break through. When one (or both!) of these things happen, should I kill one last zombie in my final moment or should I put a bullet in my brain to avoid joining their ranks? Instead of allowing my mind to wander to the desperate wails that would drive me to madness in time, I will instead focus my attention on a careful philosophical consideration of how to make the choice I cannot avoid.

1. Field exercise: The choice

There were lots of ways that the internet made people's lives better—maintaining long-distance relationships, ordering wine online, an unlimited supply of cute animal GIFs—but there was one respect in which it made everyone's lives much worse. Setting aside the so-called "alternative facts," arguments over the *facts* were a lot less interesting than they were before the internet.

Back when we were dating, we would debate for hours over the best 70s pop music. Our respective cases were built on a flimsy foundation of youthful experience bent through the funhouse mirror of time. We knew that what we claimed to remember were mnemonic malapropisms, but our ridiculous creations were even more ostentatious than the garish originals. Although Major Tom never returned to Earth on the P-Funk Mothership, it seems more appropriate to remember it that way. While questions of who copied whose sound, makeup, or antics (both onstage and offstage) were a source of unending debate then, all these issues were easily settled by the internet—"Fame" did inspire "We Want the Funk"!— just as *I* always said.

Whereas he always had an opinion on the little stuff, he was equally prone to reserve judgment about the big stuff. We dated for ten years before he finally popped the question!—But I guess that says as much about me as it does about him. Even so, once he had made the decision, it was decisive. Although I never thought of saying "no," it is hard to imagine him accepting an answer other than "yes." The puerile passion that he had brought to our little debates had taken on a more mature edge when applied to something more important—for both of us.

* * *

Our most recent debate was equally serious though we did our best to pretend that it wasn't. He was trying to fasten a 2x4 across the kitchen door. My points filled the gaps between the taps of his hammer creating a staccato conversation in counterpoint.

"You know, even their"—Bang, Bang, Bang—"nails can accelerate"— Bang, Bang, Bang—"the infection"—Bang, Bang, Bang—"they just need"—Bang, Bang, Bang—"to break the skin."

He paused in his labor and turned around with a cocky smile.

"Stop worrying," he said, "I read on the internet that *only* a bite would spread the infection—something about the saliva triggering the virus."

Now that he was facing me, I could again see the thin red line on the hand holding the hammer.

I looked at him with concern. "We should go to the stadium the Emergency Alert System was talking about on TV … they say they have a treatment for the virus."

He laughed, "A lot of good *they* did us … in any case, you shouldn't trust everything you see on TV." He stuck out his tongue before turning around to resume his work. "I'll trust my ClickHole article."

* * *

When it came time for the wedding, he insisted that we write our own vows. Mine were common platitudes. I have a hard enough time expressing how I feel in private much less in front of 300 of my closest strangers. In stark contrast to my own, his vows were uniquely personal. Although it would seem patronizing and paternalistic in any other context, when he promised that he would always protect me, the moment within which the promise was made robbed it of any potential offense and laid bare the honesty with which it was uttered.

He soon came to discover, however, that there were things from which he could not protect me. While we were on our honeymoon, we found out that my father had committed suicide. He and my mom had been divorced for years, but after the wedding—and perhaps after seeing her so happy after years of struggling without him—he had enough and just sat in his garage with the engine running. He was long gone before the car ran out of gas.

I was inconsolable, and my now-husband was livid. They never really got along and for him this seemed like one last slight. Not only did my father ruin our honeymoon, but he also ruined it in such a way that would be uniquely painful to my husband because of the degree to which it affected me. Seeing the pain in his eyes, I knew that his suffering was amplified immeasurably by his perception of my own. Even when he was able to control his voice and expression, his eyes always let me know what he was thinking.

"I would *never* be so selfish," he murmured with a disgust softened only slightly by sympathy.

* * *

The kitchen door was the last place they could get into the house, but also the last place where we could still get out. Until recently, all of the zombies had stuck to the front of the house. Since the kitchen was at the back, we had risked using that door to go foraging. He had barricaded all other points of egress (or ingress) long ago. After the most recent supply run, he returned with a couple of undead in pursuit. Apparently, they had figured out—or remembered—how to work the gate to the backyard. At first, he lied to me about where the scratch had come from.

"Oh, that little thing," he said dismissively. "I just grazed my hand on the latch, trying to get it closed before those things caught up to me."

Although his mouth was telling one story, his eyes were telling another, and I just had to look at him silently for a moment to know the truth.

Notwithstanding our best attempts to ignore it out of existence, the infection spread as we both knew it would. The thin red line darkened, stretched, and split. New branches formed and rose from his alabaster skin turning it into a rich marble. Once the transformation started, both of us knew that leaving was no longer an option. They wouldn't let him into the stadium looking like this.

Although there was less humor in our conversations, there was greater honesty. Both of us recognized that dissembling—however true to ourselves—was inauthentic given the gravity of our predicament. In particular, he kept returning to his promise to always protect me. He had killed plenty of the undead, and he had done a fine job sealing up the house. Even a large horde would have trouble getting in. That being said, the greatest threat lies not outside the house but festering latent within it. He would turn soon, and in that moment, my staunchest defender would become a mortal enemy. Regardless of how much he might try, he simply could not protect me from himself.

For all of our new-found honesty, neither of us could face up to the choice that confronted us. Letting him turn into one of them inside of our home was simply not an option. He was much stronger than me, and once he turned there would be little I could do to defend myself from his insatiable bloodlust. Since nailing up the kitchen door, zombies had started to crowd in on all sides of the house. It was as if they were dimly aware that another of their accursed kind was about to join their ranks and they waited to welcome him. Before that happened I had to kill him or he had to kill himself.

He vehemently opposed the second option. First, he wanted to hold out as long as possible. Second, he was unwilling to rob himself of even one moment with me as *him*. The longer he could hold on, the more he came to biologically resemble them. Before we lost electricity and with it any connection to the wider world, he had read about one "trick" on the internet—as crazy as it was horrific—that you could use to protect yourself at least temporarily from the zombie threat. Their bodily fluids, when spread on living skin, scrambles whatever means they have of detecting your living status and they mistake you for one of their own. Put bluntly, if I could bring myself to bathe in his gore, my husband insisted that I could walk out of here.

"You can do it!" he insisted. "You just have to hit me in the head as soon as I start to turn."

He engaged in a macabre pantomime with the hammer. "Just keep hitting as hard as you can until you've broken through." Thinking it might help without realizing how much it would horrify me, he made a simile. "It's just like the coconuts we cracked open on our honeymoon!" As I blanched, he came to his senses. "Honey," he said, "You *have* to do it. I just … I just can't."

I felt a rush of anger wash over me. "You're the one that's being *selfish* now," I protested. "Why are you putting this all on me?" He stared at me blankly though I could see the anguish in his eyes. I stared square into those eyes and said, "If you want to keep your promise, you need to find a way of doing this yourself!"

I stormed out of the room, unable to slow the carousel of emotion that was spinning out of control. I came back later that night. He lay languid, the dark lines streaked across his otherwise muscular pale torso. The rise and fall of his chest slowed with each breath, as if he were settling into a still-life that had already been sculpted. I grabbed the hammer which felt much heavier than its size would indicate and approached him not knowing if he were living or undead. As I turned to look at his face, his eyes caught me immediately. They looked into my core, fierce and bright. I cradled his head in my lap and my tears fell on his face substituting for his own. Slowly, the light in his eyes started to fade, and as it did I steeled myself for my grim task. His fierceness had become my own. I cut the Gordian knot and kept the promise he could not fulfill.

The act disassociated me from my former self. I took a knife from the butcher block and cut into the marble. I imagined his vital fluids as a kind of glitter make-up that I spread across my body as I might have done before a show in our youth. Finally, like *Alladin Sane*, I drew a lightning bolt on my face before tearing down the 2x4 and walking into the light—a new character for a fallen world. On the other side of the threshold, I was greeted as a rock star. My legions of fans welcomed me as one of their own.

FIGURE 9 Final embrace.

2. Perfect duties, imperfect duties, and Kant's view on suicide

Kant's moral theory offers some guidance as to how to make the fateful decision in the field exercise above. He distinguishes between **perfect duties** that I must always perform regardless of what I may want to do and **imperfect duties** that I may sometimes ignore in favor of what I desire. To illustrate what he means, he gives a couple of examples of each kind of duty. We have perfect duties to preserve our lives and to keep our promises. These are duties of *justice* to oneself or others. Regardless of how much you might desire to do so and for whatever reason, there is never a situation where it would be permissible to commit suicide or to lie. In contrast, we have imperfect duties to better ourselves and to help others. These are duties of *beneficence* to oneself or others. The duties are imperfect since pursuing one of them with the single-minded devotion that a zombie shows to the flesh it craves would make it impossible for you to pursue the other duty. If we spent all our time helping others, we would not help ourselves and the converse is true as well.

These two duties need not work at cross-purposes, but it is easy to see how they could in this violent world, one where you make daily choices of life and (un)death. Every time I share my limited food with a starving survivor or snatch a stranger from the jaws of the equally ravenous undead, I jeopardize my own status among the living. In contrast, barricading myself in a room with food and water in order to spend my remaining days pondering philosophical questions (an ostensibly self-edifying pursuit) would make it impossible for me to help those being devoured beyond my walls. This contains an irony not lost on me, though one I hope to minimize should this book ever find a reader.

Suppose the day comes, however, when the zombie horde gathering on the other side of my door grows large enough to break through. If I were to shoot myself with my last bullet, what would be the maxim of my action? It would seem to be something like this: "If I am sure to be devoured by zombies, then I will kill myself to escape becoming one of them." Is it permissible to act upon this maxim? Certainly, many survivors would say so. Some would probably consider suicide under such dire circumstances morally obligatory. Kant would argue, however, that this maxim would fail both the universal law and the humanity formulations of the categorical imperative. Consequently, it would be morally impermissible to commit suicide even if one were about to be rendered undead by a ravenous horde.

Admittedly, it is not immediately obvious why the suicide maxim would fail the universal law formulation. After all, the maxim would not undermine itself if everyone were to endorse it. Unlike the infected liar in the previous chapter, there is no contradiction in everyone offing themselves when faced with immanent undeath. Although no one would grant anyone else sanctuary in a world in which everyone would lie about being bitten in order to gain sanctuary, it does seem that everyone could commit suicide if they were about to be devoured without any inconsistency. If anything, we would have fewer of these wretched creatures to worry about in such a world. Kant's worry in this case has less to do with the *content* of the maxim, but rather with our *motivation* for endorsing it. The motivation, in this case, seems to be some kind of self-love, namely, one's squeamishness at the prospect of being devoured and turned into a zombie; I want to stay *me* and not turn into one of *them*. The feeling that drives us to commit *suicide* in this case, however, is the exact same feeling as the one that normally drives us to *survive* among the undead. The maxim contradicts itself when made into a universal law, not because it would be impossible to act upon it, but rather because it places our desire to remain ourselves (rather than the undead) at cross-purposes. As Kant would say, a world governed by a law that would require us to commit suicide by means of the same feeling whose purpose is to keep us surviving would contradict itself.

3. Moral value and the distinction between doing and allowing harm

Kant would argue that the above maxim also fails the humanity formulation of the categorical imperative. In order to see why, one first needs to appreciate how the distinction between ends in themselves and mere means underwrites his theory of moral value. Consider a world in which all persons have been replaced by the dead and the undead. Nothing that we survivors currently value (ample ammunition, food/water, strong walls) would matter anymore. All of these things have only *instrumental* value insofar as we can use them for a certain purpose. A bullet has no value in a world occupied exclusively by the undead since it cannot be used to defend the living. What is missing from the picture is *us*. We have *intrinsic* (moral) value for Kant because our rational nature is the source of all other (instrumental) value. In order for things to have *value*, there must be a *valuer*. Being able to value something else as the means to achieving some goal that you have set for yourself is a rational capacity. Although we survivors often say that zombies "desire our flesh," they cannot be said to *value* our flesh in the above sense. Even though individuals have succumbed to their flesh-driven desires for as long as there has been flesh to desire, there is a big difference between the philanderer and the zombies we now face. Besides the end to which the flesh is put, the zombie "desires" your flesh no more than a bullet fired from a gun "desires" to stay in motion. Both are fully determined by the natural laws appropriate to their kinds, the law of the virus (zombies) or the law of inertia (bullet).

A world without reason would be a world without value. It is a world in which the *ought* (moral law) has been entirely eliminated in favor of the *is* (natural law). It is a world in which *persons* (rational beings capable setting goals and valuing the means of achieving them) have been replaced by *things* (undead controlled by the virus). Although the undead could be of instrumental value to a person, for example using the mournful moans of a captive zombie to attract others of its kind to their final death, they completely lack the intrinsic value that persons possess. For Kant, only persons have an absolute moral worth that deserves the respect of other persons.

Although I am now talking about the moral worth of *persons* rather than the moral worth of *actions* (previous chapter), the two conceptions of moral worth are deeply connected. Recall that, for Kant, an action only has moral worth if it is done for the sake of duty. In order for your action to be morally praiseworthy, you must not only do the right thing but also you have to do it for the right reason. It is not enough that I help a survivor escape the steely clutch of an undead assailant; I must also help the person escape *because* I recognize that it is my duty to do so. If I am motivated by some other desire, for example, that the person I save will grant me sanctuary, my action lacks moral worth. Only persons are capable of considering and acting on the basis of reasons. Consequently, in order for an action to have moral worth, it has to be performed by a person who has absolute moral worth. Not only do zombies lack all moral worth themselves, but also it is impossible for their actions to have any moral worth. Although I might be happy that the moaning zombie in my pit of punji sticks has attracted others of its kind to their eternal entrapment, this is hardly a reason to praise the zombie. It is doing only what it must on the basis of the natural laws that govern its miserable kind.

If persons have an absolute moral worth, one can readily see why Kant would think that we are always obligated to preserve our lives as persons. Regardless of how desperate my circumstances and assured my fate may be, willfully depriving myself of even one last moment as a rational being is a grievous moral harm since it would be a moment that now lacks someone of absolute moral worth. If I were to commit suicide in order to avoid being devoured, I would be using myself, as a person, *merely as a means* to avoid such an unpleasant end. Much better is it, from Kant's perspective, to be devoured as a *person* than to be ignored by the undead simply because you had turned yourself into a *thing* (i.e., a corpse with a bullet in its head).

Even so, don't you end up as a *thing* in either case? If you commit suicide, you become a lifeless corpse. If you are bitten, you become a zombie. For Kant, there is no moral difference between a lifeless corpse and a zombie. Both are equally worthless. Whether I kill myself or am bitten, the consequences are the same. Why does it really matter then, from the moral standpoint, *how* the same result is brought about?

There is a moral principle, often associated with Kant's moral philosophy, called the **Doctrine of Doing and Allowing** (DDA) that can help to draw the distinction. Holding all else equal, the DDA claims that *doing* harm is morally worse than *allowing* harm to occur. For example, the DDA would hold that it is morally worse (1) to mortally wound one person so that five others can escape while the undead feast upon the one person's living though immobile body than (2) it would be to allow that person to die by abandoning them to a ravenous horde so that five others can escape this horde. It is easy to see how the DDA would also be relevant to the suicide case. While committing suicide (doing harm) to avoid joining the ranks of the undead would be morally impermissible, being bitten and turning into one of them (allowing harm) is morally permissible. Even if you ultimately end up as a morally worthless *thing*, at least you were not the one that brought yourself to that ruined state.

4. Suicide from altruistic motives

To this point, we have been considering a maxim that prescribes suicide because of self-love. You prefer to remain a rational being capable of designing and executing plans to ensure your survival, rather than to become mindless creatures governed only by an insatiable hunger for living human flesh. In order to avoid the latter fate, you willfully put an end to yourself. Although you would prefer to remain yourself, this is no longer possible. What if the motivation for suicide, however, were less self-interested and more altruistic? For example, consider this modified maxim: "If I am sure to be devoured by zombies, then I will kill myself in order to preserve the lives of those I might devour in my undeath." Would this maxim pass the universal law and humanity formulations of the categorical imperative?

Some of the explanations given above for rejecting the previous maxim do not work as well in rejecting this one. For example, since the motivation for suicide is no longer self-love, that is, your squeamishness at being devoured and joining the ranks of the undead, Kant's explanation for why the first suicide maxim could not be made a universal law no longer works. Likewise, although acting on the maxim would involve destroying a person, the person is not being used merely as a means in order to avoid an unpleasant personal fate (*you* becoming a zombie). Rather, you are killing yourself in order to help others avoid a similar fate (*others* becoming zombies). Admittedly, you would be depriving yourself of some—however short and painful—future as a rational being and you would be the one *doing* the harm, so Kant would still likely reject the maxim. Even so, could there be a moral difference between the two suicidal maxims based upon the different motivations—self-interest vs. altruism—that drives you to adopt them?

It is important to note that, in the case of the altruistically motivated suicide, your reason for committing suicide is grounded in *duty*, specifically the duty to help others that are in need. This is a duty of beneficence that Kant explicitly mentions. How could it be morally impermissible for you to commit suicide in this case, if the reason why you are doing it is because of a duty that Kant says you have? Given the way that Kant understands moral worth, furthermore, couldn't you go so far as to say that your action has moral worth since it is done for the sake of duty?

5. The problem of conflicting duties

Before going for your gun, however, recall Kant's distinction between perfect and imperfect duties discussed in the first section of this chapter. Whereas Kant believes that it is *never* morally permissible to commit suicide (perfect duty), it is *sometimes* morally permissible not to help others (imperfect duty). It seems reasonable to assume that one of the times it would be morally permissible not to help others escape an undead fate is when discharging this duty would require you to commit suicide so as to prevent yourself from becoming one of the undead from which they would have to escape. In other words, a perfect duty would, for Kant, always override an imperfect duty if the two came into conflict. If imperfect duties admit of exceptions for our *desires*, they most certainly admit of exceptions for our perfect *duties*. Put simply, duties of *justice* are always stronger than duties of *beneficence*. Likewise, following the DDA, it is more important from the moral standpoint not to *harm* people (including oneself) than it is to *help* them.

Even if the perfect duty to preserve our lives cannot be overridden for the sake of desire (not wanting to become one of the undead) or an imperfect duty (saving others from being bitten by our undead selves), what happens if this *perfect* duty comes into conflict with another *perfect* duty? Kant seemed to believe that such a scenario could never occur, but it is easy enough to think of possible scenarios, some of which you may have actually had the great misfortune of encountering while trying to survive.

Take the field exercise above for example. What if I made a promise to a loved one that I would do everything in my power to protect them from zombies, but then I find myself turning and trapped with them with no hope of rescue? If the only way to keep my promise is to commit suicide, what would I be obligated to do? If I keep my promise, then I must find a way of destroying my brain (hopefully I still have a bullet) so as to prevent myself from turning into a mindless monster that would surely disembowel my screaming loved one as they begged me to stop. If I preserve my life until I crack up, then I break my promise to protect my loved one from creatures like myself. Either way, I am going to violate a perfect duty. What am I to do?

6. W.D. Ross's solution to conflicting duties

Since Kant thought such scenarios could never occur, it is not surprising that he offers no guidance as to what to do when perfect duties conflict with one another. Thankfully, there is another philosopher, W.D. Ross, who does offer a possible solution. Although Ross approaches moral issues from a roughly Kantian perspective, he does not believe that any of your duties are "perfect" in Kant's sense of the term. Rather, Ross believes that you are subject to a large number of **conditional duties**. These are things that you ought to do as long as they do not come into conflict with anything else that you ought to do. There are any number of conditional duties that you have both to yourself and to others—to preserve your life, to keep a promise once made, to show gratitude for a kindness done for you, to help others, not to harm others, etc. When considering what you ought to do in a particular situation, you need to consider all of the conditional duties that apply to you in that set of circumstances in order to form an opinion as to what your **duty proper** is in that situation. One's duty proper can change, however, depending on the circumstances, the relevant conditional duties, or even the person considering their options.

In the above situation, when you are about to turn and are trapped with a loved one, Ross would ask you to consider all of the conditional duties that are relevant to your decision. The circumstances are straightforward. Most importantly, you are about to turn. You pose an imminent threat to your loved one but you have a duty not to harm them. You had previously promised to protect your loved one from the zombies which places you under a prior obligation. You can save them by killing yourself and ensuring you do not turn. At least in the short term, this would most certainly help them. Your loved one has shown you nothing but kindness in your ever-worsening condition, something for which you are incredibly grateful. Although you realize that under normal circumstances you would do everything you could to keep surviving and to protect them, your capacity to do either is rapidly diminishing. What would you do? Whatever you decide, after carefully considering all of the above factors, becomes your duty proper. Of course, it is just your opinion—after all, your loved one might have the opposite opinion—but this is your decision to make and your duty to discharge. Of course, in the field exercise above, the husband is unable to carry out the decision that he has made which leaves discharging the duty proper up to the loved one. In doing so, however, the spouse is carrying out the husband's wishes.

A concern with Ross's view is that it does not offer a moral decision-making procedure that fully determines what you ought to do in any particular situation. This was the great promise of Kant's view within the context of a zombie apocalypse. The two formulations of the categorical imperative were supposed to provide you with an efficient way of determining whether or not you should act upon a particular maxim. An efficient moral decision-making procedure is important when the stakes are high (life vs. undeath) and time is short (the undead knocking down your door). Unfortunately, as we have seen, Kant's view cannot deliver on its promise when perfect duties come into conflict. How can you decide between two duties when neither of them is supposed to have an exception? Ross would say that it is much more important that a moral theory be practical in the field than that it be governed by a single principle (e.g., the categorical imperative). Even if it takes a little more time to use, and its procedure is a bit less certain in its outcome, Ross's moral theory at least will not break down on you. In the field, the last thing you need is for your gun to misfire. You should expect nothing less from your preferred moral theory. Even so, it is troubling that two people could have all of the same information (about relevant conditional duties, circumstances of the situation, etc.) yet come to different decisions as to what they ought to do. It is even more troubling considering the high stakes of the decisions we are so often forced to make in this unforgiving slaughterhouse of a world. That my decision to kill myself and prevent my cracked up counterpart from devouring another person could have just as reasonably been a decision to allow myself to turn and devour them seems cruelly arbitrary. Perhaps there is some way, however, of ensuring that my opinion is more *considered* than the opinion of another even if we hold onto Ross's idea that your duty proper in a particular situation is fundamentally a matter of *opinion*. What this might be is something I will return to in the Conclusion to this book, assuming I make it long enough to write it.

Summary

Although Kant believes that it is never morally permissible to break a promise or to commit suicide, the field exercise above offers an example of where these two duties come into conflict with one another. In situations like this—regrettably common in this pitiless landscape—Kant's moral theory offers no guidance as to what one ought to do. W.D. Ross offers a solution to this problem that maintains we have duties while rejecting the idea that some duties have no exceptions. Although Ross's solution avoids the problem that Kant faces, it does so by introducing an element of subjectivism into moral decision making that raises new concerns.

Further study

- *Dawn of the Dead* (2004), [Film].
  - Offers a number of examples illustrating themes from this chapter. Just like Roger in the 1978 original, Frank is infected but humanely allowed to live out the remainder of his life before being shot by another member of the group. At the end, cornered in a wrecked van with no means of escape, C.J. blows himself up—along with a large horde of undead—so

that the remaining survivors can escape to Steve's yacht. Michael, who is bitten, refuses to get on the yacht. He stays on the dock and uses his final bullet on himself.

- Foot, Philippa. "Killing and Letting Die." In *Abortion and Legal Perspectives*, edited by Jay Garfield and Patricia Hennessey, 177–185. Amherst: University of Massachusetts Press, 1984.
  - Provides a rigorous defense of the DDA under certain conditions.

- Kant, Immanuel. *Groundwork for the Metaphysics of Morals*. 1785. Translated with introduction. Cambridge: Cambridge University Press, 2012.
  - See the Preface for Kant's distinction between natural law and moral law (4:387–388). Section I discusses Kant's conception of moral worth (4:398). Section II contains the source that inspired the opening quotation of this chapter (4:429) as well as a brief discussion of the difference between perfect and imperfect duties (4:421). Kant uses the perfect duty of preserving your life—not committing suicide—as the primary way of illustrating each formulation of the categorical imperative.

- Kant, Immanuel. "On a Supposed Right to Lie from Philanthropy." 1797. In *Practical Philosophy*, edited by Mary Gregor, 611–615. Cambridge: Cambridge University Press, 1996.
  - Contains Kant's argument for why it is *always* wrong to lie, even if the intention is to save another person's life. The title of this chapter is adapted from the title of the article.

- Rachels, James. "Active and Passive Euthanasia." *The New England Journal of Medicine* 292 (1975): 78–80.
  - Offers some classic objections to the DDA within the context of the debate over whether there is a moral difference between killing someone (active euthanasia) or letting them die (passive euthanasia).

- Ross, William David. *The Right and the Good*. Oxford: Oxford University Press, 1930.
  - See chapter 2 for Ross's discussion of how we can resolve conflicts between our duties by making a distinction between prima facie duties and our duty proper.

- *The Return of the Living Dead* (1985), [Film] Dir. Dan O'Bannon, USA: Orion Pictures.
  - Although there are many examples of suicide to avoid undeath in the annals of zombie horror, Frank's suicide by cremation furnace is a classic. Once he realizes that he is turning into a zombie and will never see his wife again, he decides to put an end to his transformation in a literal blaze of glory. Ironically, the ash that is released by his incineration spreads the infection further than he likely ever would have as a shambling corpse.

- *The Walking Dead*, [TV Program].
  - With the blessing of the group, Andrea commits suicide to avoid turning after being bitten in season 3.16 "Welcome to the Tombs."
  - A very different example is Sasha's suicide. She ingests a cyanide tablet to turn herself into an undead biological weapon aimed at killing Negan and saving Alexandria in season 7.16 "The First Day of the Rest of Your Life."

6 WHEN TO SACRIFICE SURVIVORS TO HUNGRY HORDES

How are they free of sin who are stained with human blood for the sake of that which has little worth—bodies infected from conception though not yet turned?

—DE LIBERO ARBITRIO IN TERRA MORTUIS

If they have any patina to them, the individual zombie is likely to be slow, weak, and rather stupid. These strays are easily avoided or destroyed. Unfortunately, the undead tend not to wander alone. Like carnivorous buffalo, zombies prefer to travel together, led by a kind of ravenous groupthink that grows more cunning in proportion to its numbers. Although a herd starts out as only a handful of individuals, once it identifies a target and starts moaning, these moans—like a siren's call—will attract every other zombie in earshot. This call grows ever-louder as the horde's ranks swell. As we will see in the next chapter, this is why it is so hard to maintain a stronghold. A horde, having fixed upon the object of its desire, will not cease to grow until it overwhelms what protects the living flesh it seeks to devour.

Predatory hordes of undead are a constant threat to the living and it is vitally important that survivors adopt tactics for diverting these threats from their communities when they cannot destroy the threats outright. This chapter explores some of these tactics as well as the moral dilemmas often associated with them. We will approach these dilemmas from the Kantian standpoint that has been examined over the last couple of chapters. As we will see, **hordeology**—the study of the ethical dilemmas arising from horde diversion—generates a number of problems from the Kantian perspective.

1. Horde

Imagine you belong to a nomadic community of survivors that has found a seemingly safe place to spend the night. Your group will be camping at the end of a canyon protected on three sides by sheer cliffs. Several hundred yards up the canyon from the camp there is a narrow bottleneck the size of one very large man or several of you. Next to the bottleneck lies the entrance to an adjoining ravine. You and a friend have been sent out to do some reconnaissance of the surrounding area. You have volunteered to head back up the main canyon, away from the camp, to see if there is anything that might be of use to your group of survivors. Your friend has been sent to explore the adjoining ravine. Five people have been left behind in the camp to set up tents and prepare for the evening. You are several hundred yards past the bottleneck when you spot a rampaging zombie horde in the distance hurtling toward you. The canyon is full of them—wall-to-wall—a ferocious grinder of rotting claws and jagged teeth. Your friend and the camp are too far away for you to warn them. If you stand your ground, the horde will quickly devour you. Your slight frame will not even break their stride. If you run back down the canyon, however, you can at least choose which direction the horde will go. They will follow you like a rabbit at a greyhound race. If you head through the bottleneck, the undead will flow through it and overwhelm you as well as the five other survivors who remain in the camp. If you head down the adjoining ravine, their lives will be spared, but both you and your friend will be consumed. You care deeply both for the people in your camp and your companion, but there is no way to save both. Let's call this case "Horde." What should you do? The response might seem obvious. You should direct the horde toward the ravine where only two of you will be devoured rather than toward the camp where six will be killed. Although you will be killing your friend by leading the horde down the ravine, since people will be killed in any case, isn't it better to ensure fewer people are killed?

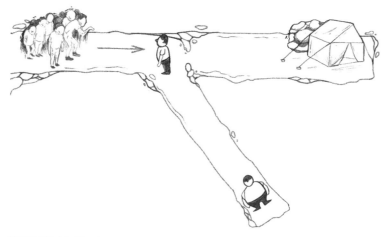

FIGURE 10 Horde.

2. Fleshy Friend

Before answering this question, consider a slightly different case. Imagine that you and your companion have finished your reconnaissance duties. Your colleague has explored the ravine and discovered that it terminates in a dead-end surrounded by sheer cliffs. After informing the rest of the camp, you and your companion are tasked with setting up a diversion that will lead the horde down the adjoining ravine, and away from the camp, in case there is an attack. On the far wall at the end of the ravine, your friend has installed a rechargeable megaphone that is connected to a walkie-talkie by an auxiliary cable. You hold the other walkie-talkie. Recorded on your smartphone are the cacophonous moans of another horde that your group was able to destroy. If you happen to see a horde entering the main canyon, you can play the recording on your smartphone into the walkie-talkie, which will draw the horde to the megaphone at the end of the ravine and away from the bottleneck that leads to the camp.

You are the look-out, positioned at the top of the canyon above the bottleneck, which gives you a good view of the main canyon as well as the smaller ravine that branches off of it. Imagine that your companion is now standing next to you, at the top of the canyon, after having installed the megaphone and climbed out of the ravine below. Looking toward the main canyon, both of you see a horde rapidly approaching the bottleneck which leads to your camp. You push "play" on your smartphone and activate your walkie-talkie, but you only hear your phone's tiny speaker, not the megaphone below. Someone forgot to charge the megaphone! The solar cell is sitting next to you but it won't do anyone any good now. Both of you watch helplessly as the horde continues its inexorable advance toward the unsuspecting members of the camp below. You hear the moans start which indicates that they have locked onto the settlement for their next meal. Recall that the opening from the main canyon leading to the community is quite narrow. If only you had a sizeable boulder, you could probably block the opening for a period of time—at least long enough to warn the folks in the camp of the imminent threat.

You turn to look at your companion. He has wanted to slim down which is why he volunteered to install the megaphone and walkie-talkie combo, figuring the exercise of climbing up and down would do him some good. Notwithstanding his intentions and recent exertions, however, he is still a quite portly fellow. To be frank, he is a mountain of a man, the size of a boulder himself. If you were to push him over the edge, he would wedge into the narrow opening between the main canyon and the ravine. His already tenderized frame would not only provide a generous feast for the ravenous horde, but it would also stop moaning and attracting new zombies as it gorged on his ample flesh. During the time it took the horde to consume his eviscerated body and reopen the bottleneck, the members of the community—warned by your companion's cries as he fell to his death—would have time to mount a collective defense of the bottleneck. Even if you were willing to sacrifice yourself—an option for which you have no particular desire—it would be for naught. You are more bones than flesh at this point. Besides not being able to fill the gap, your thin frame would be a paltry snack for the horde below, a mere appetizer that would drive them even more quickly toward the main course that lies ahead.

FIGURE 11 Fleshy Friend.

Is this situation, let's call it "Fleshy Friend," significantly different from Horde? If you think directing the horde to kill your companion is morally permissible, but pushing your companion so that the horde kills him is morally abhorrent, then it is absolutely vital to find some morally relevant difference between the two cases.

As you might recall from the last chapter, some philosophers draw a moral distinction between doing harm and allowing harm to occur. According to the Doctrine of Doing and Allowing (DDA), holding all else equal, doing harm is worse than allowing harm to occur. Both Horde and Fleshy Friend involve doing harm. In the case of Horde, doing harm is the *only* thing that you can do. Either you kill the five people in the camp by leading the zombies their way or you kill the one person in the ravine by directing the zombies toward him. If *all* you can do is harm, it seems plausible that you ought to do the *least* amount of harm, that is, direct the horde toward your partner in the ravine. In Fleshy Friend, however, you have a choice between doing and allowing harm. By pushing your colleague to his death, you are *doing* harm to him. Conversely, if you do nothing, you merely *allow* the horde to consume the five survivors in the camp. Perhaps, this constitutes the moral difference between the two cases. Whereas we cannot draw a moral distinction between doing and allowing harm in Horde, we can draw such a distinction in Fleshy Friend. According to the DDA, wouldn't *killing* your friend be worse than *allowing* the five encamped survivors to be devoured? Are we really "holding all else equal" though? After all, aren't *five* people being eaten alive morally worse than *one* person being eaten alive?

Applying the DDA in these cases will only make sense through the lens of moral *rights*. In the Kantian ethical tradition, persons possess rights and these rights denote the kinds of things that we ought or ought not to do to persons. As mentioned in Chapter 4.6, philosophers talk about two kinds of rights. In the first category are *negative* rights, which refer to things that we *ought not* to do to other people, or that they ought not to do to themselves. For example, if someone has a right to life, then we ought not to kill that person and, for someone like Kant, they also ought not to commit suicide. Many of the moral rights that people are familiar with from the political realm—at least before society ceased to exist—fall into this negative category, for example, life, liberty, and property. For those that subscribe to a Kantian theory of moral rights, society is not necessary for these rights to exist. These rights are *natural* in the sense that you possess them by virtue of being a "person" in the Kantian sense. To be a person, you must be a rational agent capable of recognizing what you ought or ought not to do.

In the other category are *positive* rights, which refer to things that we *ought* to do for other people or for ourselves. For example, if someone has a right to aid then we ought to help them when they are in need of it. Both negative and positive rights can alternatively be overridden or violated. A right is *overridden* when it is outweighed by other rights-based considerations. If you have a choice between aiding five people and aiding one person, holding all else equal, it seems as if you should aid the five people if you cannot aid everyone. For example, imagine a situation where a zombie is approaching one trapped and defenseless person and another zombie is approaching five trapped and defenseless people (don't worry about *why* they are trapped and defenseless). For this scenario, you can destroy one zombie or the other zombie, but unfortunately you cannot destroy both zombies. Here it would seem that five positive rights to aid *outweigh* the positive right of the one to aid. Put differently, the right to aid of the one is *overridden* by the rights of the five. In contrast, if you chose to aid the one instead of the five, the positive rights of the five would be *violated*. Their rights outweigh the rights of the one, but this moral fact is ignored when you destroy the zombie descending upon the one instead of the other zombie approaching the five.

What is true of positive rights is true of negative rights as well with a caveat, one that is central to understanding why the DDA applies in the case of Fleshy Friend: negative rights are *stronger* than positive rights. Additional moral justification is required to *kill* someone (negative right), then is required to *allow* someone to die (positive right). In fact, one might think that no number of positive rights could outweigh the negative right to life of an innocent person. Put differently, perhaps one's obligation to help others—regardless of how many or how much they could be helped—would never justify killing an innocent person. This does not entail, on its own, that doing harm is *always* worse than allowing harm. Even if killing an innocent person is always wrong, there could still be cases where allowing an innocent person to die is equally wrong. In such cases, the DDA would not apply. For someone who accepts the existence of negative and positive rights, however, there could also be *some* cases where doing harm is worse than allowing harm.

Here is a possible **criterion for applying the DDA** using the language of negative and positive rights: The DDA applies in those cases where a negative right exists and is not overridden and a positive right either does not exist or is overridden. Let's start by considering Horde. Both your friend in the ravine and the people in the camp have a negative right to life. They are all innocent persons—moral agents—that must be treated as ends in themselves according to Kant. Holding all else equal, it would be wrong to kill anyone. The problem is that you *must* kill someone. You do not have a choice on *whether* to kill, but rather only on *who* to kill. In this case, the five negative rights of the survivors in the camp would *outweigh* the one negative right of your friend in the ravine. Although negative rights exist, they are *overridden*—namely, the negative right of your colleague. Using the criterion above, the DDA would not apply, and this seems to fit the case since there is no option to merely *allow* harm.

Let us now turn to Fleshy Friend. Again, it seems as if everyone has a negative right to life. Likewise, the people in the camp have a right to aid. The crucial difference is that in order to *aid* them, you would have to *kill* your portly partner by pushing him into the bottleneck. Your friend, however, is an innocent person. Just as it would be wrong for you to *kill* the innocent people in the camp, for example, by pushing boulders down on them from above, it would be wrong for you to *kill* your friend.

What about the positive rights to aid of those in the camp? Aren't these being violated if you don't save them from the army of zombies descending upon them? Let us assume, for the sake of argument, that the ravenous undead have no positive rights to their living flesh. Here it is important to remember that negative rights are stronger than positive rights and the negative right to life appears to be the strongest of all. In this case, your burly buddy's negative right to life *overrides* the positive rights of the people in the camp. Fleshy Friend meets the above criterion for applying the DDA. Pushing your friend into the bottleneck (doing harm) is worse than watching as the horde devours the encamped survivors (allowing harm).

As mentioned above, however, just because the DDA applies in this case does not entail that the bare difference between doing and allowing harm always makes a moral difference. Consider a variation on Fleshy Friend where the camp doesn't exist at all, but the hungry horde is nonetheless approaching the bottleneck below. Both you and your companion are at the top of the canyon looking down at the army of undead approaching the bottleneck. For whatever reason—maybe you want to take his gear—you intend for him to die. Unbeknownst to your colleague, you are about to push him from behind. In the first case, you push him into the canyon, much as you do in Fleshy Friend. In the second case, however, as you approach, he loses his balance. If you do nothing, he will fall into the bottleneck below. If you reach out a hand to steady him, however, he will stay on the ledge. Both the *consequences* of pushing him and doing nothing are identical: your chum falls into the bottleneck, his body serving as zombie chum for the approaching horde. What is equally important, however, is that your *intentions* are the same as well: you want him to die so that you can take his gear. In this case, it seems hard to believe that whether you *do* harm (push) or *allow* harm (let fall) makes a moral difference. Let's call this scenario "Selfish Survivor."

In both cases, your companion has a negative right to life that is not outweighed by any rights-based considerations. In fact, since the camp does not exist, their positive rights could not even in principle compete with his negative right to life. For the same reason, their positive rights could not outweigh his positive right to aid. We will again assume for the sake of argument that the voracious appetite of the horde does not place you under an obligation to feed it, that is, the horde possesses no positive rights. Even so, the man whose possessions you covet still possesses a positive right. This is obvious in the second case where he is teetering and you could easily come to his aid by steadying him. Even in the first case, however, he possesses a positive right. As you are pushing him into the canyon and he teeters on the precipice, you are under an obligation to pull him back from the edge. When you push him, you are violating both a negative and a positive right that are not overridden. When you allow him to fall, you are violating a positive right that is not overridden. Most importantly, however, the above criterion for applying the DDA is not met in these cases and so the bare difference between doing and allowing harm does not make a moral difference in Selfish Survivor.

While we don't need to worry about cases where the criterion for applying the DDA is not met and our intuition tells us that allowing harm is *no worse* than doing harm (e.g., Selfish Survivor), the conscientious survivor should worry about cases where the criterion for applying the DDA is met but our intuition tells us allowing harm is *worse* than doing harm. If there are such cases, then the DDA won't provide us with a reliable rule for determining what we ought or ought not to do when faced with the moral dilemmas that horde attacks too often generate. Given how quickly one must typically make a decision, and the high stakes that are involved, discovering a reliable rule is all the more pressing.

3. Spur

Let's go back in time to when your companion was setting the diversion at the end of the ravine, a spur off of the main canyon. Your friend has finished installing the megaphone and is headed back. You turn around to see with terror that a ravenous horde of undead is now barreling toward the bottleneck that leads to the camp. If you do nothing, the undead will devour the five survivors in the camp. You are too far away to warn them. In addition to drawing the zombies away from the camp, the megaphone is supposed to warn your friends of the undead threat so that they could either defend the bottleneck or escape back up the main canyon. The only other option you have is to activate the megaphone and start playing the moans at full volume. This would draw the horde down the spur, away from the community, but would ensure that your companion is devoured instead. He is too far away for you to warn him to start climbing and by the time he sees the horde it will be too late. What should you do ... or not do? Let's call this case "Spur."

FIGURE 12 Spur.

Say you are seriously considering activating the megaphone and let's assume that it's actually charged this time! If you do nothing, you are only *allowing* the horde to devour the survivors in the camp. Unlike Horde, you aren't actually leading them there. If you flip the switch and play your smartphone, however, you will be *killing* your friend by redirecting the horde down the ravine. Consider the criterion above for applying the DDA. Both your friend and the survivors in the camp have a negative right to life. The people in the camp have a positive right to aid which places you under an obligation to prevent them from being devoured. At the same time, however, their positive right would be outweighed by your friend's negative right to life since the latter is the strongest right of all. Everyone has a negative right that is not overridden and positive rights do exist—the people in the camp have them—but their rights are overridden by your friend's negative right to life. According to the above criterion, the DDA would apply in this case. Doing harm (activating the megaphone and killing your friend) would be *worse* than allowing harm to occur (the horde devouring the encamped survivors). Your gut reaction to this case, however, was likely the very opposite, namely, that doing harm is *better* than allowing harm to occur. If this is the correct moral judgment, then it is important to find an ethical justification. Put in terms of the above cases, what is the moral difference between pushing your colleague in Fleshy Friend and activating the megaphone which draws the horde that devours him in Spur? Aren't you doing harm in both cases so that you can save five others who would otherwise be devoured?

Here it might be helpful to go back to basics and consider what someone like Kant would say. He might ask: "What is the maxim behind your action?" It would probably be something like the following: "If I can save several lives by sacrificing one life, then I will sacrifice the one life." The question then becomes whether your maxim will be consistent with the categorical imperative. Consider the life of the one using the formulation of humanity as an end in itself. Are you treating this one person—your companion—*merely* as a means to achieve some other end? At first blush, it certainly seems like you are. In both Fleshy Friend and Spur, don't you intend those hungry harbingers of undeath to devour your companion so that you can save the community from their ravenous onslaught?

Something called the **Doctrine of Double Effect** (DDE) should lead us to reconsider our answer to this question. The DDE traces its lineage all the way back to St. Thomas Aquinas in the Middle Ages. It holds that we can draw a moral distinction between (i) the intended consequences of an action and (ii) the consequences that are merely foreseen but not intended. These two different kinds of consequences are the "double effect." Put simply, the DDE holds that it may be permissible to bring about a harm that is *foreseen* as the effect of one's action as long as that harm is not itself the *intended* effect of one's action. There are four conditions for applying the DDE:

(1) Considered independently of its harmful effect, the act is not wrong in itself.

(2) The agent intends the good effect and does not intend the harmful effect—either in itself or as a means to the good effect—though this harmful effect can be foreseen.

(3) There is no other way of achieving the good effect without causing the harmful effect.

(4) The good effect outweighs the harmful effect.

Let's start with Spur. With respect to (1), although theft, rape, and murder might be wrong in themselves, simply activating a megaphone is morally neutral even if it leads to a harmful effect in this particular circumstance. When it comes to (2), the agent clearly intends the good effect—the community being spared from the undead horde—though it is unclear whether the harmful effect is intended by the agent. Is your companion's gruesome demise merely foreseen or is it intended as a means to achieving the good effect? To answer this question, consider what you would do if your companion had finished hiking back up the ravine and was standing next to you on the canyon ridge rather than exposed to the horde in the ravine below. It stands to reason that you would still activate the megaphone which suggests that you don't really intend for your companion to be devoured. Even so—and this is where (3) is relevant—under present circumstances you cannot save the community without sacrificing your companion. He is, in fact, trapped in the canyon spur with no hope of rescue from the clutches of the onrushing zombie horde. Finally, with (4), assuming that the community is full of fine people and your companion is a fine fellow as well, the many fine people saved by your action outweighs the, admittedly, grisly consequences for your buddy. Although you might feel terrible for your friend, activating the megaphone in Spur meets all four of the above conditions and would be justified according to the DDE.

Does Fleshy Friend meet the four conditions as well? One potential difference between the two cases is that it seems as if you really do intend to kill your companion in Fleshy Friend. His bountiful body is the only thing that stands between the hungry horde and the terrified members of the community. Whereas in Spur his violent death is not necessary to save the community—the horde would be trapped safely at the end of the canyon spur with the moaning megaphone—in Fleshy Friend the death of the man himself is absolutely necessary to achieve your desired end. Returning to Kant, this also seems to be a clear example of where you are using your friend merely as a means. He is being treated as nothing more than a hunk of meat to occupy the horde until the other survivors are able to mount a defense. Like you, this is a fate he would presumably not choose for himself. Fleshy Friend does not meet condition (2) above for applying the DDE since you do intend his death. It also stands to reason— at least *Kantian* reason—that Fleshy Friend also violates condition (1) for applying the DDE. The act of *pushing* your colleague off a cliff to his gory death below would be wrong in itself for someone like Kant. Even though the other two conditions are likely met—there is no way of producing the good effect (saving the community) without the bad effect (your friend's grim demise) and the former outweighs the latter (more people are saved)—insofar as the first two conditions are not met, the DDE would not apply in the case of Fleshy Friend.

4. Loop

It seems like we are making some moral progress. The DDA was able to explain the moral difference between Horde and Fleshy Friend, but was unable to explain the apparent moral difference between Fleshy Friend and Spur. At this point, we invoked the DDE to explain the moral difference between Fleshy Friend and Spur. There is another case of horde diversion, however, which seems morally identical to Spur but for which the DDE would claim a moral difference.

Consider Spur again, but with one small difference. Instead of the ravine terminating in a both literal and figurative "dead end," it continues back around to the camp. Neither your partner doing the reconnaissance, nor the survivors in the camp noticed the narrow path that connected the end of the ravine to the end of the canyon behind the camp. Although human eyes can overlook such things, nothing escapes the notice of the undead, especially with numbers as great as this horde. Just as life used to "always find a way" before the outbreak, the virus now always finds a way to end it—or at least turn it into something far different from its former self. As in Spur, your companion has completed installing the megaphone and has started back. From your vantage point at the top of the canyon, you are able to see for the first time the connection between the ravine and the camp. You realize that diverting the horde up the canyon spur will not actually save the people in the camp, but will only momentarily delay the massacre as the horde works its way around to the unsuspecting victims. Unbeknownst to him, however, your friend is now standing right next to the narrow opening that leads to the camp. In fact, his ample frame almost completely obscures it.

Disappointed, you turn around to see—with sudden dread—the horde rapidly approaching the bottleneck. Now that you know the main canyon and the ravine are connected, activating the megaphone would, under normal circumstances, not do the camp any good. The horde would be upon them almost as quickly as if you had done nothing at all. Since your friend happens to be next to the opening that leads to the camp, however, things are far from *normal* and you are faced with a horrific choice. If you activate the megaphone, the horde will be led down the ravine until it barrels into your friend. With the time it takes the horde to eat through his bountiful flesh and with the amplified moans from the megaphone warning the camp, the survivors will escape through the bottleneck and back up the canyon. Alternatively, if you do nothing, the horde will careen through the bottleneck, devouring the camp, before turning to your friend for dessert. Let's call this situation "Loop." What should you do?

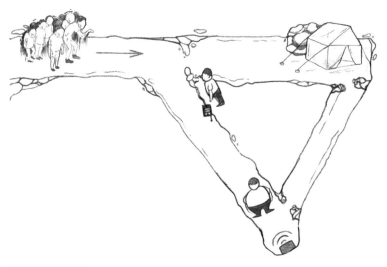

FIGURE 13 Loop.

At first glance, it seems hard to explain why this situation would be *morally* different from Spur. If it is morally permissible to activate the megaphone in Spur—which it seems to be—then it should be permissible to activate the megaphone in Loop as well. Why should the newly discovered path from the ravine to the main canyon make a moral difference with respect to the fate of your partner? Everything else about the two cases remains the same. If there really is no moral difference between Spur and Loop, we should expect the DDE to apply equally in both cases.

As you will recall from above, we used the DDE to draw a moral distinction between Fleshy Friend and Spur. What would the DDE have to say about Loop? Is it different from Spur? Let's go through each of the criteria for applying the DDA. Starting with (1), in both cases, simply activating the megaphone is morally neutral even if it leads to a harmful effect in this particular circumstance. Likewise, with respect to (3), you cannot save the community without sacrificing your companion. Similarly, when it comes to (4), the good effect (five survivors in the camp saved) outweighs the harmful effect (one companion devoured). If there is a difference between the two cases, it will lie with (2). The key question is the following: Do you intend the good effect (five saved) and not the harmful effect (one devoured)—either in itself or as a means to the good effect—though this harmful effect can be foreseen? In Spur, when you activate the megaphone, the same result would be brought about regardless of whether your friend is in the ravine or not. Of course, you would prefer that he were not there. His death is *unnecessary* for the end you intend to achieve by activating the megaphone, namely, saving everyone in the camp by drawing the horde down the adjoining ravine. In stark contrast, however, the death of your friend is absolutely *necessary* for the end you hope to achieve by activating the megaphone in Loop. If it were not for your friend's burly body blocking the narrow path that leads from the ravine to the canyon, the ravenous horde would complete the loop and devour everyone in the camp. Your friend must be exactly where he is and be devoured by the horde in order to save everyone in the camp from their otherwise violent demise.

5. Second Horde

Although the DDE would claim a moral difference between Spur and Loop, there is good reason to think the cases are morally identical. According to the DDE, as long as there is a narrow path connecting the ravine to the camp, it is morally *impermissible* to let loose the hungry horde on your partner. If this path does not exist—perhaps a real, rather than a human boulder blocks the way—it suddenly becomes morally *permissible* to let loose the ravenous scourge on your unsuspecting friend. Why should this little bit of path have an impact on the *moral* permissibility of killing your friend? This is a strange result, one which should make us reconsider whether this narrow path leads us astray from the moral standpoint.

In order to bring these various cases in line with our considered judgment, we need a way of morally distinguishing between Spur/Loop on the one hand and Fleshy Friend on the other. A potential moral difference between Spur/Loop and Fleshy Friend is your agency with respect to the fatal sequence that leads to your companion's death. In Spur/Loop, it seems as if you are merely *redirecting* a threat that already exists. That hungry horde is already hurtling toward the community of survivors. By activating the megaphone, you are simply attracting the horde down a different path that leads, unfortunately, to your colleague's tasty torso. In Fleshy Friend, however, you *initiate* the fatal sequence that leads to your friend's death. Even if by some miracle he were to survive the initial fall, he will soon be devoured by the horde hurtling toward his broken body. Although it may be permissible to redirect a fatal sequence to save more lives, perhaps it is not morally permissible to initiate a fatal sequence with the same goal.

Even if there is a clear distinction between initiating and redirecting harm, this does not entail that this distinction always makes a moral difference. Consider one final case. Take the situation in Loop again, but imagine that the narrow path extends past the ravine into *another* canyon. As in the original case, a voracious horde of the undead, in the main canyon, is rapidly approaching the bottleneck that leads to the camp. If you do nothing, the horde will devour the five encamped survivors. If you activate the megaphone, however, the horde will be led down the adjoining ravine occupied by your companion. Let's assume he is a bit closer to you this time, but is still in the ravine. He is far enough from the narrow path that leads to the camp, however, that no one—or *thing*—on that path would notice him. As you are considering whether or not to activate the megaphone, you see a *second* horde approaching the ravine, through the narrow path, leading from the other canyon. This horde, left unimpeded, will also devour the survivors in the camp. The camp is facing destruction on two fronts! If you were to activate the megaphone, the first horde would chase your friend back to where the narrow path meets the ravine. There, his ample frame would block—just as in Loop—the narrow opening to the path that leads to the camp. In the time it would take the second horde to devour his beefy body, the other survivors would have the opportunity to escape through the bottleneck. Let's call this case "Second Horde."

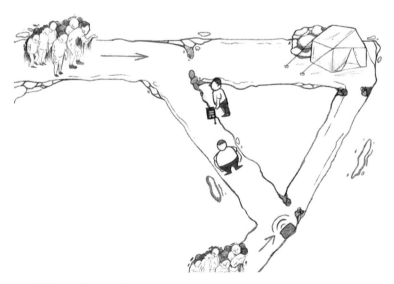

FIGURE 14 Second Horde.

This situation contains elements of both Fleshy Friend and Spur/Loop. By activating the megaphone, you are using the first horde to *push* your friend toward the second horde. Just like Fleshy Friend, you *initiate* a fatal sequence, namely, indirectly pushing your friend to his death at the hands—and teeth—of the second horde. What's crucial is that you aren't redirecting the *second horde* to kill your friend; rather, quotes this passage as well in the Summa Theologica you are redirecting your *friend* to the second horde and by doing so *initiating* a new fatal sequence. Morally, this should be no different than Fleshy Friend. Even so, the situation also contains elements of Spur/Loop. You are redirecting an existing threat—the first horde—toward your friend in the ravine so as to save the survivors in the camp. If it is permissible to redirect a fatal sequence in Spur/Loop, why shouldn't it be permissible here as well? Redirecting the threat in Second Horde, however, also initiates a fatal sequence that is morally similar to Fleshy Friend. If it is impermissible to initiate a fatal sequence in Fleshy Friend, shouldn't it be morally impermissible here as well?

What are conscientious Kantians to do? The philosophical distinctions at their disposal—the DDA, negative vs. positive rights, the DDE, initiating vs. redirecting a fatal sequence—are together unable to explain all of the above cases. Put differently, there does not seem to be a single rule or even a set of rules that the Kantian can rely upon to resolve the ethical dilemmas that arise in cases of horde diversion. Given how little time the agent has, as well as the high life and (un)death stakes involved, we should consider looking elsewhere for a more practical approach.

* * *

Thankfully, there is another approach—utilitarianism—for which hordeology does not vex at all. Although we will discuss this position at greater length over the next couple of chapters, for present purposes, suffice it to say that your portly partner would not fare well under utilitarian thinking. Utilitarianism would counsel to do whatever produces the most overall happiness. Even though this post-apocalyptic existence is hardly a life of luxury, people are generally happier *surviving* than being *consumed* alive by the undead. Insofar as saving the *five* people in the camp would produce more overall happiness than saving your *one* friend, the utilitarian would say to sacrifice your friend. Whether you are doing or allowing the harm to your friend, intending or foreseeing it, is irrelevant to the utilitarian. All that matters is the amount of happiness produced or unhappiness, for example, the abject suffering of being devoured and turning, which is prevented.

Summary

Although Kantian moral theory might be able to deal with simple horde scenarios, the undead rarely leave us with simple choices. As the situations grow more complex, the Kantian struggles to defend the moral distinctions they depend on when making decisions in the field. Most importantly, there seem to be cases—like Second Horde—against which all the moral weapons in the Kantian arsenal are ineffective. We need to look elsewhere for a theory that will allow us to make sound moral judgments regardless of how complex the undead threat might be.

Further study

- Augustine. *On Free Choice of the Will. 389.* Translated with introduction. Cambridge: Cambridge University Press, 2010.
  - In Latin, the title is *De libero arbitrio* and contains the passage that inspired the quotation at the beginning of this chapter. In the original, Augustine asks, "How indeed are they free of sin in the sight of Divine providence? They have been stained by human blood for the sake of things [human bodies] which should be held of little worth" (I.5.13.39–40). Aquinas quotes this passage as well in the *Summa Theologica* when presenting the DDE (II.II, Q. 64, Art. 7).

- Cathcart, Thomas. *The Trolley Problem or Would You Throw the Fat Guy Off the Bridge?* New York: Workman Publishing, 2013.
  - A short and partially fictionalized overview of a few central trolley cases that also provides most of the relevant philosophical background to the cases.

- Edmonds, David. *Would You Kill the Fat Man?* Princeton: Princeton University Press, 2014.
  - A lengthy but very readable discussion of all the most important trolley scenarios with additional philosophical and historical/biographical context.

- Foot, Philippa. "Killing and Letting Die." In *Abortion and Legal Perspectives*, edited by Jay Garfield and Patricia Hennessey, 177–185. Amherst: University of Massachusetts Press, 1984.

- The criterion for applying the DDA, discussed above, is taken from this article. She also adopts the very strong position on the negative right to life that is reflected in this chapter.

- Foot, Philippa. "The Problem of Abortion and the Doctrine of Double Effect." *Oxford Review* 5 (1967): 5–15.

  - In its original form, the threat was a not a zombie horde barreling down a canyon but rather a trolley barreling down a track. The above article spawned the vast "trolleyology" literature and contains the trolley-based examples of Horde (Trolley) and Fleshy Friend (Fat Man) above.

- Gliesberg, Brian and Kielpinski, Gerald. *Surviving the Zombie Outbreak: The Official Zombie Survival Field Manual.* Detroit: Aquarius Press, 2011.

  - See chapter sixteen for a number of different zombie diversion techniques.

- Kamm, Francis. *Intricate Ethics.* Oxford: Oxford University Press, 2007.

  - This book introduces the original version of Second Horde for which the author uses a tractor. The tractor is moving down a path toward five trapped people simultaneously with a trolley barreling down on them (pp. 136–138). The only way of saving the five is to use the trolley to "push" a heavyset man in front of the tractor which will kill him. The book contains a plethora of other ingenious trolley scenarios.

- Kant, Immanuel. *Metaphysics of Morals.* 1797. Translated with introduction. Cambridge: Cambridge University Press, 1996.

  - For his discussion of natural rights, see the first part of the book, the "Doctrine of Right."

- Rachels, James. "Active and Passive Euthanasia." *The New England Journal of Medicine* 292 (1975): 78–80.

  - This article contains the example that serves as the basis for "Selfish Survivor" above and poses several objections to the DDA.

- Thomson, Judith Jarvis. "The Trolley Problem." *Yale Law Journal* 94, no. 6 (1985): 1395–1415.

  - This article contains the original trolley-based versions of Spur and Loop as well as a discussion of Fat Man (Fleshy Friend above).

- *The Walking Dead*, [TV Program].

  - Season 2.2 "Save the Last One" contains a zombie diversion and an ethical choice similar to Fleshy Friend. When Shane sacrifices Otis to the pursuing horde by shooting him in the leg, he does so in order to save himself as well as Carl for whom he has retrieved life-saving supplies.

7 HOW TO MAXIMIZE PLEASURE IN A WORLD OF FLESH-CONSUMING ANGUISH

Destroying the living or undead may be said to be conformable to the principle of utility when the tendency this destruction has to augment the happiness of a survivor community is greater than any it has to diminish it.

—PRINCIPLES OF POST-APOCALYPTIC MORALS AND
LEGISLATION FOR SURVIVOR COMMUNITIES

As mentioned at the end of the last chapter, the utilitarian would not be troubled by hordeology. If killing one person will save the rest of the community from the clutches of the undead, then that is what should be done. The same is true of the undead. If destroying them will augment the happiness of the community, then they should be destroyed. Things aren't always so clear-cut though. Zombie search and destroy missions can put survivors at unnecessary risk for infection. Likewise, if your community is fending off the undead, it is not always so easy to figure out which of the various actions you *could* perform *would* actually bring the greatest happiness, or ensure the least unhappiness, for your community. This chapter will examine different utilitarian procedures for determining which act you ought to perform in order to ensure the overall happiness of your community.

1. Field exercise: The horde

Thinking that others were doing *their* jobs, I had focused on doing *mine*. Tasked with cleaning up the camp, I had been listening to "Changes" on my headphones to keep my mind both occupied and distracted. The camp lay at the dead-end of a canyon protected on three sides by sheer rock cliffs. If the fall did not destroy a zombie, it would break every bone in the creature's body leaving it totally immobile though still dangerous—a land mine of infection. This had happened at some point in the past, and I was walking among these twitching mounds of decomposing flesh, to finish what the cliffs had started. In addition to being prudent, it also seemed like the right thing to do. After destroying the brain with a staff I had carved for this purpose, I dragged them into a pile that we could later burn. On the fourth side of the canyon, lay a narrow bottleneck that only a few people could pass through at a time. If necessary, we could defend the bottleneck ... assuming we had sufficient warning to do so.

I looked up from my grim work and saw them just as Bowie was counseling me to "turn and face the strange"—a massive horde squeezing itself through it leading to our camp. They not only ran through it, but trampled over one another in their blind desire to devour us. When they began to pile up at the bottom of the bottleneck—a writhing but immobile mass of rotting arms and legs—the undead scurried up the walls and over, like cockroaches through a hole. As their preternatural movement closed the physical distance between us, it created an uncanny valley across which I could no longer see myself. They were more virus than human, infection propagating by turning nature against itself.

Only seven of us had made it this far. Two had been tasked with setting up a diversion and activating it if they saw a horde approaching. Apparently, something had gone wrong. There had been no diversion and we received no warning. Although the mass of the horde had been delayed by the bottleneck itself, the vanguard was upon us in an instant and quickly divided us from one another. In the little time I had, I tried to take stock of the situation, and decide what to do.

The "warrior" of the group, as he liked to refer to himself, was living up to his moniker. He swung a shaolin spade: a six-foot long staff with a bell-shaped blade at one end and a crescent-shaped blade at the other. Like a whirling dervish, turning and thrusting like a piston, he popped their heads off as soon as they got within a few feet of him. Champagne plumes of gore rained down as their bodies formed a ring around him. This macabre circle, however, soon trapped him as two zombies broke through the perimeter and pinned him against the far side. Without him, it seemed unlikely that those of us that remained would be able to defend ourselves for long.

FIGURE 15 Zombies attacking survivors.

I started running toward him—my staff over my head—when I saw two zombies approaching what would have been our "medical tent" if we had either a doctor or more than one tent. This sight stopped me in my tracks. One member of our group who had taken ill was lying unconscious inside. She wasn't bitten and her condition wouldn't be life-threatening in a more civilized time. In the miserable present, however, she was totally immobile. Without the conveniences of modern medicine, her common cold had advanced to pneumonia and would kill her if she was not allowed time to recover. She was a farmer, just the kind of person we would need were we ever fortunate enough to rebuild the world again. Our rifle was also in the tent, but it would do her little good given her condition.

I changed direction and was poised to take out both ghouls when I spotted the last two members of our group. A single zombie approached two small children huddled together for protection. Both were healthy and mobile, but were nonetheless just as defenseless as the woman in the tent. Although they were not my own, I had grown with time to love them as if they were. Their utter dependence on me had created a bond that generated its own obligation. Anyway, in a world in which so few are left alive, aren't all that remain my sister or my brother, my daughter or my son? Don't these familial bonds strengthen in inverse proportion to our dwindling numbers? I called to the children to run to me, but they could not break free of their debilitating terror.

Whereas the children were frozen by fear, I was frozen by indecision. Should I save the warrior? Doing so would make it more likely that we—however many of us remain—would survive in the short-term, since he was best suited to eliminate the current threat. The rifle in the tent would also help right now, but—more importantly—without the farmer our long-term future was dim. Assuming we did survive the present, at some point we would need to start building for our future happiness. The leftovers of a lifeless society could last only so long. Even though the farmer was necessary to rebuild this world and the warrior was required to defend it, what point was there in building something if there was no future generation to enjoy it?

My options overwhelmed me, and the undead took the opportunity to make my choice for me. The warrior released his own plume of gore as the two attackers tore into his carotid arteries simultaneously. I then turned to see the tent fall, its occupant offering no resistance. I closed the gap with the children as quickly as I could. Dropping my staff and pulling them from the ghoul's grasp, I simultaneously kicked it in the head. As it staggered backward, I dropped them to the ground and kicked my staff back into my hand. I twirled around and punched it through the eye with an ease that comes only through habitual action. It dropped—now truly lifeless—to the ground.

The children were screaming and crying, but there was no time to comfort them. The rest of the horde was rapidly descending upon us.

I forced the kids to the back corner of the canyon where at least we would be safe on two sides. Looking around wildly, my eye caught a narrow opening in the rock that we had all missed before. Like an optical illusion, its secret was only revealed from this single perspective. This time, without hesitation, I dragged both of them through the opening in the rocks, their feet hardly touching the ground. The horde closed in behind us, but the opening was so small that the mob was flummoxed by its own bloodlust. No more than one zombie at a time could fit behind us, but as soon as one started to push into the opening a second would pull it out in its uncurbed desire to consume us first.

Leaving this undead paradox behind, I pulled the children toward the opening on the other side. We were in a ravine. Looking up, in the far distance, I saw two figures on top of the canyon wall. Both were small though one was noticeably larger than the other. They were the two charged with looking out for the camp—a task they failed miserably. "Damned cowards," I muttered to myself as I picked the children up. Not knowing if I would be able to control my anger if I confronted the men and not knowing how long it would take the horde to resolve its paradox, I decided to strike out on my own.

At this point, my bug-out bag is simply a part of me. I only take it off to sleep and had it on during the attack. The children had also been integrated into my contingency plans. In addition to the basic survival necessities, I also have a sling I fashioned to carry them. They rotated between walking and being carried as I continued walking ceaselessly from the day—to the evening—and through the night. I feared stopping in the open terrain and kept at it until the following morning.

When dawn broke, I saw an object twinkling in the distance. A shipping container lay at the edge of an abandoned settlement and had all of life's basic needs—bottled water, canned food, etc.—pouring out of it. Before the American government fell, it used to resupply isolated communities like this one, cut off by the undead from the rest of the country, with periodic shipments delivered by helicopter. I was suspicious. There was a lot of value here, but the labels on what lay outside had faded to blank strips of white. If this was a trap, the hunter had long abandoned it. I put the child on my back down on ground and handed the other a bottle of water from inside the container. Our long journey had, at least temporarily, come to an end.

2. Three tenets of utilitarianism

The protagonist in the above story wants to do what's best for the camp *overall* which reflects utilitarian thinking. All versions of utilitarianism agree upon three basic tenets. The first is **hedonism**. Although I discussed the view briefly in connection with moral naturalism in Chapter 2.4, here I will dig deeper into some of the challenges it faces. To review, hedonism is the view that pleasure is the *sole* intrinsic value, that is, the only thing that is valuable for its own sake. The basic argument in favor of this position is that everything you value, is valued either because it brings you pleasure itself or is a means toward pleasure (or the avoidance of displeasure). Take one of the least pleasurable tasks one might be asked to perform in a survivor community, namely, finishing off incapacitated undead and burning their bodies. Why do we value the proper disposal of the undead? This activity brings no pleasure in itself, assuming one does not possess a sadist streak, but the still-twitching bodies of the undead pose a constant threat for further infection. If one were headed to the restroom and stumbled into their snapping teeth in the dead of night—like a steel jaw trap lying in wait—you might end up being infected and devouring the rest of your camp as it slept. Even if the proper disposal of the undead does not bring pleasure in itself, it avoids a great deal of potential displeasure in the future.

Are there other things besides pleasure that are intrinsically valuable, for example, knowledge of the world, friendship, or aesthetic enjoyment? In order to answer this question, we need to consider whether or not each of these would still be valuable even if it neither produced pleasure itself nor was a means toward pleasure. Let's start with knowledge of the world. Regardless of whether it has been discovered or not, the virus either has a cure or it doesn't. Assume for the sake of argument that it does not. Is this knowledge valuable? It certainly does not bring you any pleasure to know that the scourge will continue until there are none left to scourge. It is also hard to see how this knowledge might be the means toward some other pleasure. If this knowledge is valuable, it could serve as a counterexample to hedonism. It is unclear, however, whether it is valuable. I can only assume that many of us would prefer to remain in ignorance if the alternative is the crushing hopelessness that comes with knowing that the virus is incurable. Let's assume, however, that you nonetheless find this knowledge to be valuable—perhaps it produces a stoic calm. This doesn't entail that *all* knowledge is valuable. What if you are the lookout at the top of the canyon, but your day was far less exciting than our stories thus far made it out to be. With nothing to do, you spend the day counting all of the boulders in the canyon below, say all 1,977 of them. Is this knowledge *valuable* in any way? Even if the task of counting kept your mind occupied, it is hard to find any worth in the final product. Knowledge of the world, in and of itself, does not seem to be valuable. Its value is always relative to something else and the utilitarian would claim that "something else" is happiness. The stoic calm, referred to above, produced by the knowledge that there is no cure, could be considered a form of happiness. After all, the stress and anxiety of uncertainty are now behind you. We will discuss the idea that there could be different *forms* of happiness at greater length below.

What about friendship? Here, again, it is important to consider an instance of friendship that neither produces pleasure nor is the means toward pleasure. Would such a friendship be valuable? Consider Fleshy Friend from the previous chapter. What if your portly partner is a perpetual hindrance, always getting into trouble—trapped in canyon spurs, bottlenecks, and the like—requiring that you constantly rescue him from the clutches of the undead? If this relationship brought you nothing but grief, would it be valuable? Does friendship unaccompanied by pleasure, either in itself or as a means to it, even constitute what we would consider "friendship"?

Alternatively, a friendship might cause *only* pleasure but still be morally worthless. What if you took great *joy* in the troubles and travails of your companion—an intense *Schadenfreude*? When he finds himself in trouble, more often than not, it was of your own making, that is, you are the one sending him into canyon spurs or dropping him into bottlenecks before swooping in to rescue him at the last minute. He might deeply value your friendship and greatly appreciate your constant assistance, but the whole relationship is really a sham. You are manipulating him the whole time. Isn't this wrong at some level? If so, it would serve as a counterexample to hedonism, since it suggests that something else must be valuable besides pleasure.

Finally, consider aesthetic enjoyment. Although there is little of this to be had in a devastated world with neither art nor culture, there is still the beauty of nature when unblemished by the undead. This is something that I never fail to appreciate in the fleeting moments it is afforded to me. Does this enjoyment count as "pleasure"? What exactly do we mean by the term? The utilitarians, Jeremy Bentham and J.S. Mill, whose views we will examine at greater length below, offer different answers to this question. By "pleasure," Bentham means only *sensuous* pleasure: the pleasure you feel when eating a scavenged chocolate bar or the pleasure a zombie might feel when consuming your flesh. Although this is an issue we will revisit in the next chapter, let's assume for the time being that at least some zombies are capable of feeling this kind of pleasure. If this were the only kind of pleasure that the utilitarian cared about, it would seem that the existence of a fully satiated zombie, overflowing with the bloody offal of its most recent victim, would be preferable to the existence of a starving though nonetheless rational survivor. Mill would point out, however, that it is rare to find a survivor wishing to switch places with a zombie even if she is fully convinced that the zombie is more satisfied with its lot than she is with hers. Is it not better to be a survivor *unsatisfied* than a zombie *satisfied*? With a moment's reflection—of which the zombie is incapable—you should recognize that your zombie self would be missing out on quite a bit that seems valuable. We survivors are rational beings who are capable of experiencing things like aesthetic enjoyment which is itself a **higher-order pleasure** that zombies would seem incapable of experiencing. The satiated zombie above only experiences the **lower-order pleasure** associated with sensuous activities like eating. Far from being a counterexample to hedonism, aesthetic enjoyment can actually help to illustrate the value of higher-order pleasure for creatures like us. Returning to the concept of human flourishing introduced in Chapter 2.4, this kind of pleasure is a form of rational activity, and for someone like Mill makes the survivor's life preferable to the zombie's undeath. Even so, one might worry that expanding the definition of "happiness" to include the aesthetic, intellectual, and the social might be taking it too far away from actual pleasure and closer to something like a cultivated state of mind. Expanding the definition too much would have all the benefits of theft over honest labor since anything valuable in itself—that would otherwise pose a counterexample to hedonism—simply becomes part of our conception of happiness.

The second tenet of utilitarianism is **altruism**. This holds that one ought to weigh one's own pleasure or happiness equally with the happiness of others when determining what you ought to do. There is no special feature that I possess by virtue of being me that makes my pleasure more important, from the moral standpoint, than your pleasure. When determining what I ought to do, I cannot consider only my own happiness. Assuming you are affected by my action, I have to consider your happiness as well as the happiness of everyone else that might be affected by it equally. In some cases, my happiness might well be outweighed by the happiness of others if I am really weighing each individual's happiness equally with my own happiness. An interesting consequence of hedonistic altruism is that I need to take into account the pleasure/pain of *all* sentient creatures that would be affected by my action when determining what I ought to do. If (some) zombies feel pleasure/pain, their interests—not only survivor interests—matter as well. Although we may give greater weight to the higher-order over the lower-order pleasures, the lower-order pleasures that zombies might feel are not morally irrelevant. The lower-order pleasure of the zombie (consuming living flesh), furthermore, must be weighed equally with the lower-order pleasure (consuming chocolate bar) of the survivor. For the utilitarian, what matters from the moral standpoint is not the *individual* but rather the *pleasure* the individual feels. Another interesting consequence of hedonist altruism is that our personal relationships are largely irrelevant to moral action. The fact that the protagonist in the above story has a personal relationship with the two children should not affect their calculation of what to do. The pleasures/pains of the children need to be weighed equally with those of everyone else in the scenario.

The final tenet of utilitarianism is **consequentialism**. This holds that one ought to produce the most overall good, where the "most overall good" is understood in terms of the most happiness or pleasure. Although not all consequentialists are utilitarians, for example, you may not believe that pleasure is the sole intrinsic good, all utilitarians are consequentialists. It is here that one can notice the biggest differences with Kantian ethical theory. Whereas the *Kantian* would hold that it is unjust to kill one innocent person just to save five others—as one is tempted to do in Fleshy Friend—the *utilitarian* would hold that the greater injustice is to allow five innocent people to die when you are in a position to save them. Whereas the Kantian would hold that killing the one violates his right to life, the utilitarian would hold that recognizing rights prevents us from being altruistic. Rights preclude us from weighing everyone's interests equally since we can no longer view the interests of the five as outweighing the interests of the one. Finally, the Kantian would hold that the utilitarian view totally ignores the intrinsic moral value of things like promises. If breaking a promise produces the same amount of happiness as keeping a promise, the utilitarian would see no moral difference between the two actions. Going a step further, if breaking a promise actually maximized overall happiness, that is what the utilitarian would require. Returning to Fleshy Friend, what if you had promised your companion, prior to leaving the camp, that you would watch his back and keep him safe? Instead of *watching* his back, the utilitarian would require that you *push* him in the back to save five others. The fact that utilitarianism ignores these so-called "backward-looking reasons" (i.e., actions in the past, like promising, that place you under obligations in the future) is often seen as a weakness of the view. The utilitarian would likely respond, however, that we are simply conditioned into thinking that promising is morally right by repeatedly seeing the bad consequences of breaking promises. At root, the reasoning is utilitarian and once we recognize this, we will be able to see that there could be individual cases where breaking a promise is morally justified, for example, pushing your companion off the cliff in Fleshy Friend.

Consequentialism is sometimes phrased in terms of the slogan, "the greatest good for the greatest number," but this slogan is ambiguous as to which "greatest" ought to be greatest. Put in utilitarian terms, should we maximize the amount of happiness or the number of happy people? As every survivor knows, resources are scarce and are just getting scarcer. Imagine I had more people trapped with me right now. I have enough supplies for ten people to barely survive the amount of time that I will live in relative comfort. Which situation is better: one person living happily for a period of time—at least as happily as one can live alone and surrounded by the moans of the undead—or ten people just scraping by for that same period of time?

Let's assume, for the sake of argument, that the challenges that face the three tenets of utilitarianism can be overcome. This still leaves the problem of how the agent ought to act upon these three tenets when actually facing down the undead. This is the problem that the protagonist in our story faces and the next section articulates a possible solution.

3. Bentham's act utilitarianism

Although other figures in the history of philosophy anticipated certain aspects of utilitarian thinking, Bentham was the first to codify these into a single ethical system. Bentham subscribes to **act utilitarianism**. This view holds that an act is objectively right if no other action the agent could perform would produce better consequences. For any particular situation, I need to calculate which of my actions, of all the actions I could perform, would produce the most overall happiness, weighing everyone's happiness equally. Bentham offers a procedure for carrying out this calculation.

The agent should start with a particular action and a particular person whose interests seem most immediately affected by the action. Consider (1) the value of each pleasure produced by the action relative to this individual, (2) the value of each pain produced by the action relative to this individual, (3) the value of each pleasure produced by the first pleasure relative to this individual, and (4) the value of each pain produced by the first pain relative to this individual. There are a number of different features that one should take into account when determining the "value" of each pleasure/pain. To list a few, one must consider the intensity and duration of the pleasure/pain, how certain or uncertain it is that pleasure/pain will be produced, as well as how near or remote the pleasure/pain will be to the individual who experiences it.

Assume that you have accurately calculated the value of each individual pleasure/pain as well as of the pleasures/pains that it would produce. At this point, the agent should (5) sum up the values of pleasure and pain to give the good tendency (if pleasures greater) or bad tendency (if pains greater) of the action relative to the individual in question. Finally, the agent must (6) repeat the above process for each individual whose interests are affected by the action to determine whether the tendency of the action is good on the whole or bad on the whole, that is, taking into account all of the individuals affected by the action.

Let us return to the story above. Start by considering the action of saving the "warrior" by destroying his two attackers. Without a doubt, if you were to save him, he would be happy and this happiness would likely be intense and last at least until the next attack. His happiness is fairly certain and is quite close to him. You are destroying attackers he is already grappling with, not bombing a distant horde that might at some point threaten him. Unlike a drug where the immediate pleasure is followed by the pain of withdrawal, the happiness he feels will likely generate more happiness, or at least relief, assuming that he survives the overall attack. There are cases of warriors growing despondent and depressed in the absence of zombie hordes to destroy, however, the withdrawal from adrenaline being just as painful as from heroin. Since both the woman in the tent and the two children would be devoured, one can safely assume that the pain they would feel would be just as intense, if not more so, than the happiness of the warrior. If they are fortunate, and quickly lose consciousness as they are being consumed, their pain should be short and no pains/pleasures would follow upon the void. Here, I pass over, until Chapter 10, the question of whether the pains/pleasures you might feel are still *yours* after conversion. The pain while still living is *certain* and no pain could be *nearer* than that of being eaten alive. Now, what about the effect his survival would have on your own happiness?

Before you could answer this question or any of the others asked above, the zombie horde will have made the decision for you much as they did in the above story. Bentham's act utilitarian decision procedure is totally *impractical* for the split-second decisions of life and (un)death that most survivors must make on a daily basis. Although this amount of careful contemplation might be appropriate to a Philosophy classroom or a legislator's office, neither exists anymore in this fallen world.

Bentham's own response to this worry is to say that we must always keep the procedure in view even if we are not using it for every decision. It is unclear, however, exactly what this would mean. How can we "keep it in view" without actually taking the (copious) time to use it? As an act utilitarian, what would be the principle of one's decision making if not the **principle of utility**—the prescription to produce the most overall happiness—as applied through this decision procedure? It seems there is little guaranteeing that our decision would be *exact*, by Bentham's lights, if we do not go through the procedure. Consequently, our choice is between an *impractical* decision procedure and an *inexact* moral judgment, neither of which is very appealing.

4. Mill's rule utilitarianism

One way of avoiding the impracticality of act utilitarianism is to hold that the principle of utility should not be used for choosing individual *actions* but rather for choosing the *rules* for action. In other words, instead of asking whether one's action produces more overall happiness than any other action one could perform, one should ask whether the rule for one's action would tend to produce more overall happiness if followed than if ignored. J.S. Mill subscribes to the **Greatest Happiness Principle** which holds that actions are right insofar as they tend to produce happiness and are wrong insofar as they tend to produce unhappiness. By "actions" he means *types* of actions (e.g., helping those in need) instead of *specific* actions (e.g., helping this warrior, or helping this farmer). **Rule utilitarianism** holds that the rightness of an act is fixed, not by the degree to which the act produces overall happiness, but by the happiness produced by the relevant moral rule, or that most or all members of a type of act are being performed. For rule utilitarianism, the principle of utility is a *meta-rule*. It helps us choose the rules that would go into a moral code, but it is not itself one of the rules that is chosen. Whereas an act utilitarian would evaluate individual actions by direct appeal to the principle of utility, the rule utilitarian would ask what rule the act would fall under where the rule is a rule because it has been justified in terms of the principle of utility.

For example, take the following candidate for a rule: "Kill people from whose deaths you would personally benefit." If that rule were part of the moral code, what would the effect be on overall happiness? Although it might be tempting to think that everyone would benefit from a rule that prescribed killing for personal benefit, consider yourself on the wrong end of the knife. If this were the rule, you—and everyone else with anything of potential value—would live in constant fear of violent death. Are people generally happy or unhappy when they live in a constant fear of violent death? If you are anything like me, you are very unhappy living the way we do in this post-apocalyptic wasteland. Returning to Chapter 3, getting out of this poor, nasty, brutish, and short condition is the very function morality is supposed to serve. Far from constituting part of a moral code, this "rule" would seem to undermine morality itself.

What if we went the other way with our rule? Consider this alternative: "Don't kill innocent people." Since people are perhaps *most* unhappy when they live in a constant fear of violent death, including this rule in our moral code would go the furthest toward helping to ensure people's happiness (or at least the minimization of their unhappiness). We could use similar reasoning to justify any number of rules: tell the truth, keep promises, help others in need, etc. A rule would be justifiably included in our moral code just in case following that rule would tend to have a positive impact on overall happiness (or would minimize unhappiness). In each case, we would use the principle of utility to select the rule, but the principle of utility would not itself be one of these rules.

The rules included in our moral code are themselves action guiding. This constitutes the crucial difference between act and rule utilitarianism. According to the latter view, the agent could determine what to do just by following whatever moral rule is relevant in that situation rather than calculating out the relative utility of every possible action she could perform. For example, in the story above, the relevant rule would seem to be to help others in need. As long as the protagonist is protecting the living from the zombie onslaught (regardless of who it is and in what order), they are doing what they ought to do according to the rule utilitarian. In principle, the protagonist would be able to make a decision much more quickly using rule rather than act utilitarianism.

Although one might notice strong similarities between the rules that a rule utilitarian would include in an ideal moral code and the duties that a Kantian includes in her moral code, the ways in which these rules are justified are very different. Whereas the rule utilitarian includes these rules because of the good *consequences* of following them, such considerations are irrelevant from the Kantian standpoint.

It is important to note that even if breaking the rule, in a particular situation, would produce more overall happiness, the rule utilitarian would say that one should still follow the rule. Taking an example from the previous chapter, whereas the act utilitarian would say you ought to push your portly partner in Fleshy Friend to his grisly demise, the rule utilitarian would hold that this would violate the rule that you ought not to kill innocent people. The fact that the rule utilitarian does not allow you to violate the rule when doing so would promote overall happiness— in this case saving the five survivors in the camp from their own grisly demise—is one of the main objections to the view. If the *rule* chosen using the principle of utility is more important than the *principle of utility*, how can this really be considered a form of utilitarianism? Isn't it rather a form of rule-worship? If you violate the rules whenever doing so would produce more happiness, however, then aren't you just an act utilitarian? The rules no longer seem to play any role and you would again face the problem of calculating the consequences of each individual action you could perform before deciding what to do.

The situation grows even more difficult when one considers that rules within the moral code could also come into conflict. For example, in Fleshy Friend, there are at least two relevant moral rules. There is the rule not to kill innocent people which would counsel against pushing your friend. On the other hand, there is the rule that says that one ought to help others in need which would counsel to save the encamped survivors from the oncoming horde. What should the conscientious rule utilitarian do? Mill himself suggests that when the rules conflict, one should do whatever produces the most overall happiness. If this is what you do, however, then there is no effective difference between act and rule utilitarianism whenever the rules conflict. You would make direct appeal to the principle of utility to determine what you ought to do just as the act utilitarian does.

Another possible solution, however, would be to use the rules themselves to resolve these conflicts. Perhaps we can create a hierarchy of rules based upon the relative impact that following each rule has on overall happiness. For example, while helping others generally has a positive impact on overall happiness, one might reasonably think that not killing them has an even *more* positive impact. As suggested above, people tend to be *most* unhappy when they live in constant fear of violent death. If you use this hierarchy, then you should *not* push your colleague in Fleshy Friend since not killing innocent people would be the higher-order rule in the hierarchy. Of course, there would still be a problem when higher-order rules conflict. For example, if you were ever faced with the horrible choice of having to decide between killing two perfectly innocent people, this approach would be of little use.

Although rule utilitarianism promised to overcome the calculation problem that act utilitarianism faces, it would seem that we have come a full circle and the rule utilitarian position actually faces problems very similar to the Kantian position. Far from delivering us from the problems the Kantian faces, utilitarianism returns us to them again albeit through a different route. Both the Kantian and the rule utilitarian have difficulties determining what they ought to do when the duties/rules come into conflict with one another. As we have seen, instead of being the exception, such conflicts are all too common in this violent world. If we cannot find a reliable way of resolving such conflicts, Ethics will ultimately offer little guidance in the zombie apocalypse. This is a problem I will tackle one last time in the Conclusion of this book.

Summary

Unlike the Kantian, the act utilitarian would have little difficulty deciding what to do in hordeology cases. There are typically only two possible actions and the probable impact of each action on overall happiness— one devoured vs. five devoured—is relatively straightforward. It is easy to think of other situations, however, where the choices are multiplied and the impact of each possible action on overall happiness is difficult to calculate. If the horde is diverted to your camp, you will have to decide—in a split second—who to save and in what order. Rule utilitarianism offers a more efficient decision-making procedure, but like the Kantian approach, it runs into problems when two or more rules conflict with one another, a common problem in our violent world.

Further study

- Bentham, Jeremy. *An Introduction to the Principles of Morals and Legislation.* 1789. Edited with introduction. Oxford: Oxford University Press, 1970.
  - Defends the three tenets of utilitarianism and presents his act utilitarian decision procedure. It inspired the work quoted at the beginning of this chapter.
- Brandt, Richard. "Some Merits of One Form of Rule Utilitarianism." *University of Colorado Studies* 3 (1967): 39–65.
  - Distinguishes between act and rule utilitarianism. It also discusses the above strategies for avoiding the problems that rule utilitarianism faces.
- Brooks, Max. *The Zombie Survival Guide.* New York: Three Rivers, 2003.
  - On p. 36, recommends the shaolin spade as one of the most effective hand weapons when battling zombies in open spaces.
- Cooper, Angel and Devlin, William. "Back from the Dead." In *The Ultimate Walking Dead and Philosophy*, edited by Wayne Yuen, 63–82. Chicago: Open Court, 2016.
  - Discusses various examples of how consequentialist reasoning shows up in *The Walking Dead*. Playing off Mill's Greatest Happiness Principle, the authors introduce the "Greatest Survival Principle" which holds that actions are right if they promote survival for the greatest number; wrong if they produce the reverse of survival.
- Delfino, Robert and Lesinski, Lea. "Carol's Transformation." In *The Ultimate Walking Dead and Philosophy*, edited by Wayne Yuen, 175–187. Chicago: Open Court, 2016.
  - Discusses the differences between act and rule utilitarianism using some of Carol's actions in *The Walking Dead*.
- Mill, John Stuart. *Utilitarianism.* 1863. With related remarks from Mill's other writings. Indianapolis: Hackett, 2017.
  - See chapter II for the Greatest Happiness Principle, Mill's distinction between higher-order and lower-order pleasure, as well as his endorsement of rule utilitarianism.

- Yuen, Wayne. "Carol Didn't Care." In *The Ultimate Walking Dead and Philosophy*, edited by Wayne Yuen, 193–203. Chicago: Open Court, 2016.
  - In addition to discussing Bentham's act utilitarianism, it illustrates the view's strengths and weaknesses within the context of *The Walking Dead*.
- *The Walking Dead*, [TV Program].
  - There are several episodes that illustrate utilitarian reasoning, or at least the "Greatest Survival Principle" mentioned above. For example, there is Shane's refusal to put the group at risk to save a smaller number of survivors in season 1.2 "Guts" and his sacrifice of Otis to save the greater number in season 2.3 "Save the Last One."
  - The Governor also applies consequentialist reasoning when dealing with Rick's group in the prison. See season 3.7 "When the Dead Come Knocking." His reasoning, however, ignores the altruism tenet of utilitarianism since he does not weigh the good of the individuals in Rick's group equally with the good of the individuals in his own group. In this same season, Rick rejects consequentialist reasoning when he refuses to sacrifice Michonne to the governor to save the group. See 3.17 "This Sorrowful Life."
  - In season 4.4 "Indifference," Carol offers utilitarian reasoning to justify killing two other survivors who were infected with a deadly and highly communicable strain of the flu.

8 ARE ALL ZOMBIES EQUAL?

The day may come when the infected may acquire those rights which never could have been withholden from them but by the hand of tyranny. It may one day come to be recognized that black spider veins, a desire for flesh, and tears of blood are reasons insufficient for abandoning a sensitive being to the caprice of a human tormenter. What else is it that should trace the insuperable line? Is it the faculty of reason, or perhaps the faculty of discourse? But the cracked up are beyond comparison more rational, as well as a more conversable, than an infant of a day or a week or even a month old. But suppose it were otherwise, what would it avail? The question is not, can they reason? Nor can they talk? But, can they suffer?

—PRINCIPLES OF POST-APOCALYPTIC MORALS AND LEGISLATION FOR SURVIVOR COMMUNITIES

Most survivors, or at least those that have made it long enough to be reading this book, do not give destroying zombies a second thought. It is either us or them and we—the living—are the only ones that matter from the moral standpoint. The received view has also been, up to this point, the default position of this book. We will now interrogate this assumption not only to see if zombies might be morally considerable but also, if they are, whether they are all *equally* morally considerable. As any survivor knows, not all zombies are the same. There are those for whom infection has taken hold—the "cracked up"—but are not yet undead. There are the "moaners" who are undead and simply ravenous. Finally, there are other undead zombies that seem to be developing capacities that make them similar to survivors and may even possess gifts that the living do not. These are the so-called "talkers." To determine whether or not it is wrong to kill zombies, we first need to determine why it is wrong to kill *us*. Put differently, why are survivors morally considerable? Is it because we are biologically human ... or persons ... or conscious ... or have the capacity to feel pleasure and pain? As we will see, answering this question is surprisingly difficult, but doing so will help us to determine whether and to what extent zombies are morally considerable as well.

1. Field exercise: Trapped

Walking down the sidewalk, rifle pointed ahead, I had been paying so much attention to potential threats around and above me, that I overlooked what lay below me. Flush with the sidewalk, a steel cellar door had been left open. The crunch of my ankle turning came a split-second before the searing pain. Looking around in agony, I slowly realized that I couldn't have fallen into a better place. It was the well-stocked commercial kitchen for a restaurant that must have been upstairs. The windows were all barred at street-level and the heavy hatch doors, once closed, could be latched from behind. Save for a dumbwaiter, the cellar doors were the only way in or out.

The space was divided in half. On one side was a small office with a messy desk and an old TV. Next to the office was a large walk-in fridge. On the other side was the kitchen itself with the dumbwaiter. The fridge was well stocked, and there were plenty of dried/canned goods in the kitchen. Since the locals don't trust the tap water in these border towns, there were also pallets of bottled water in the corner. When I arrived, I was surprised that the electricity was still running. Like the rest of the town, it looked like the cooks had just picked-up and gone. Turning on the TV, President Mentemuro explained:

> It isn't true that the border has been abandoned! Believe me ... we're going to take care of the incredible men and women who live up north. We've spent a lot of money ... *a lot* of money. They even have electricity up there. Ask anyone. When the mainstream media says those gringo cockroaches are infesting our country, they're lying. *Lots* of people are saying we're winning again.

Sitting back in the office chair with my wounded ankle elevated and on ice, I contemplated the metamorphosis I had ostensibly undergone by crossing the border and reflected on how appropriate it was that I found myself in a restaurant kitchen. Although I appreciated Mentemuro keeping the lights on, if anyone had infested this place, it had to be me.

The next few weeks were great, but they were also listless. I just sat around all day and watched the tube as if the apocalypse had never happened. Mentemuro provided steady entertainment and the fridge held all I could eat. He seemed to be the only thing broadcast anymore until an infected Latino guy sparked an outbreak at one of his rallies that claimed the old man and shattered Mexico's own sense of cultural superiority. The powers that be soon decided their remaining power was better spent elsewhere.

Without electricity, there was neither refrigeration nor entertainment. Without refrigeration, my diet was limited to rice and beans. The lack of ice also forced me to notice that my ankle had not really improved and, if anything, had grown worse. Without entertainment, my attention was drawn to the horde of zombies—all colors of the rainbow—that I could see shuffling outside the basement windows. With my likely broken ankle, there was no hope of making a run for it. I was stuck in a once gilded cage that had lost its luster.

As the hours turned to days and the days to weeks, I reconsidered Mentemuro's comparison though I still refused to include myself within it. Were the constant moans and scratching that surrounded me different in kind from the chirping and humming of cockroaches in the walls of a squalid home? Although the zombies were larger, wasn't this place infested all the same?

Since I could not escape through *them*—without joining their ranks—I resolved to bring them to *me*. I would turn the kitchen into a "roach motel" of sorts—they can check in, but they can't ever leave. The dumbwaiter was the key since only one "roach" could enter at a time. As soon as the weight of one zombie was in the box, the door closed automatically and brought *it*—the personal details of gender now seem inappropriate—down to the basement kitchen. As the door opened, I welcomed each like a bellhop *cum* exterminator—smile on my face and muzzle to their head. After removing the ruined corpse, a counterweight took control, the upward journey ending with a loud bell and an open door that attracted the next guest. Eventually, I would welcome them all before checking out myself.

I enjoyed releasing these creatures from their miserable existence, but as the bodies piled up in the disused fridge, my happiness grew more important than their release. The sense of intoxication didn't last long, however, and soon soured into a hangover of unfulfilled desire. I waved my gun at the pile: "Do you even feel it?" I asked aloud. "Why do you need them to?" my mind whispered back.

I began to experiment … First, I devised a snare—fashioned out of kitchen twine I had woven into a rope—that would catch them as soon as they left the dumbwaiter. I tied one end to a sturdy pipe above the opening to the dumbwaiter and at the other end tied a noose. I placed this in front of the door so that it was slightly larger than the opening. As long as they led head-first, and they always did, the head went right through the noose leaving them hanging upright, feet slipping and sliding on the charnel floor. They were still dangerous but immobile. Deciding it would be best to save what little ammunition remained, I instead created a rudimentary spear by taping a kitchen knife to a broom handle. Thrusting from a safe distance, I soon discovered a difference between the *undead* and the infected *living*. Those that were moaners couldn't care less about my pokes and prods. They kept their glassy eyes fixed on the prize—my luxuriant flesh. In contrast, there were those who had recently cracked up but were still alive. They snapped and grabbed much like the moaners, but they would also scream in pain when I cut them and then shield the fresh wound from my searching blade. I took my time with them since they offered double the pleasure of the undead ghoul. I could cut and slice away until the living—and screaming—creature finally expired at which point its undead self would resurrect for a final merciful release.

Once replicated enough, even my experiments devolved into a chore. I didn't *enjoy* what I was doing as much as I *needed* to do it … I was addicted. With repeated torture, the infected had lost almost all their power to please. The want of their screams became far more disagreeable than torturing them was pleasant. Despondent, I dragged the last corpse to the dormant walk-in freezer that served as a silent mausoleum of undead flesh and bone. Covering my mouth and nose to avoid the musty stench—not unlike a cockroach nest—I tossed the desultory parts into the dark abyss where they could join their rotting brethren.

As the saying goes, when one door closes another opens. Likewise, as soon as the freezer had slammed shut, I again heard a knocking coming from the dumbwaiter. Approaching the door, the knocking stopped replaced by a mournful moan:

"Fleeeeaaaash!"

Taken aback, I stammered "What are you?"—my hoarse voice sounding less human than the one to which I was responding.

"The paaaaiiin ..." the voice in the dumbwaiter trailed off.

I opened the door, but instead of lunging at me, the creature crouched in the dumbwaiter—its eyes glimmering in the darkness.

"I *neeeed* your fleeeeaaaash ..." Cautiously, it pushed its clawed hand out of the dumbwaiter. I grabbed my spear and held it at the ready. The zombie found the noose and *she*—she deserves this much—gently placed it around her neck as she slid out of the dumbwaiter. Looking up at me, she was crying tears of blood.

I could tell she was old. Her face was completely desiccated—bones, tendons, and broken parchment for skin. She must have fully converted in the first days of the outbreak. Although ancient for a zombie, when the tears touched a patch of skin, they soaked in and released a warm blush that briefly revealed the youthful beauty she possessed when turned.

FIGURE 16 Zombie with noose.

"Noooo moooore," she pleaded. Her eyes sparkled with intelligence and searched my face for some sign of empathy.

"Kiiiillll meeee ..." she whispered. Her final words cut me to the bone: "Weeee coooome here for thiiiissss."

With that, she stepped lithely toward the floor and hung slowly turning in the air—like a ballerina—her pale toes standing *en pointe* above the pool of blood and gore. Although she could no longer speak hanging from the noose, she continued to mouth "kill me" with what remained of her lips and jaw. When her body stopped turning, she opened her mouth wide as if to moan, but instead all I heard—for the first time in months—was total silence. The scratching and moaning—my constant torment—had ceased. I looked out the windows and all of the feet had stopped shuffling and were completely still. This respite lasted but a moment until it was broken by a single thunderous moan. All of the zombies surrounding my refuge were moaning together at the same pitch, creating an enormous sonic beacon that gathered the undead to itself.

I was crying when I thrust the knife through her skull. Not only would I never escape this place, but I was doomed to serve the undead, releasing them from an addiction that deepened my own. Every action has a reaction and, with each thrust of the spear, I sacrificed a shred of my humanity which transformed into a final measure of their own.

2. The human criterion

Consider the following—perhaps surprising—argument: (1) It is wrong to kill an innocent human being. (2) A zombie is an innocent human being. (3) Therefore, it is wrong to kill a zombie. At first blush, the argument appears to be valid. The conclusion (3) seems to follow from premises (1) and (2). If we assume that it is wrong to kill *all* innocent human beings and a zombie is an example of an innocent human being, then it would be wrong to kill a zombie as well. If the argument is valid, then the only remaining question is whether or not it is sound, that is, are the premises true?

It might be tempting to challenge the truth of the second premise. How could a bloodthirsty, murderous, undead monster be considered *innocent*? They are violent vectors of infection. Just because a creature is violent, however, does not entail that it is morally responsible for what it is and does. By what criteria can zombies be considered *guilty* for what they have become? All of us carry the virus—it is not our choice—and the infection treats us all differently. When bitten, some of us turn immediately while for others it takes time to crack up. If you are fortunate enough to avoid being bitten, it is a law of nature that you will convert once you die. Unless your brain is destroyed in time, undeath gets us all in the end. Since our collective fate is unavoidable, however, we cannot be held morally responsible for becoming what we must become.

What do we mean when we talk about a "human being" in the above argument? If we intend to draw a distinction between ourselves and the undead, it can't just be a matter of appearances. After all, they look like us, albeit in a more desiccated state. It is equally difficult to draw the line at infection since *all* of us are infected. The difference between zombies and survivors is a matter of the degree to which the infection has taken over. Have you cracked up or not? Have you died and fully converted into the undead? In each of these cases—survivor, cracked up, undead—we are talking about someone *biologically* human. Just as we are all infected, we also all have twenty-three chromosomal pairs. If the above argument means "biological human being" when it uses the term "human being," then premise (2) would seem to be true. Zombies are innocent biological human beings. At the same time, however, one might have reservations about premise (1). Why is it morally wrong to kill something that has twenty-three chromosomal pairs? Most of us have no qualms at cutting off a recently bitten limb in order to stem the acceleration of the virus. Even though the limb is biologically human, it seems permissible—if not obligatory—to destroy it when an accelerating viral load is posing a threat to the larger human organism. More importantly, just because the cracked up and the undead are both biologically human, does this mean it is wrong to kill/destroy them? Why is this *biological* fact *morally* relevant? If we mean "biological human being" in both premises (1) and (2), then although the argument would be valid it now seems unsound since premise (1) appears to be false. It is far from obvious that it is wrong to kill something simply because of some biological feature that it possesses.

There is something else, however, that we could mean by "human being" in the above argument. Instead of referring to *biological* humanity, we could instead be referring to *moral* humanity. A moral human is a biological human that is capable of making and responding to moral claims. This is Kant's conception of a *person*, something we first discussed in Chapter 4.4 and which we will return to again in the next section. If what we mean by "human being" in the above argument is "moral human being," what would the implications be for the argument? Again, if we mean the same thing by "human being" in each of the premises, then the conclusion would follow. The argument would be valid. Would it be sound? It now seems much more obvious that premise (1) is true. Once the moral component is built into our conception of human being, it is easy to see why it would be morally wrong to kill one. To use Kant's approach, to kill a person would be to rid the world of something that has unconditional moral value, an action that is wrong in itself. What about premise (2)? Are zombies *persons*? Are they capable of making and responding to moral claims? The only possible candidate would be a talker, for example, the final zombie from the field exercise above. Such cases are rare, however, and for the most part zombies are wholly controlled by the virus whose only master is the natural law to propagate in as many human hosts as possible. With all executive functions controlled by the virus, we cannot consider either the cracked up or undead moaners morally responsible for their violent actions. With the personhood criterion, a lack of moral responsibility entails a lack of moral considerability. Neither the cracked up nor undead moaners are capable of making and responding to moral claims. Although they are *biologically* human, they fail to be *morally* human. It appears that premise (2) is false.

Some philosophers, however, try to tie the two conceptions of humanity to one another. If the ability to make and respond to moral claims is an *essential* feature of being human, then just because some human individuals fail to have this feature for some reason—being too young, or being a zombie—this should not be grounds for saying they are not morally considerable. The ability to make and respond to moral claims should not be used as a filter for sorting humans. All humans should be morally considerable since they are all members of a kind—a species—for whom the ability to make and respond to moral claims is an essential feature. This view is called **speciesism**. It is also deeply misleading since it intentionally conflates the two conceptions of humanity we have gone to great lengths to keep separate. Although all moral human beings are biologically human, not all biological human beings are morally human. If the ability to make and respond to moral claims really were an essential feature of humanity, then every single human would need to have this capacity in order to count as a member of the species. Just as a sample of virus that does not affect executive function would not be a sample of the virus that caused the outbreak, so too a creature that cannot make and respond to moral claims would not be a human being. The speciesist is faced with a difficult choice. Either the young, the senile, or zombies are not *human*—since they fail to possess this ostensibly essential feature—or the speciesist is wrong about what the essential feature is. The latter seems more plausible. What we, the small child, the senile, the cracked up, and the undead all share in common is that we are *biologically* human—we all have twenty-three chromosomal pairs regardless of our viral load.

Returning to the above argument, the only situation where both of the premises would be true is if we meant *different* things by "human being." Whereas premise (1) is true if we mean "moral human being," premise (2) is true if we mean "biological human being." In this case, however, the argument would itself be *invalid*. The conclusion would not follow from the premises since the argument itself would rely on a *fallacy of equivocation*. In this case, it would be an equivocation on the meaning of "human being." Consequently, the argument is either (1) invalid but the premises are true, or (2) at least one of the premises is false, rendering the argument unsound.

Even though the above argument cannot establish that it is wrong to kill zombies—or young children for that matter—it could contain the seeds of a more promising approach. In particular, we should examine Kant's personhood criterion for moral considerability. Although Kant would draw a moral distinction between survivors and zombies, we should only accept this moral distinction if his personhood criterion can first account for our obligations to other survivors.

3. Kantian personhood and rights

As you might recall from Chapter 4, for the Kantian, what makes a survivor morally considerable is that she is a rational and autonomous agent, capable of recognizing and being motivated by the moral law. Survivors are "ends in themselves," persons that possess an unconditional moral value that make them worthy of respect. Zombies, however, are "mere means" or things whose value, if any, derives from the value that a survivor places in them, for example, being a source of pleasure in the above story. Even so, Kant would disagree with the actions of the protagonist. To paraphrase, Kant would say that he who is cruel to zombies will also become hard in his dealings with living persons.

A moment's reflection will show that this is strange reasoning for Kant to deploy. The idea seems to be that we should not be cruel to zombies—

torturing them for our pleasure—because of the *consequences*, namely, that doing so would make it more likely that we will be cruel to other survivors. Kant's ethical theory, however, holds that the consequences of an action are morally *irrelevant*. Kant is concerned wholly with the *motive* behind an action, that is, the nature of your maxim, not the *consequence* that might follow from it.

If he were being honest, Kant would have to admit that there isn't anything wrong *in itself* with torturing zombies, assuming, of course, that we always mean the same thing when we use the term "zombie." As the above field exercise suggests, however, we can potentially mean many different things by this term. For Kant, "moaners," undead and ravenous, would not be morally considerable. This is not because they are moaning, undead, or ravenous, but simply because they are neither rational nor autonomous. They are controlled wholly by an infection that recognizes only the natural though not the moral law.

Perhaps more troubling, Kant would also hold that there is nothing wrong in itself with what the protagonist does to those that have cracked up but are still living. These individuals are *sentient*, they feel pleasure and pain. When we prick them, not only do they bleed, but they also *suffer* because of it. As the opening quote makes clear, and as we will see below, this constitutes the central difference between the Kantian and the utilitarian standpoint. Whereas the Kantian does not believe that the capacity to feel pleasure and pain is morally relevant, the utilitarian holds that this capacity is of central moral importance.

Despite the utilitarian concerns, which we will deal with in Chapter 8.5, there are concerns about whether Kant's criteria would adequately cover *all* survivors and whether it might also cover *some* zombies. When it comes to the former, what about small children or the very old? Although small children might develop into fully fledged members of the moral community capable of making and responding to moral claims, until a certain level of mental maturity, they simply do not possess these capacities. Does this mean they are not morally considerable according to Kant's personhood criterion? Likewise, consider the elderly—some senile and suffering from dementia—who are no longer capable of making and responding to moral claims. Would it be morally permissible to euthanize them in order to avoid the kinds of surprise conversions discussed in the field exercise from Chapter 4? Kant could have problems if his view covers too *few* of the individuals we believe should be morally considerable.

To push things a bit further, what about the protagonist and the talker in the story above? Even if the protagonist possesses rationality sufficient to still have some dim view of the moral law, the individual's moral humanity is so compromised that they seem to have lost nearly all autonomy. Although Kant would likely insist that the protagonist can still be held morally responsible, as mentioned above, he also recognizes that agents can harm themselves in a way that makes it more difficult for them to follow the moral law. Could an agent debase herself to such an extent that she is no longer capable of recognizing what she ought to do and is driven wholly by external impulse, for example, an insatiable sadism like the protagonist above? What of the talker in the above story who recognizes that she cannot withstand her desire for living human flesh but nonetheless wants to be rid of this desire? Does this zombie's will show her to be more of a *person* than the protagonist?

One concern with Kant's personhood criterion of moral considerability is that it is all or nothing. Either you are a person or you are not. Depending on where you draw the exact line between person and non-person, you could end up with some strange results. Some zombies might end up being *persons* (ends in themselves) while some survivors might end up being *things* (mere means). Another approach is to hold that there is a certain set of features that define what a person is and the more of these features you possess the more "person-like" you are. Here are some possibilities:

(1) Consciousness
(2) Reasoning
(3) Self-motivated activity
(4) Capacity to communicate
(5) Presence of self-concepts
(6) Self-awareness

Most survivors possess all of these features. Even the protagonist in the above story whose (Kantian) moral agency was compromised is a person in all of the above senses. Again, there could be a question about the very young or the very old. Even in these cases, however, we would want to say that they possess at least *some* of these features. If we believe that personhood is a sliding scale, then the strength of the rights that a person possesses could correspond to one's position on this sliding scale.

The connection between personhood and rights is very clear from the Kantian perspective. Rights entail making and responding to moral claims. Your negative right to life is a claim on me not to kill you (and vice versa). Your positive right to aid is a claim on me to help you when you are in need (and vice versa). For the Kantian, only individuals who are capable of making and responding to moral claims—persons—have rights. The more person-like you are the stronger your negative and positive rights are.

Moaners would possess few if any of these features. Whatever conscious subjectivity they possess is residual and quite limited. It is just enough to identify and pursue whatever living flesh they sense. Although hordes are much more effective than individuals in overcoming the barriers that lay between them and the survivors they seek to devour, this is more the result of sheer numbers and the collective activity of a hive mind more than the reasoning power of any individual ghoul. The moans of your individual zombie, furthermore, are limited to signaling others to a location where they can likewise devour the living. Unlike survivors, they cannot communicate a wide variety of concepts in a wide variety of ways. Moaners, meet few, if any, of the conditions for being a person and so would lack any of the rights of persons as well.

The cracked up, though still living, present a different case. Although their reasoning and communication powers are not that different from the moaners, they are conscious since they feel pleasure and pain. As the above story illustrates, they also have a self-concept sufficient for them to recognize themselves as the subject of harm when they are being tortured. Since they still lack a number of capacities that full persons possess, their corresponding rights would be weaker than our own. When the rights of actual persons come into conflict with the rights of quasi-persons—for example, you are defending yourself from someone who has cracked up and is trying to devour you—your rights, the rights of an actual person, should take precedent. In this example, it would be morally permissible for you to destroy the brain of your attacker even though they are innocent and meet many of the conditions of personhood.

Things become even more complicated with the talker in the above story. She not only meets all of the above conditions, but she meets some of them in ways that we, the living, are incapable. Not only can she communicate with the protagonist verbally, but she also has the ability to communicate with the hive mind telepathically and direct their activity. If personhood is on a sliding scale, and she demonstrates abilities associated with personhood that we do not possess, then would she be *more* of a person than your average survivor? Is she more valuable from the moral standpoint than we are?

Setting aside such troubling questions for the moment, one might consider another, admittedly remote, possibility that also raises difficulties for the personhood criterion of moral considerability. With the complete collapse of civilization, it now seems quite unlikely that a cure will ever be found. Even so, what if we were to find a cure so that zombies could be turned back into persons (either living or undead)? Like the talker from the field exercise, perhaps *all* zombies will eventually develop back into individuals that meet all above conditions of personhood. Assume that all *actual* zombies are *potential* persons. Do potential persons have the same rights as actual persons? This would greatly complicate the post-apocalyptic moral landscape. We have already established that all zombies, regardless of their violent bloodlust, are still innocent biological human beings. Although being a biological human being carries no moral import, is it wrong to kill zombies simply because they are potentially persons? Put more generally, just because something is a *potential* X, does that mean that it has all the rights of an *actual* X? Back before the world fell, potential voters, for example, children, did not have the rights of actual voters, namely, the right of those that had reached voting age to vote. In this post-apocalyptic landscape, potential warlords, for example, small-time bandits, do not have the rights of actual warlords, namely, to command strongholds and marshal their garrisons into battle with other warlords or the undead. Just because something (e.g., a zombie) is potentially something else (e.g., a person) does not entail that the former has the rights of the latter.

Even if potential persons do not possess the rights of actual persons, it still seems like *some* though not *all* zombies are actual persons. It might also be the case that some of these zombies are more person-like than some survivors which raises troubling questions of moral considerability. Returning again to the standard with which we began, before we can determine whether or not zombies are morally considerable, we have to find a criterion that adequately explains why it is wrong to kill other survivors. It is unclear, however, whether the personhood criterion, even when viewed on a sliding scale, can explain why the very young or the very old deserve moral consideration equal to other survivors.

4. Conscious life criterion

Assuming that *final* death is a misfortune—an open question for many survivors—what makes it so? It cannot be the impact that your death would have on your fellow survivors. Like me, many of us are holed-up alone defending ourselves against armies of undead. Assuming that you still value your life under such conditions, death would be a misfortune for you even if no other survivor was aware of the fact that you had died. Perhaps, the misfortune is loss of your future *biological* life when you fully convert into one of the undead. After the infection takes over, however, you do live on for some time albeit cracked up and ravenous. Even after you *die* biologically, you continue a biologically *undead* existence. Most survivors, however, see little value in continuing to exist as a bloodthirsty monster whether living or undead. What really makes death a misfortune is the loss of your future *conscious* life. If your situation is anything like my own, you probably do not value your *present* conscious life— one dominated by loneliness and fear of (un)death—but you persist nonetheless. Why is that? Hope is the last to die and it is what keeps most of us going in this living nightmare. What we almost universally hope for is a future when we can enjoy a world freed from infection. Enjoying such a world, however, requires having a conscious life. What we value, and what would make death such a misfortune, is the loss of this *future* conscious life. It also explains why killing a survivor is the worst thing you could do to them. While knocking another survivor out—perhaps to steal their weapons—does harm to them by depriving them of their present conscious life as well as their weapons, killing them does far worse since you are also depriving them of all future conscious life.

What do all of the problematic cases of survivors share in common with folks like you and me? Whether you are a young child, an elderly person suffering from dementia, or someone whose own moral agency has been compromised by relentless sadism, you are still the subject of a conscious life. Perhaps, we could even make this the criterion for moral considerability within an otherwise Kantian ethical framework. If you are the subject of a conscious life, then you have a right to life, and it is wrong to kill you. This sets the bar for having rights much lower than Kant would, but it allows us to extend rights to all of the different types of survivors who fail to be Kantian moral persons.

Although being the subject of a current conscious life seems sufficient to have rights, what really makes it wrong to kill this individual is that you would deprive them of a future conscious life. Of course, if this criterion for rights is to work, then this future conscious life must be one of *value* to the individual at risk of losing it. If it turns out—as seems likely—that there is no cure, then our future conscious lives may ultimately be *worthless*. Would you look forward to an ever more desperate existence, always competing with other survivors over increasingly scarce resources, while also perpetually battling the swelling hordes of undead for your continued survival?

Turning now to zombies, an interesting feature of this view is that most if not all zombies would have a right to life as well. Even though her life was not of value to her, the talker in the field exercise above was painfully conscious of having one. If her desire for human flesh could be cured or curtailed, perhaps she would even find her future conscious life one worth experiencing. Assuming that was the case, then killing her would be wrong since she would have a future conscious life of value. Let's assume for the sake of argument that all zombies—if their brains are spared long enough—will develop into a zombie like her. If so, then all zombies, if they have a future conscious life of value, would have a right to life. The cracked up are sentient and so we know that they already have a current conscious life. What about when the cracked up fully convert into undead moaners? Even if moaners lack consciousness, they would have a *future* conscious life once they develop into their final form (e.g., the talker in the story). If one accepts this account for the wrongness of killing, then it seems as if there really won't be a moral difference between killing survivors and killing zombies. In each case, assuming there is a future of value, you would be depriving an individual of the future goods of consciousness.

One might still try to draw a moral distinction between zombies and survivors, however, by claiming that what matters is not that they have a future conscious life of value to *them*, but rather that they have a future conscious life similar enough to *our* own. However, what constitutes "our own"? Is it you or me? Is it the elderly suffering from dementia? Is it the survivor addicted to torturing zombies? In each case, the conscious life the individual has to look forward to will be very different. If we insist on drawing a moral distinction between the future conscious lives of zombies and our own future conscious lives, then we will be forced to draw moral distinctions among survivors as well.

Although *all* survivors have a current conscious life, *some* zombies do as well (cracked up and fully developed undead). If one holds that being the subject of a conscious life is sufficient for having a right to life, then it seems we will not be able to draw a clear moral distinction between survivors and zombies. The distinction is even harder to draw if all those that have a future conscious life also have a right to life since it seems as if all of us—whether zombie or survivor—would meet this criterion assuming we have a future of value.

5. Utilitarianism and zombie euthanasia

Perhaps utilitarianism will offer a way of drawing a moral distinction between survivors and zombies? Although we already covered the utilitarian view of zombies at some length in the last chapter, what's most important to remember for present purposes is that the utilitarian believes that anything *sentient*—that feels pleasure and pain—is morally considerable. This means that the cracked up are morally considerable as is the talker in the field exercise who self-reports her own *pain*.

As mentioned in Chapter 7.2, the utilitarian does allow us to draw distinctions between different kinds of pleasure and pain. The higher-order pleasures that a survivor might value (e.g., those associated with friendship or mental cultivation) would be of greater value than the mere lower-order pleasures that a zombie experiences (e.g., the satisfaction of a swollen belly full of human flesh). Although any lower-order pleasure that a survivor might feel (e.g., the visceral sadistic pleasure of the field exercise's protagonist) would have to be weighed equally with any lower-order pleasure that a zombie might feel, a survivor's higher-order pleasure would outweigh a greater amount of a zombie's lower-order pleasure. This would give us reason to prefer (some of) the interests of survivors over those of zombies.

Although this might seem to not only explain what makes survivors morally considerable, but also why their pleasures/pains are of greater moral value than the pleasures/pains of zombies, if the pleasures/pains are of the *same* level, then they deserve *equal* moral consideration. The addiction of the protagonist is not different in kind than the addition of the talker. Both of them have a desire for a lower-order pleasure that they cannot control. Also, whatever higher-order pleasures/pains the talker might feel must be weighed equally with the higher-order pleasures/pains of any survivor. In fact, given the strange abilities she seems to possess, perhaps she is capable of feeling forms of pleasure/pain that make our higher-order pleasures appear lower-order from her perspective. For example, perhaps she feels a pleasure of friendship from communing with the hive mind of the horde that goes far beyond the kind of pleasure that we feel in our human friendships.

Let us not forget, however, what she *really* desires. She wants to be euthanized since undeath—and her insatiable appetite for living human flesh—has grown insufferable. Would there be a utilitarian argument for granting her wish? As long as euthanizing her produces more overall happiness, or perhaps more appropriately prevents more pain than the alternative, then it seems as if it would be morally obligatory. The problem, however, is that the apocalypse is miserable for almost *everyone*. Survivors suffer under a constant fear of violent undeath and zombies suffer under a constant hunger for the living that cannot be satisfied. Since everyone is unhappy, by this reasoning, the best action would be to euthanize everyone since this would greatly reduce overall unhappiness in comparison to the status quo where everyone suffers.

Even so, a lot of survivors do not want to die even though they are miserable. Doesn't it seem wrong to kill these survivors even though doing so would reduce the amount of unhappiness in the world? What the utilitarian standpoint is missing is something we have discussed at length in connection with Kant, namely, a conception of rights. Once you factor rights into the picture, then euthanasia is only permissible when it reduces overall unhappiness and does not violate anyone's rights. Assuming that an individual can renounce their rights, for example, the talker in the field exercise who wishes to die, then it would be permissible to kill them in order to reduce overall unhappiness. This also explains why it is wrong to kill miserable survivors who do not wish to die. Although killing them would reduce overall unhappiness, it would violate their rights which they have not renounced.

Do we now have a way of morally distinguishing between survivors and zombies? Not really since the above example assumes that both survivors and zombies have rights. What we need to show is even if zombies have a strong right to life, one that they do not renounce, that killing them would still be morally permissible in most cases. This would be a powerful argument against the zombie rights supporter since we will have granted him everything that he wants but still showed that he is wrong that we ought not to kill zombies.

Above, I mentioned the possibility of finding a cure. Let's go a step further and assume, for the sake of argument, that *you* are the cure. Your blood holds the antibodies necessary to eradicate the virus that ultimately causes undeath. Perhaps, you are unaware of this, but you awake one morning in a field hospital to find your body connected by tubes to the body of a zombie in an adjoining cage. A doctor tells you that you were rescued from the Zombie Reconversion Society who had kidnapped you and plugged you into this zombie against your will. The doctor explains your special gift and says that if you stay plugged into the zombie for nine months that you will eradicate the infection that wracks his body and he will fully recover into a living person. If you choose to unplug yourself, then it will cause the zombie's final death. Apparently, the transformation, once started, must be completed. There is no going back to undeath. Of course, it's not the zombie's fault that you are connected to him. It was the Zombie Reconversion Society that did this to you. Are you morally required to stay plugged into the zombie for nine months? Although it would be **supererogatory**—going above and beyond the call of duty—were you to do so, most survivors would likely say that you are not morally *obligated* to do so. Even assuming that the zombie has a strong right to life, a right as strong as yours, it still seems at least morally *permissible* for you to unplug yourself from him even though this effectively sentences him to final death.

Consider another situation where we will again assume that the zombie has a right to life that is as strong as yours. What if you were trapped in a room with someone who has just turned and is much stronger than you? They are totally consumed by their bloodlust and are doing everything in their power to devour you. The zombie is now on top of you and is about to chomp into your supple flesh. Your dagger is at the ready. Either you can destroy its brain or you can allow yourself to be devoured. Again, the zombie is innocent. It is not up to the zombie that it is what it is. All of us are infected and although a bite will accelerate the process, it is not up to us when we will crack up. Even assuming that the zombie has a strong right to life, it seems like it is morally permissible for you to defend yourself and kill it. You cannot be morally obligated to sacrifice your life to satiate a zombie's appetite. Let's assume that it will tear you apart to the point that you cannot reanimate. Even if a cure were on its way, promising to eventually turn your ravenous killer into a healthy human being, it still seems morally permissible to defend yourself. You cannot be morally obligated to allow yourself to be killed just so that this zombie can eventually become what you once were—a moral person.

We have considered situations where you were forced to save a zombie and where your life was in danger from a zombie. Even assuming that the zombie is completely innocent and has a right to life as strong as your own, it still seems morally permissible to kill it in both cases. Finally, let us consider a couple of other situations which, as survivors, we have likely found ourselves within. Let's say you are trying to fortify your house from the undead and do everything you possibly can to secure your home. You close and lock all of the doors and windows, nail wooden planks against all of the openings, and place blackout curtains against the wooden planks so that no interior light will alert the undead to your presence. What if, after all your precautions, a zombie still manages to break in? Assume that a cure is on its way and the provisional government will reach your home in nine months. Are you obligated to let the zombie wander around downstairs in the interim, as you are barricaded upstairs with your supplies? Would it be permissible for you to retake your home by force, destroying the undead ghoul that lurks below? You didn't invite the zombie into your home. In fact, you did everything in your power to prevent it from getting in. Just because it managed to get in, regardless of your best efforts, does that mean you are obligated to let it stay? Although it would again be supererogatory, were you to be so hospitable, we seem hard pressed to say that you are obligated to be so accommodating.

What if you had not been so careful? What if you had left your windows and doors open for a bit of fresh air—after all, it can get quite stuffy holed-up in your stronghold—and a zombie happened to wander in? You have no desire to host a zombie, but you did nothing to prevent it from finding its way inside your home. Again, it is not the zombie's fault that it has found itself in your house. We may even assume, as we did before, that a cure is just nine months away. Are you morally required to allow the zombie to remain in your home for nine months just because you did nothing to prevent its entry? If you believe that it is morally *permissible* to kill the zombie in this situation, even assuming the zombie has a strong right to life, then it would seem it is morally permissible to kill a zombie in most situations where we would be inclined to do so. Consequently, even if zombies are just as morally considerable as survivors are, that is, possess a strong right to life, this does not entail on its own that it is morally wrong to kill them.

Summary

Although it may appear not only ridiculous but also dangerous to ask if zombies are morally considerable, the question grows more difficult to answer the more one reflects upon it. The various reasons one might give for why it is wrong to kill survivors—being biologically human, possessing reason, having a conscious life, feeling pleasure and pain—are either features that not all survivors possess or are features that at least some zombies possess. Even if we assume that zombies have a right to life that is as strong as any survivor, however, it still seems morally permissible to kill them under most circumstances.

Further study

- Bentham, Jeremy. *An Introduction to the Principles of Morals and Legislation*. 1789. Edited with introduction. Oxford: Oxford University Press, 1970.
  - See p. 311 for the passage that inspired the quotation that opens this chapter.
- Carey, M.R. *The Girl with All the Gifts*. London: Orbit, 2014.
  - Whereas first-generation zombies (directly infected by a fungal disease) are irrational and driven solely by their desire for living flesh, second-generation children (born of infected mothers) are rational and can be educated though they retain an uncontrollable desire for living flesh. The book was made into a movie of the same name in 2016.
- Cohen, Carl. "The Case for the Use of Animals in Biomedical Research." *New England Journal of Medicine* 315 (1986): 865–870.
  - Adopts Kant's view that rights entail the ability to make and respond to moral claims, but also defends speciesism in order to show that *all* human beings have rights (regardless of their moral abilities) while animals do not.
- *Fido* (2006), [Film] Dir. Andrew Currie. USA: Lions Gate Films.
  - The movie is set in a world where zombies are controlled through the use of electronic collars that transform them into docile menial labor. They are non-threatening and can follow basic directions. If the collar is deactivated, however, their bloodlust reemerges.
- Grant, Mira. *Feed*. London: Orbit, 2010.
  - The zombies in her world exhibit a kind of hive mind. The virus starts to reason when it gets enough hosts in the same location. Like President

Mentemuro, the most virulent anti-zombie people in her world are the racists, sexists, and homophobes of the world that existed prior to the outbreak.

- Greene, Richard. "The Badness of Undeath." In *Zombies, Vampires, and Philosophy: New Life for the Undead*, edited by Richard Greene and K. Silem Mohammad, 3–14. Chicago: Open Court, 2010.
  - Using lower-order pleasures, argues that the life of a zombie could still be quite enjoyable from the zombie's perspective. As long as the zombie experiences these lower-order pleasures, the zombie would be morally considerable.

- Hinzmann, Jeffrey and Arp, Robert. "People for the Ethical Treatment of Zombies [PETZ]." In *The Walking Dead and Philosophy*, edited by Wayne Yuen, 179–193. Chicago: Open Court, 2012.
  - Contrary to what is claimed in this chapter, the authors argue that walkers, or "moaners," meet the utilitarian's criterion for moral considerability.

- *In the Flesh* (2013–2014), [TV Program] BBC.
  - This TV Series is set in a world where a cure has been found. Although the undead remain undead, through regular injections of a drug, they regain all of their cognitive abilities and the personalities they once had. Since the undead still appear different from the living, they face systematic discrimination even though the outbreak is over. The basic idea was also adapted into a movie, *The Cured* (IFC Films, 2017).

- *Land of the Dead* (2005), [Film] Dir. George Romero. USA: Universal Pictures.
  - The fourth of Romero's *Living Dead* films and the one where the cognitive development of the zombies is most apparent. These rational capacities were foreshadowed, however, in Romero's previous film: *Day of the Dead* (1985). The zombie "Bub," in the earlier film, exhibits many of the same abilities as the lead zombie "Big Daddy" in the later film though to a lesser extent. In *Land*, the zombies exhibit not only individual rationality, but also a capacity for collective action that is far more developed than the humans they devour.

- Littmann, Greg. "Can *You* Survive a Walker Bite?" In *The Walking Dead and Philosophy*, edited by Wayne Yuen, 17–27. Chicago: Open Court, 2012.
  - Although walkers are not conscious humans, he argues that they should be considered equivalent to conscious animals.

- Marion, Isaac. *Warm Bodies*. New York: Atria Books, 2010.
  - Set in a world where there are two kinds of zombies: "Fleshies" and "Bonies." The former are recently turned, retain some measure of

their humanity though they are rather dim-witted, and can relive the experiences of those that they infect by eating their brains. The latter are older zombies and are as ruthless as they are rational. It turns out that the power of love, however, can convert Fleshies back into living human beings. The book was turned into a movie of the same name in 2013.

- Marquis, Don. "An Argument That Abortion Is Wrong." In *Ethics in Practice: An Anthology*, edited by Hugh LaFollette, 141–150. Oxford: Wiley-Blackwell, 2014.
  - Argues that it is wrong to kill an adult human being primarily because it deprives the individual of the future goods of consciousness. For the same reason, according to the author, abortion is morally impermissible in most cases. He also argues against both the biological humanity criterion for wrongness of killing and the inference that because an individual is a potential person, they have the rights of an actual person.

- Mogk, Matt. *Everything You Ever Wanted to Know about Zombies*. New York: Gallery Books, 2011.
  - Although it is claimed above that "moaners" are not sentient, he argues in chapter ten of his book that even these zombies must have sensations—at least a kinesthetic sense—in order to be locomotive. The neuropathy in the undead could only cause a loss of sensation without eliminating it entirely.

- *The Return of the Living Dead*, [Film].
  - For a zombie experiencing suffering similar to the talker in the above field exercise, see the female half-zombie who pleads for brains to ease the pain of being dead. The zombies in the film also possess at least instrumental rationality, for example, placing an order to police headquarters to "send more cops" for them to eat.

- Rachels, James. "The Morality of Euthanasia." In *Matters of Life and Death*, edited by Tom Regan, 49–52. New York: McGraw-Hill, 1986.
  - Provides both the utilitarian argument for euthanasia and the rights-based modification mentioned in Chapter 8.5.

- *Ravenous* (2017), [Film] Dir. Robin Aubert. Canada: Les Films Séville.
  - This film depicts zombies that seem to have communicative and rational powers that are minimally different from and perhaps even supersede the powers of the humans that struggle to survive.

- Regan, Tom. "The Case for Animal Rights." In *In Defense of Animals: The Second Wave*, edited by Peter Singer, 13–26. Oxford: Wiley-Blackwell, 2005.
  - Argues for a conscious life criterion for having rights. This criterion would entail that human beings and animals have equal rights.

- Singer, Peter. "All Animals Are Equal." In *Animal Rights and Human Obligations*, edited by Tom Regan and Peter Singer, 148–162. Englewood Cliffs, NJ: Prentice-Hall, 1989.
  - The inspiration for the title of this chapter which offers a utilitarian argument for why the interests of animals should be weighed equally with the interests of human beings.
- Thomson, Judith Jarvis. "A Defense of Abortion." *Philosophy and Public Affairs* 1, no. 1 (1971): 47–66.
  - Assumes that fetuses have a strong right to life, but then shows how abortion is still morally permissible in most cases. The various examples in Chapter 8.5 are adapted from this article.
- Walker, Seth. "I Want You to Survive." In *The Ultimate Walking Dead and Philosophy*, edited by Wayne Yuen, 31–44. Chicago: Open Court, 2016.
  - Discusses Regan's conscious life criterion for inherent value within the context of *The Walking Dead*.
- *The Walking Dead*, [TV Program].
  - That all survivors are infected is revealed in season 1.6 "TS-19."
  - Lizzie does not see a moral difference between humans and walkers, something which leads her to kill her sister—so that she will reanimate—and ultimately leads Carol to kill Lizzie to protect the remaining survivors. This all comes to a head in season 4.14 "The Grove."
- Warren, Mary Anne. "On the Moral and Legal Status of Abortion." *The Monist* 57, no. 1 (1973): 43–61.
  - She criticizes the argument in Chapter 8.2 as it is deployed by those who support the pro-life position in the abortion debate. After distinguishing between biological and moral humanity, she rejects the biological humanity criterion for having a right to life. She defends the personhood criterion for having a right to life, but holds that personhood exists on a sliding scale (see Chapter 8.3). Since fetuses lack most if not all of the characteristics that a person possesses, whatever rights they possess are outweighed by the rights of actual persons (e.g., the pregnant woman).
- Wellington, David. *Monster Island*. New York: Thunder's Mouth Press, 2006.
  - Gary, the antagonist of the novel, is a zombie who has managed to maintain his rational will and comes to value his future. Although he originally identifies with the survivors, after one of them shoots him, he embraces his new powers, including a telepathic connection with other non-rational zombies that he can control.
- Whitehead, Colson. *Zone One*. New York: Anchor Books, 2011.
  - This post-apocalyptic world includes both aggressive zombies—for whom survivors use the pronoun "it"—and "stragglers" who are caught in a

behavioral loop from their previous lives but are not aggressive. Survivors assign these zombies pronouns based on their gender.

- Yuen, Wayne. "Carol Didn't Care." In *The Ultimate Walking Dead and Philosophy*, edited by Wayne Yuen, 193–203. Chicago: Open Court, 2016.
  - From the standpoint of moral considerability, he argues that walkers are like animals.

9 THE RESPONSIBILITIES OF STRONGHOLDS TO THE UNPROTECTED LIVING

If it is in our power to prevent a survivor from being devoured
without sacrificing anything of comparable moral significance—
e.g., being devoured ourselves—we ought, morally, to save them.

—FAMISHED HORDES, AFFLUENT STRONGHOLDS,
AND MORALITY

This chapter considers a practical example that should be familiar to any survivor who has lasted long enough to read this book. When living in a stronghold, you must regularly decide whether or not to let new people in. If you have plenty of resources, trust the people trying to get in, and do not already have a lot of mouths to feed, the decision might be an easy one. As the armies of the undead grew, however, an increasing number of strongholds were overrun which left the remaining survivors scrambling for safety in the few strongholds that remained. Often, there were more survivors than a stronghold could adequately care for or defend. This is when the question of whether to let additional survivors in becomes more difficult to answer. After first examining an argument for why you should *not* admit additional survivors under these circumstances, we will examine what the Utilitarian and the Kantian would say.

1. Field exercise: Drowning in the dead

"How long do you think we can last, *all* of us, *together*?" I asked Gary.

"It's hard to say, depends on how much food and water they have on them," he replied. "I don't think we should let them in though … they're too many."

"Are you talking about the survivors or the undead?" I replied grimly. I had called Gary to the roof once I spotted it: a dark line slowly growing, in both length and thickness, on the horizon. As the sun started to rise in the east, its shadow stretched westward, through the shantytown, revealing distended individuals while portending the destruction that lay in store.

We had at least a hundred survivors camped around our fortress. It had been an agricultural warehouse before the outbreak which is what made it so valuable afterward. As the pandemic worsened and

FIGURE 17 Approaching horde.

government services faltered, the company had spent some additional money protecting their property. They had installed an eight-foot chain-link fence topped with razor wire. The windows and doors had been boarded up save for a single loading dock which was secured by a heavy-gauge steel door on rollers. The company had fitted an aluminum ladder to the loading dock, allowing for access, but it could get kicked away in case of a horde attack. Since the dock itself sat four feet above the ground, there was no way a horde could create enough leverage to break through the door regardless of its size.

Up to this point, we had drawn a distinction between those that had started out inside the fortress, mostly warehouse workers and their families, and those who had come looking for sanctuary. We called it BYOR: "bring your own resources." We would let you come in and trade, cool off from the scorching sun, and keep a look-out for zombies from the roof. When night fell, however, you were expected to head back out to the shantytown until the next morning. The only exceptions were people who looked like they needed to be quarantined. For them, we had a special cage in the middle of the warehouse to make sure they were safe before releasing them into the shantytown.

Although day had broken, Gary had not yet opened the dock door which allowed us a few moments to consider our options before panic set in. Unaware of the threat that loomed on the horizon, people were already banging on the door, demanding to make some morning trades.

Gary continued, "We're like any other store back in the old days. You come, you do your business, and you leave. Nobody should expect to stay."

"There's no way they'll survive this," I replied. "If we don't open the door, they're going to be devoured."

"I know it sounds harsh, but that's *their* problem, not *ours*." Gary took on a soothing tone that belied the import of his words. "If we let them in here, our supplies won't last for long. Right now, we have enough to last us months, maybe even a year. If we go silent—blackout curtains, no noise—eventually the horde will lose interest or find easier prey. We need *time*, but we won't have it if we let everyone in."

"You let me in!" I replied, my voice barely concealing my growing anger. "I needed help and you gave it to me. Why do they deserve any less?"

Gary looked me in the eyes. "Well, you had a functioning helicopter when you got here ... if we had any fuel for it. After that, we put you and your friends in quarantine, just like everyone else. I didn't treat you any different." Gary looked down before continuing. "The kids took a shine to you. If it had been up to me …"

He broke off, but didn't need to finish. I knew his mind. The soldiers I arrived with had obvious talents and were easily repurposed as guards. I guess I got to stay because of the kids, but I had taken a shine to them as well. Their story was all too common: One of the workers had been bitten while bringing her two small children back to the warehouse during the outbreak. When she turned, and was subsequently destroyed, the kids were orphaned. The other workers had little skill or interest in caring for them. During the days I was in quarantine, however, they had been my constant companions: sneaking me food, playing games with me outside the cage, and sleeping—with their stuffed animals—beyond the bars since I sang them to sleep.

I was torn from my reveries by the desperate yelling below. It hadn't taken long for the folks outside to realize why we hadn't opened the door. A low-pitched rolling thunder preceded the horde—thousands of shuffling feet mixed with moans—a cacophony that was building to its crescendo descended on us.

One man tried negotiation, "I'll give you everything I have—guns, fuel, batteries—just let me in!"

A woman played on our sympathy, "Just take my baby!" she pleaded, holding it aloft. "They'll rip her to shreds!"

Another man attempted to rally the others to enter by force, "Screw them! They've been fleecing us for weeks. Let's blast our way in! Who's with me?"

A crack rang out. Gary had shot the man in the head. Putting the rifle aside, Gary looked below and yelled through the megaphone we also kept on the roof, "Listen up! Instead of trying to get in here—which isn't going to happen—you had better work on creating a defensive perimeter. You have enough weapons already. We'll try to take down as many as we can from up here."

Split between resignation and hope, in the few minutes they had remaining, the people of the shantytown broke down their rickety structures to fashion a makeshift wall against the fence. Behind this, they created a couple of firing lines. By the time they had finished fashioning their meager defense, the roar had grown deafening and we could make out individual zombies in the distance.

As the horde barreled across the last stretch before the fence, Gary was screaming "Hold! Hold! Hold!" into the megaphone which was nearly drowned out by the din. Before he could yell "Fire," however, we heard screaming and shots from *inside* the warehouse. The sound of gunfire caused the shantytown survivors to start firing haphazardly themselves.

As I suspected, resistance was futile. The horde passed through our exterior defenses as a wave would wash through a sandcastle. I briefly saw people being torn limb from limb before disappearing into the sea of decay. The surge of dead and dying finally broke upon the loading dock—quickly building on itself—pushing against the once secure but now groaning door below.

One of the guards climbed out onto the roof with the kids in tow. Following him was just a handful of other survivors. Everyone had grabbed what they could in terms of weapons, food, and water, but most everything of value had to be abandoned.

The guard—visibly shaken—tried to explain, "That guy in quarantine … I had just turned my back for a moment … one of the kids must have unlocked the door … he was on us before we knew it."

I didn't appreciate him blaming the kids for his mistake, but there was no time to argue. We could already hear monotonous thumping on the other side of the roof hatch and the sea of undead below would soon break through the main door.

Our only means of escape, at this point, was a zip line that connected the roof to a pile of boulders on the opposite side of the warehouse about 100 yards past the fence. From there, a small group might escape detection as long as it moved quickly. One-by-one we went down the zip line, over the sea of undead, and disappeared into the rocks. The guard took one of the kids and the rifle after which I took the other child along with the megaphone.

When I reached the bottom, I handed my cargo to the guard who vanished with both children through the boulders. I looked back at Gary, the last one on the roof, as he connected his carabineer to the zip line. Just as he was about to step off, I cut the line with a pair of pliers. In the distance, I could see Gary was livid—screaming at the top of his lungs—while gesticulating wildly. He wouldn't last long up there, but for the moment his cries carried over the din of the undead, gathering them to him and away from us.

As I turned and escaped into the rocks, I thought to myself that Gary had to understand. Whereas I at least had my bug-out bag, including a pair of pliers, all Gary had was, well … Gary: a drain on limited resources that the rest of us could ill-afford. I know it sounds harsh, but at the end of the day, isn't it really *his* problem not *ours*?

2. The case against helping unfortunate survivors

The philosopher Garrett Hardin would compare a community's stronghold to a lifeboat which has a limited amount of space and resources. Assume that you already have as many people in your lifeboat as it was designed to hold. What if there were twice as many people outside, clamoring to get in to escape the sea of undead that threatens to envelop them? If you were to let everyone into your lifeboat, it would quickly sink. As in the story above, there are not space and resources sufficient to sustain everyone for long. Even if you could fit a fraction of these unfortunate survivors inside of your lifeboat, you would lose your "safety factor," that is, your margin for error—both in terms of space and resources—that you have to ensure that everyone else in your lifeboat will survive unforeseen events. For example, what if some communicable disease other than the infection was to break out within the stronghold, but you were too packed together and had too few medical resources to combat it? By letting *anyone* else in, you are putting *everyone* else at risk. The only solution, when a wave of undead is imminent, is to batten down the hatches, and wait out the storm.

When too many people enter into a community for which space and resources are limited, these things of value become scarce, and there is an increased threat that people will take more than their fair share. As you might recall from Chapter 3, this is the foundational problem that motivates contractarianism. In the closed environment of the overcrowded lifeboat that we are envisioning, preventing the selfish overuse of resources— consuming more than your fair share of rations for fear that others will do the same if you don't do it first—becomes a constant concern. As Hardin would say, in a crowded stronghold of less than perfect survivors, mutual ruin is inevitable if there are no controls. This is called the **tragedy of the commons**. The "controls" in question, however, grow increasingly more difficult to implement as space and resources grow scarcer.

You may think that this response is cruel. What about the baby in the above story? Doesn't she deserve to live? If you don't like the result of the calculation above, you should always feel free to switch places with someone outside of the lifeboat. The baby's mother will surely be happy for her daughter to take your place rather than being consumed by the undead horde. This will also have the positive effect of ensuring that the guilt-ridden are eliminated from the fortress making it easier for the group to make these difficult decisions in the future.

If we continue to make these difficult decisions *correctly*, that is, denying entry to outside survivors, this will eventually lead to fewer and fewer living demanding to come aboard. What is effectively the *overpopulation* of the living among the sea of undead will be dealt with naturally, namely, the living being devoured and joining the ranks of the undead. Those that nonetheless survive on the outside will do so because they were ultimately strong enough. For example, instead of coming to our fortress to seek shelter, perhaps they create a self-sustaining stronghold of their own. If we continue to accept survivors into our fortress, however, the need will never end, and our stronghold will eventually be overwhelmed from within. This is the worst possible outcome for *all* survivors whether in the stronghold or outside of it.

3. Utilitarian Greater Moral Evil Principle

Let's assume, for the sake of argument, that the suffering of being eaten alive and then violently converting into the undead is a *bad* thing. Under this assumption, consider the utilitarian Peter Singer's **Greater Moral Evil Principle** (GMP): If it is in our power to prevent something bad from happening, without thereby sacrificing anything of comparable moral significance, we ought, morally, to do it. What would it mean to sacrifice something of comparable moral significance with the bad thing that is about to happen to the survivors outside of your stronghold? It would mean sacrificing to the point where you would be no better off than the survivors you are trying to help, namely, being eaten alive and violently converting yourself, or something morally equivalent to this. This principle reflects all three tenets of utilitarianism. What is morally bad is something *painful*, for example, being devoured by the undead, and we are asked to consider how much pain we would have to endure in order to alleviate someone else's pain. The focus on pain here is consistent with hedonism, the idea that pleasure—or, in this case, the absence of pain—is the sole intrinsic good. We are asked to weigh our own pleasure/pain *equally* with those who are suffering. This is consistent with altruism. Finally, GMP prescribes that we ought to *maximize* happiness—or, in this case, minimize unhappiness—by acting in a way that minimizes overall suffering. This is consistent with consequentialism. What might move you to accept GMP? Consider the following example:

Let's say that there is a small child trapped on a pile of boulders, not unlike those in the above story, being approached by a zombie who is clumsily but steadily climbing up the rocks toward her. You are armed with a shaolin spade at the bottom of the rocks and could easily scramble up, destroy the zombie, and rescue the child, if you desired to do so. There is little risk to you and you would be preventing something significantly bad, using our above definition, from happening to the child. Are you obligated to do so?

I think most of us would say that we are obligated to save the child and our intuition seems to support GMP. Assuming that the zombie itself is a moaner—non-sentient and so morally inconsiderable from the utilitarian perspective—the decision seems like a proverbial no-brainer. Nothing bad will happen to you and you will be preventing something very bad from happening to the child. Although it might inconvenience you to some extent—you will have to clean the coagulated blood and brain matter off of your spade—this sacrifice seems insignificant in comparison to the harm that would befall the child otherwise.

What if you were a bit further away? For example, assume you were on top of the stronghold and would have to take the zip line down to save the child. As long as you are still in a position to save the child, does the extra distance matter from the moral standpoint? It is hard to see how it would make a moral difference. Although the extra distance might make some difference when it comes to whether you *will* help the child, it doesn't make any difference when it comes to whether you *ought* to help the child.

Alternatively, what if there were other people on top of the stronghold, for example, Gary from the story above, unwilling to go down and save the child? Would this reduce your moral obligation to do so? Again, it is hard to see how it would. Just because others do not fulfill their moral obligations does not minimize or reduce your own. Her cries call out to all of you and just because others are not *willing* to answer the call does not in any way minimize or remove your moral *obligation* to do so.

Up to this point, your sacrifice has been negligible. What if the stakes were higher and instead of one zombie shambling up the rocks there were a hundred? At what point would you have to stop slaughtering zombies and save yourself instead of the child? Assuming that you could continue decapitating the undead with your shaolin spade indefinitely, wouldn't you be obligated to do so until such point that you couldn't without succumbing to their onslaught? In other words, it seems like you are obligated to sacrifice until such point that you would be sacrificing something—being eaten alive and painfully converting—morally equivalent to the harm that would befall the child were you to run away and allow her be swallowed by the sea of undead.

Before going further, however, let's consider Gary's view. Why is it that he is unwilling to save the child? He would likely argue that after destroying the moaners that threaten her, you would need to bring the child into the stronghold, which eats into our collective "safety factor." Allowing her inside, according to Gary, would violate the moral obligation you already have to those inside of the fortress. Even if bringing the child into the stronghold might place some additional strain on internal resources, however, it is hard to believe that the sacrifice involved would be equivalent to the harm the child would otherwise endure: being painfully devoured—helplessly suffering and dying on the hot rocks—before finally reanimating. From the perspective of GMP, Gary's moral judgment is indefensible.

Taking the example in a slightly different direction, what if there were a hundred children outside your walls under threat from the undead. At what point would you no longer be morally required to bring them into your stronghold? According to GMP, the answer would again be when doing so would require a sacrifice equivalent to the harm that would befall the remaining children. It is only when things become equally desperate inside of the stronghold—those inside are no better off than those outside—that it would be morally permissible to stop admitting newcomers. Things would have to be quite desperate indeed, however, given the terrible plight of those who remain at the mercy of the undead. The bar that GMP would set is far above anything that Gary would recognize.

The central objection to GMP is that it is too demanding, for example, that I would be required to admit children into the stronghold until those inside were no better off than the children who remained outside. In response to this worry, Singer proposes a more *moderate* version of

GMP: if it is in our power to prevent something bad from happening, without thereby sacrificing *something* morally significant, we ought, morally, to do it. The key difference between this formulation and the stronger one is that what is morally required of you is no longer a sacrifice that is *comparable* to the suffering you hope to alleviate, but rather only *something* morally significant. Whereas reducing those in the fortress to a starving approximation of the pain those outside its walls must feel as they are feasted upon would clearly be something morally significant, it is less clear whether admitting a small number that might eat—both literally and figuratively—into one's safety factor but would otherwise cause no harm would likewise be a morally significant sacrifice. Although Gary seems unwilling to make even this amount of sacrifice, Singer believes that it should strike us as morally uncontroversial. Singer does not introduce the more moderate version of GMP to defend it—he still thinks the stronger version is the correct one—but rather to show that most of us (e.g., Gary) fail to fulfill our moral obligations even according to this far less demanding standard.

4. Kantian stronghold ethics

The Kantian view on our obligations to the survivors outside our stronghold falls somewhere in between Hardin's and Singer's positions. Whereas Hardin believes our obligations are non-existent and Singer holds that they are very strong, the Kantian would hold that we have some obligations to those outside our walls, though he would hold that these obligations are not nearly as demanding as Singer thinks that they are.

According to Onora O'Neill, the fundamental differences between Kantian and the utilitarian positions lie in their moral scope and precision. The Kantian position has more limited scope—the actual maxims that the agent forms—but much greater precision using the formula of humanity as an end-in-itself. In contrast, the utilitarian position has much greater scope—all possible actions the agent could perform—but far less precision because of the problem of calculating the consequences of every possible action.

To flesh this out, one can see three basic differences between the Kantian and utilitarian views: (1) Although the Kantian is strictly bound to performing or not performing some actions, unlike the utilitarian, the Kantian is not committed to working indeterminately through all our possible actions and all their possible consequences. (2) Whereas the utilitarian ought always to perform the specific action that will produce the most overall happiness, or prevent the most overall suffering, the Kantian does nothing wrong as long as their acts are not unjust and are reasonably beneficent. (3) While utilitarians must compare *all* available acts to see which one has the best consequences, the Kantian need only consider the maxims that *actually* occur to them to see if these maxims can take on the form of categorical imperatives.

Put in terms of stronghold ethics and the GMP, the problem for the utilitarian would be that there is so *much* suffering and so *many* possible survivors that we could help. As in the field exercise above, when there are too many survivors begging for sanctuary and you cannot grant it to them all without reducing those already inside to a level no better than those outside, you have to make choices and those choices quickly grow complicated. For example, do I let in the man with resources or do I let in the defenseless baby assuming that I cannot let in both? For each possible action, I would have to work out the impact on overall happiness of performing and not performing the action before I could determine what to do. As discussed in Chapter 7, this is simply impractical given what little time we have to make these life and (un)death decisions in our constantly violent world.

Instead of focusing on actions and their consequence, the Kantian position focuses on our actual maxims and two types of duties: *justice* and *beneficence*. Whereas duties of justice require that we *never* act on a maxim that treats another survivor merely as a means, duties of beneficence require that we *sometimes* act on maxims that foster the ends of other survivors. What it means to treat a survivor merely as a means is to include them in a plan of action to which they, in principle, could not consent. What it means to foster the ends of other survivors is to help these individuals pursue the plans and goals that they have set for themselves.

How does the Kantian view apply to the context of stronghold ethics specifically? Let's first consider duties of justice that are relevant to stronghold situations. If you are inside a fortress and there is a rationing scheme in place to extend resources, it would be unjust to take another survivor's rations. To do so, would be to treat the other survivor merely as a means toward your own end, namely, a full belly. Alternatively, consider the duties of justice that you might have to those outside your walls. In the field exercise, it would be unjust if the stronghold was in fact "fleecing" those that came to trade. This would be a good example of treating the survivors in the shantytown merely as a means to your own end, namely, to increase your own resources at their expense. Gary's action of killing the man who made the accusation, furthermore, is itself a clear instance of injustice. He is using the man merely as a means, an *example* to dissuade others from taking action against the stronghold.

There are also duties of beneficence that would apply to survivors both inside and outside a stronghold. Although there is a perfect duty *never* to be unjust to other survivors, there is only an imperfect duty *sometimes* to be beneficent. This raises the question of *who* I should help. When answering this question, the Kantian holds that putting people in a position to pursue their own ends is more important than sharing ends with those who are already in a position to pursue their own ends. For example, consider you have a choice between helping the child outside the fortress who is about to be devoured and helping Gary to take stock of all available resources inside the fortress. Although you may take the same joy as Gary in completing a methodical inventory, this is presumably something that Gary can do himself. If you do not help the child who is about to be devoured, however, she will not be able to pursue *any* of her future goals or plans. There are no rational ends to be pursued once you have joined the ranks of the undead (except, perhaps, for talkers). Consequently, it seems as if the Kantian would say that you should help the child.

What makes the Kantian view different from the utilitarian view is that you are not obligated to *constantly* alleviate the suffering of others as long as doing so does not require you to sacrifice anything of comparable moral significance. As mentioned in the previous section, the utilitarian view could require you to reduce yourself to a level no better than the survivors that you are trying to help. In contrast, the Kantian requires only that you be *reasonably* beneficent—that you help some survivors some of the time—where the priority is helping those that could not pursue any of their own ends were you not to help.

When it comes to the more limited scope of the Kantian view, it is important to note that you need only evaluate the maxims that you actually form. Unlike the utilitarian view, distance can have a role to play here. For example, you may only form maxims to help people within the immediate vicinity of your stronghold, for example, inside the stronghold or in the shantytown. If there are too many people in your shantytown and you cannot help them all, the maxim that you form might be more selective, for example, "I only help children who are about to be devoured by the undead." Not only would acting on such a maxim discharge a duty of beneficence, but it also prioritizes beneficence as the Kantian prescribes. Unlike the armed adult survivor outside your walls, the child is not capable of defending herself. If you do not help her, she will surely be devoured and so will be unable to pursue any of the goals that she has—or would have—for her life. Although the armed adult survivors outside your walls would surely benefit from your assistance in their fight against the undead, they are capable, in principle, of pursuing this end themselves. Even if they are nonetheless slaughtered, as they are in the above field exercise, the Kantian would hold that you have done your duty as long as you have been reasonably beneficent—that you have helped some people some of the time—for example, by rescuing the mother's child. Rescuing her child would be to act upon the maxim that you have endorsed which likewise discharges your duty of beneficence.

Summary

Whereas Hardin holds that we have *no* obligations to those outside of our stronghold, the utilitarian and the Kantian disagree. For utilitarians like Singer, our moral obligation is very *strong*. We are required to help those outside our fortress until doing so would place those inside in a position no better than the situation that those outside are facing, that is, being eaten alive. Although Kantians like O'Neill would hold that we ought never to be unjust either to those inside or outside our fortress, our obligation to help those outside our fortress is far weaker than what the utilitarian envisions. We are only required to help some of these survivors some of the time, though we must give preference to those under threat of being eaten alive since they will not be able to pursue any of their goals once they have turned into zombies.

Further study

- Arthur, John. "Famine Relief and the Ideal Moral Code." In *Ethics in Practice*, edited by Hugh LaFollete, 563–570. Malden, MA: Wiley-Blackwell, 2014.

- Coins the phrase "Greater Moral Evil Principle" (GMP) to refer to the principle that Singer deploys when establishing our obligation to alleviate global poverty. Arthur rejects the strong version of GMP since it ignores the moral entitlements we have to our earnings while still endorsing something like the more moderate version of GMP with respect to those closer to us.

- Brooks, Max. *World War Z: An Oral History of the Zombie War*. New York: Crown, 2006.
  - Although operating typically at a geopolitical level, it includes several examples that touch on issues of stronghold ethics, for example, both Israel and South Africa respond to the outbreak through fortified enclaves where access is strictly controlled.

- Hardin, Garrett. "Lifeboat Ethics: The Case against Helping the Poor." *Psychology Today* (September, 1974): 800–812.
  - Compares developed countries to lifeboats with limited resources and developing countries to those that are drowning at sea hoping for rescue.

- *It Comes at Night* (2017), [Film] Dir. Trey Edward Shults, USA: A24.
  - This film depicts a stronghold situation on a smaller scale. After quarantining the father of a family to ensure he is not infected, one family allows another into their secluded home during an outbreak. Because of quarrels over resources and mutual distrust, the situation deteriorates until everyone is either dead or infected.

- *Land of the Dead*, [Film].
  - This film contains the best zombie-horror example of a situation similar to the one described in the field exercise above. The wealthy and powerful live in a luxury high-rise called "Fiddler's Green" while the poor live in post-apocalyptic squalor outside of it.

- Ma, Roger. *The Zombie Combat Manual: A Guide to Fighting the Living Dead*. New York: Berkley Publishing, 2010.
  - See chapter three which deals with conditioning and preparation. Like the field exercise above, the "combat report" for this chapter discusses a stronghold ethics case involving a grocery store that has closed its gates to prevent being inundated by a desperate mob of the living.

- Moosa, Tariq. "Babes in Zombie Land." In *The Walking Dead and Philosophy*, edited by Wayne Yuen, 231–242. Chicago: Open Court, 2012.
  - Uses the example of starving children fending off a zombie horde to illustrate that, in this post-apocalyptic hellscape, we have an obligation not to *create* new children but rather to help those that already *exist*.

- O'Neill, Onora. "Kantian Approaches to Some Famine Problems." In *Matters of Life and Death*, edited by Tom Regan, 285–293. New York: McGraw-Hill, 1980.

- Discusses Kantian duties of justice and beneficence to those suffering due to famine. Covers both the obligations that individuals *within* famine-stricken regions have to one another and the obligations that individuals *outside* these famine-stricken regions have to those trying to survive within them.

- Singer, Peter. "Famine, Affluence, and Morality." *Philosophy and Public Affairs* 1, no. 1 (1972): 229–243.
  - Introduces (what Arthur later calls) GMP as a way of explaining our moral obligations to those that are starving due to famine in developing and war-torn countries. The quotation that opens this chapter is a post-apocalyptic adaptation of GMP. The original article also considers a number of objections, in addition to the central objection mentioned above, that one might pose to GMP.

- *The Walking Dead*, [TV Program].
  - Starting in season three, the show depicts many different stronghold communities. Typically, these strongholds are governed by contrasting ideologies that affect the way they deal with their own populations as well as the other stronghold communities.

10 WHAT ARE YOUR OBLIGATIONS TO UNDEAD LOVED ONES?

When your lordship has decided for himself, what remains unchanged, which at the last judgment shall receive the things done in his body; your lordship will easily see, that the body he had, when an embryo in his mother's already infected womb, when a child fleeing the undead, when a young man fighting them, when a bedridden old man dying of a bite, and at last, which he shall have after his resurrection as the undead; are each of them his body, though none of them be the same body.

—LETTER TO THE LORD BISHOP OF WORCESTER ON UNDEATH AND FINAL JUDGMENT

Even if zombies are not full-fledged persons, is there still some morally relevant sense in which my zombie self would be the same person as I am? If so, can my zombie self be held morally responsible just as my living self is? The same questions arise with respect to other survivors. Are they the same people after they have turned? Are they still morally responsible? What about moral considerability? Do I have the same obligations to those that have turned as I had to them before they turned? This chapter will first consider questions of personal identity and moral responsibility raised by the apocalypse. This will be followed by a discussion of what obligations we might still have to those that have turned, especially those to whom we are closest.

1. Field exercise: The children

From the tricycles abandoned in the front yard to the swings squeaking in the wind out back, we knew immediately we had found our new home. Before I could even check the house for zombies, the kids were screaming for joy and chasing one another across the playground. These childish reminders of a lost world usually broke my heart, but seeing them imbued with the boundless energy for which they were intended momentarily lifted my spirits.

Looking at them playing on the swings—warm sun filtering through the concertina wire the previous family had installed atop their picket fence—I thought that we were finally safe. Nothing could have been further from the truth. The undead had not pursued us, but undeath had found us just the same.

In our rush to escape the previous attack, I had not checked them as thoroughly as I should have. Cooper was the first to show symptoms, and Karen followed soon thereafter. The decline was slow, which afforded me the luxury of self-deception. At first, it was just a loss of appetite, but what kid doesn't experience that from time to time? During the night, they whimpered and wanted to cuddle with me instead of staying in their cribs, but isn't it normal that they wouldn't want to sleep alone in a new home? They were each running a temperature, but wouldn't that be expected if they were fighting off a cold?

"You'll be fine … You just caught the sniffles from someone in the old camp," I reassured them … and myself.

Yet, over the weeks that followed, I never caught their "cold" even though they slept with me every night. I was not yet willing to acknowledge it through action, but I nonetheless knew that it had to be what I feared most. At the end of the second week, my fears were confirmed by the first narrow lines showing on their pale hands and faces. They were like two porcelain dolls, the cracks revealing lives as fragile as the toys they now resembled. They grew increasingly lethargic and wasted away for lack of food. At night, they would cry weakly in my arms as I tried to comfort them. Eventually, their personalities evaporated as the infection sapped their youthful spirit leaving only listless husks. They were turning simultaneously—the infection providing a final gift—as neither would be left to suffer a life alone without the other.

That last night, I put them back in the cribs that they had not slept in since the first night. I made sure to give Cooper his favorite bunny and Karen her tattered bear. They had made the journey as well and would have to see the children through what remained. Although they were burning up, they were so feeble that they didn't fuss as I tucked them in. Sensing me above them, they turned their faces to me, eyes that could no longer see blindly searching for some measure of comfort. Their tiny fingers, covered with thin lines, reached toward my sobbing face. I grasped their hands and drew them close, a final kiss on the cheek, tears falling and mixing with their tears of blood.

I sat with my back against the door and my head in my hands. Although I still desperately desired it, I couldn't risk letting them sleep with me in case they converted while I slumbered. On the other hand, I also couldn't bring myself to finish them. I had tried a couple of times as they slept—my knife trained above their tiny forms—but I could never summon the courage necessary to defeat my own impossible dreams.

I awoke in the morning to banging on the other side of the door and airy, high-pitched moaning—"*Aaaahhhh!*"—wailing voices that had

FIGURE 18 Undead children and indecision.

not yet changed. I unsheathed my knife and steeled my nerve for the grisly work that lay ahead. They were no longer Cooper and Karen, but something else entirely: an undead trap for the next family that might happen upon this place.

As I struggled to stand, the banging was replaced by a squeaking. *Seeesaaawww … Seeesaaaww … Seeesaaawww.* The springs were sighing as the children jumped in their cribs. I could also make out … *giggling?* "*Haaahhh …. Haaahhh … Haaahhh …*" It may have just been the effect the bouncing had on their ability to moan, but it sounded, from where I was sitting, as if they were *enjoying* themselves.

My heart battled my mind into a stalemate of indecision. "Even if they aren't the same in every way, maybe there is some sense in which they are," I allowed myself to hope. Putting my ear to the door, I heard voices that sounded like Cooper and Karen. It was as if their youthful energy had been restored in undeath. Reason replied, "They are the undead. You would destroy any other without a second thought." I did have second thoughts though … and they weren't just like any other zombies. They were *mine* and I still *cared* for them. Whatever cruel will I had mustered for my grim task soon dissolved, and then resolved into my prior affection. They sensed me. I heard scratching and moaning on the other side, or was it *whimpering?* I knew what they needed … and what I needed to do. Their future wouldn't include me, but at least *they* still had a future, one that my love compelled me to deliver.

2. Personal identity

As in the field exercise above, survivors frequently hesitate to kill loved ones after they have turned. At the same time, however, survivors will often kill themselves when they are about to turn to avoid joining the ranks of the undead. Why is that? Would you really be killing your loved one after he has turned and do you, the survivor, return in some meaningful sense when reanimated?

Presumably, you hesitate to kill your loved ones because you still think it is *them* in some meaningful sense, for example, in the above story, Cooper and Karen. If you don't hesitate to kill them, then it must be because you don't think they really are themselves anymore, but rather some undead counterpart that serves only to threaten the living. The reasoning in the case of suicide is similar, though more prejudicial toward undeath. You resolve to kill yourself since either *you* don't want to turn into one of the undead, or you don't think it will be *you*, but you don't want there to be some undead counterpart of yourself that will endanger other survivors.

Implicit in these decisions is a conception of *personal identity*, a view of what makes you or your loved ones the *same* over time. There are several candidates for what personal identity consists in, and this section will consider a few possibilities: body, organism, and consciousness.

One view is that sameness of a *person* consists in the sameness of their *body*. At first blush, this seems plausible. You have the same body today as you had yesterday and if you were bitten today and turned tomorrow, then you would have the same body tomorrow as well. This would explain why you hesitate to kill your loved ones, namely, they still *look* like your loved ones. It could also explain why you might want to destroy yourself before turning, since your body would persist even after you turned.

A moment's reflection shows that there are a lot of problems with a bodily continuity view of personal identity. As the quote that opens this chapter makes clear, our bodies are changing all of the time. The children in the above story do not have the same bodies at the end of their illness as they had at the beginning. They have wasted away. Likewise, we are constantly shedding and replacing cells in our bodies. If a zombie were to bite you, is the part that is consumed still you, since it was your body, or does it now belong to the zombie?

Things get stranger once considered from the perspective of the opening quote, which deals with final judgment in Christianity. If what is judged is your resurrected body, at what point of your body's existence will you be judged? Is it your body when it died but before it was resurrected as one of the undead? What if you were a marauding cannibal who was later killed by the undead? Both the cannibal and his victims would have claim to the same *body*—or at least the tastiest parts of it—when resurrected for final judgment. In contrast, if what is judged is your undead counterpart, what relationship does it have to your living self who committed the crimes, for example, cannibalism, for which you are to be judged? Your undead self, especially if previously devoured by the undead, is also often missing body parts that our living selves possessed—arms, legs, really anything save the head—which means we are no longer the same persons according to the bodily continuity view. If so, then how could one's undead body be judged for the crimes one committed when alive? These are all vexing questions according to the bodily criterion view of personal identity.

Another possibility is that sameness of person consists in sameness of *organism*, in our case a human animal. According to this view, you just are a particular human animal. Returning to the opening quote, what the fetus, the child, and the man all share in common is that they are the same animal, the same organism, over time. The *matter* that is united to this organism—cells and such—comes and goes, but the *organism* persists. Also, when the organism dies, you cease to exist. Consequently, if your loved one were to fully convert into one of the undead, they would cease to exist as well. You should have no qualms finishing off a converted loved one since they really aren't your *loved one*—a particular human animal—any longer. Finally, there is no problem with resurrection at final judgment as there was for the bodily criterion. Presumably, God could resurrect your living human animal even if the matter united in that resurrected animal were different from the matter it possessed when it died.

At the same time, however, there are some concerns that one could raise for the organism criterion of personal identity that points the way toward our final account. What if your loved one has not yet fully converted into a moaner but is still cracked up? They are ravenous and non-rational but nonetheless living. Should you hesitate in killing your loved one since they would still be the same living *organism*? Is the fact that they are still the same living human animal sufficient to make them the same person? To answer this latter question, consider a situation where the organism has died but you might be tempted to call the individual the same person. What if you are bitten, subsequently lose consciousness, and awake fully converted as one of the undead? When I say *you* awake, I mean the same rational being with the same memories as that of your living self. You are no longer a living human animal, but have you also ceased to be *you*?

If you think there is some important respect in which your undead self is still you, the continuity of *organism* view cannot be the whole story when it comes to personal identity. What seems to be missing from this story is the role that continuity of *consciousness* plays in the continuity of the person. Perhaps, sameness of person is just the sameness of a rational being, regardless of what instantiates that rational being (body, organism, etc.). Your personal identity would extend back as far as your consciousness extends, through memory, to any past action or thought. Insofar as both my cracked up loved one and her undead counterpart are non-rational and lack consciousness—a moaner—they would *not* be my loved one. Insofar as a zombie retains rationality and consciousness of her former life—a talker—she *would* be my loved one. The consciousness criterion of personal identity explains both why we hesitate to kill a loved one who has turned—"maybe *she's* still in there somewhere"—and why survivors commit suicide for fear of *themselves* becoming the undead. It is not the exact same body as our living selves and the organism dies. The only thing to truly fear is your rational being—your consciousness—awaking in an undead form with a painful hunger for human flesh that you will never satisfy.

As one might suspect, however, the consciousness criterion for personal identity faces some problems as well. Go back to the opening quote of this chapter. The old man who is dying of a bite might remember, before turning, being a younger man fighting zombies. According to the consciousness criterion, this would entail that the old man is the *same* person as the young man. This younger man fighting zombies, furthermore, might remember being a child running from zombies. This would entail that the young man is the *same* person as the child. By the transitivity of identity, the old man would be the *same* person as the child (since they are both the same person as the young man). What if the old man, however, does not remember being the young child fleeing zombies? According to the consciousness criterion, this would mean that they are *not* the same person. Consequently, the consciousness criterion generates a contradiction inasmuch as the old man both *is* and is *not* the same person as the child.

Another worry with the consciousness criterion is that it seems to entail that if you remember doing something then you were the person doing it. What if someone has a *false* memory? For example, it has been rumored that some zombies relive the experiences of those whose brains they consume. Assume that one of these zombies is consuming the brain of its victim and remembers being the victim attempting to flee that zombie. Does this entail that the zombie is identical to its victim? Wouldn't that be contradictory? That seems to be what the consciousness criterion entails since personal identity extends as far as memory extends. One might insist that only true memories should count as part of your consciousness, but what makes something a "true" memory? If the answer is that what you remembered happened to *you*, but "you" are just your consciousness, then it being part of your consciousness would make it your memory. If you make appeal to some criterion outside of your consciousness for a memory to be yours, then you will have abandoned the consciousness criterion of personal identity.

A final worry for the consciousness criterion is similar to a worry the bodily criterion faces. Just as your body is always changing so too is your consciousness. Whereas your body constantly creates new cells and sheds old ones, your mind is constantly thinking new thoughts and forgetting old ones. The thoughts, including memories, of which consciousness consists are transient. If your consciousness is never the same at any two moments, you are never the same *person*, but at best, according to the consciousness criterion, only the same kind of *persons*.

None of these criteria for personal identity are satisfactory on their own, but perhaps some combination of them would produce a better result. Of the three options, the consciousness criterion seems most important when it comes to *personal* identity. It is hard to see how a body or an organism without your thoughts, memories, and desires could still be *you*. At the same time, however, we need a way of accounting for false memories as well as gaps in memory. A suggestion would be to look at the one thing that your living and your undead selves seem to share in common, namely, the same *brain*. It is the brain that must be destroyed to put an end to a zombie and if consciousness continues in undeath, this would have to be the thing you share with your undead self. What would make a thought *yours* is that it was thought by your *brain*. Any memory that was a part of your consciousness without having originally been thought by your brain, for example, a memory a zombie might have after consuming someone else's brain, would fail to be *your* memory. In order for a memory to be genuine, the same brain must be involved in the original experience and the memory of it. Likewise, if the brain was involved in some experience but fails to have a memory of that experience, that is, there is a gap in your memory, you can still tie yourself to that experience based on the identity of the brain that had the original experience. Since brain cells come and go as well, what I mean by "brain" in this context is a certain functional organization of brain matter that makes the brain the *same* brain. Stated differently, what's important is not the stuff—specific brain cells—that the brain is made up of as much as the way this stuff is organized. It has to be put together in such a way that it functions in the exact same way as the brain you now possess. If *this* is destroyed by a bullet or eaten by a zombie, then *you* are destroyed as well.

Although it is possible that zombies are enjoying conscious lives just like the ones they had when living, the impact of the virus on their brains and behavior make this unlikely. It seems much more likely that the cracked up and the moaners have brain structures significantly different from their living selves. Even though the brain remains active for both the living and the undead, the functional organization of the brain matter must be so affected by the infection that their conscious lives, such as they are, would be very different from what they enjoyed while living. The situation may be different for talkers, however, if their brains have returned to a functional organization similar enough to their living selves. According to the account we are considering, if your loved one's consciousness really is *trapped* inside a bloodthirsty zombie, as long as they have the same brain, they would be the same person.

3. Are the undead morally responsible?

What is required in order for you to be morally responsible for what you do? Based on what we have discussed in previous chapters, there seem to be at least two necessary conditions: (1) an understanding of what you ought or ought not to do (moral reasoning), and (2) the ability to do what you know you ought to do (autonomy).

Although the Kantian and the utilitarian have different criteria for moral *considerability*—personhood vs. sentience—they have similar criteria for moral *responsibility*. Notwithstanding their disagreements over what an individual ought to do, they would have to agree that an individual who is incapable of understanding what they ought to do and then acting on that knowledge cannot be morally responsible for what they do. Put differently, whereas the Kantian would hold that the only individuals who are morally considerable are those that are morally responsible (persons), the utilitarian would hold that all individuals capable of feeling pleasure and pain (sentient) are morally considerable. Even so, both sides would agree that only persons can be morally responsible.

How does *personal identity*, the topic of the previous section, relate to *moral personhood*? Survivors continue to be the same people over time as long as their brains are intact and are connected in the right kinds of ways with their conscious experiences. They are also moral persons as long as they are autonomous and capable of moral reasoning. It seems unlikely that either the cracked up (living and ravenous) or the moaners (undead and equally ravenous) are the same people as they were before they turned. Their brains have undergone such a dramatic change that whatever consciousness they have is likely totally discontinuous with the consciousness they had when living. These zombies also fail to be morally responsible for their actions. They lack moral agency and are governed solely by the virus.

What if these admittedly bloodthirsty zombies were somehow conscious and maintained the memories of who they were before they turned? As long as their brains are intact as well, they would be the same "people" based on the account of personal identity we have been considering. Even so, they would fail to be the same "people" from the moral perspective. Even if a zombie had some of the features listed on the sliding scale of personhood discussed in Chapter 8.3, this would at most entitle them to a modicum of moral *consideration*. They would still lack moral *agency* and with it moral *responsibility*. For Kant, moral personhood is all or nothing. Although we would be obligated to their living counterparts while they were still moral *persons*, we would have no obligations to zombies as mere *things*. Arguably, the children in the field exercise above, whether living or undead, fail to be moral persons in the Kantian sense. We do not hold small children morally responsible for their actions because we do not take them to be full-fledged moral agents, and the same would be true of their undead counterparts. As I have tried to emphasize, this Kantian view of moral agency (reason + autonomy) seems to be required for moral responsibility whether or not one subscribes to Kant's ethical theory.

The talker from the field exercise in Chapter 8.1 offers the most interesting case since she, unlike the cracked up or the moaners, seems to have a rational *will*. Does this mean she is a moral "person" in the Kantian sense? Assume that she recognizes what she ought not to do, in this case, that she ought not to consume the living. Let's further assume that she is capable of acting in such a way that she does not do what she knows she ought not to do. For example, in the field exercise, she chooses final death over continuing her pursuit of living flesh. It is unclear whether she chooses this fate because she recognizes it is what she ought to do or if it is because she simply wishes to avoid the pain of being undead. For Kant, she would be doing something wrong in either case—committing suicide—assuming that she actually is a moral person.

Even if she were a Kantian moral person, however, should we hold her morally responsible for choosing final death? Given her physical and psychological condition, could she have done other than what she did? If not, can she be held morally responsible for what she did? The **Principle of Alternate Possibilities (PAP)** claims that you are morally responsible for what you have done only if you could have done otherwise. To understand this principle, as well as the problems with it, consider a modification of the field exercise from Chapter 2.1. To refresh your memory, this was a situation where a hunter had captured an innocent person to feed to two undead children:

(1) Assume that you are the hunter and have resolved to capture a living human being and feed him to the undead children. Let's also assume that *nothing* will sway you from this decision. As you are about to set out to hunt, a woman steps out of the shadows with a gun and threatens to shoot you as well as the kids if you do not come back with someone to sacrifice to the children. In other words, the woman with the gun is telling you to do what you have already decided to do. The threat has no impact on you—again *nothing* would change your mind—so even if the woman with the gun had said "If you feed someone to these kids, I will shoot you," you would have continued on all the same even though you, and those you care most about, would have gotten a bullet for your effort. In this case, it seems like you are morally responsible since you act on your previously formed intention to capture a living human being to feed to the children. At the same time, however, the case is not a counterexample to PAP since you are not deprived of alternate possibilities. You are *unreasonable* and nothing—including a gun to the head—would have prevented you from doing *whatever* you chose to do.

(2) Consider the same situation except that you are so impressed by the threat that you totally forget you had previously resolved to hunt a living sacrifice. Put differently, this is a situation where you are eminently *reasonable*. Unlike the previous example, the threat *does* deprive you of alternate possibilities. Since you are reasonable, you cannot do other than what the woman demands. You still head out to hunt, but you do so simply because of the threat. This is not a counterexample to PAP, but rather illustrates it in action. You are deprived of alternate possibilities and also released from moral responsibility. You do what you do because you are coerced to do so.

(3) This situation is somewhere in between the first two. You have resolved to hunt on behalf of the undead children. Subsequently, the woman threatens to kill you and the kids if you do not do what you have already resolved to do. You are again reasonable, and would have been moved by the woman's threat if it were to do anything other than what you have already decided to do. Since you have already resolved to hunt a living sacrifice, you go ahead and do so. You act on your previously formed intention to hunt on behalf of the children, but are deprived of alternate possibilities since you would not have acted contrary to the woman's demands. If you think that the protagonist is nonetheless morally responsible in this case, then it would be a counterexample to PAP. You are deprived of alternate possibilities, but are nonetheless morally responsible for your action.

You might still be skeptical of how I described the hunter's psychology. Again, consider yourself in their shoes. Aren't you still *coerced* since you *know* that if you don't hunt down a living sacrifice for the kids then you are all going to get shot? You might think that there isn't any way of cleanly separating what the woman with the gun wants and what you want. If this is your view, consider one final variation on the above cases.

(4) You form the intention to hunt down someone to feed to the children. Like the second and third cases above, you are also reasonable, so you would comply with whatever the woman with the gun told you to do. The only difference is that the woman never steps out of the shadows to threaten you with the gun. If you failed to go out and hunt on behalf of the undead kids, she would have compelled you to do so, but there is no need for her to threaten you since you do it of your own volition. Although you are still deprived of alternate possibilities—you would have complied with her threat had she deemed it necessary to threaten you—you are nevertheless morally responsible for your action. This would seem to be a decisive counterexample to PAP.

The point of these cases is to show that an individual can still be morally responsible even if they could not have done otherwise than what they did. Coercion is only going to morally excuse an individual when it is the *reason* why the individual does what they do, as it is in the second example above. Assuming that the talker from Chapter 8.1 is deprived of alternate possibilities, should we hold her morally responsible or not? If not, in what way is she acting from coercion? No one is holding a gun to her head. She chooses the noose by her own volition.

It is important to note that coercion can be *external*, as it is with the woman with the gun, but it can be *internal* as well. For example, the protagonist as well as the talker in Chapter 8.1 are both *addicted* to the point that they are deprived of alternate possibilities. Each also recognizes that they are compelled to do what they do because of their addiction. They do what they do—torturing the undead or feasting on the living— even though they don't wish to have the desires that control them. To be morally responsible, according to the account under consideration, is for one's action to come from the will that one wishes to have. Since neither of these addicts wishes to have the will they have, they fail to be morally responsible. In fact, the talker's wish not to have the will she possesses is clearly expressed through her decision to commit suicide.

If the talker is not morally responsible, however, then we still lack an example of a zombie that is morally responsible. We have already established that the cracked up and moaners are not morally responsible for their actions and if fully developed zombies—talkers—always act on the basis of wills they do not wish to have, they would likewise not be morally responsible. Of course, the same would be true of at least some survivors as well, for example, the protagonist who destroys the talker in Chapter 8.1.

4. Care ethics

Returning to the field exercise for this chapter, imagine yourself again in the shoes of the protagonist. You care deeply about these children and have done your very best to protect them from harm. Over time, you have built a very special bond with them, a bond that undeath has been unable to break. The other ethical theories we have examined would have difficulty accounting for your moral feeling. Contractarians would hold that you are not obligated to the children since they can neither benefit you if you followed the rules nor harm you if you failed to do so. In fact, it would seem that regardless of whether they are turned or not, the contractarian holds that you do not have any direct moral obligations to the children. Even so, in the above story, you still feel a special bond that seems morally relevant.

Utilitarians are altruists, and so they must reject the idea that such bonds are morally relevant. Likewise, once the children are undead and no longer sentient, the utilitarian would say that they are not even morally considerable. This is a point upon which the Kantian and the utilitarian would likely agree. According to the Kantian view, furthermore, since Cooper and Karen are not autonomous moral agents, they would fail to be persons and so would be mere means—*things*—that are not morally considerable in themselves. Whatever duties of justice and beneficence we might have to other persons would not extend to the zombie children.

If you felt like the protagonist in the field exercise, the other ethical theories we have discussed thus far would strike you as woefully inadequate. There is, however, another ethical theory that does a better job of capturing the protagonist's moral attitude. Whereas Contractarian, Kantian, and Utilitarian views rely on abstract moral *principles* to guide our actions, **care ethics** asks us to focus more on our *feelings* as a guide to what we ought to do. These feelings arise organically from the network of personal relationships we cultivate with other individuals. The relevant emotions that constitute "care"—sympathy, empathy, love, etc.—reflect the nature of these relationships. The moral life consists of attending to these relationships, caring for these individuals, and responding to their needs. These relationships are more important, from the moral perspective, than abstract prescriptions to respect the terms of a social contract (Hobbes), to follow the categorical imperative (Kant), or to act in accordance with the Greatest Happiness Principle (Mill).

Whereas care ethics asks us to focus on the *particular* relationships we actually have with those that we care about when determining what we ought to do, the other ethical theories we have examined could be seen as encouraging us to adopt an impartial *universal* perspective that ignores these particular relationships when determining what we ought to do. This more universal perspective, however, could be viewed as question begging insofar as it simply assumes that what is at the heart of care ethics is morally irrelevant. The impartiality ignores, furthermore, an important feature of our moral lives, namely, the partiality we feel toward our family and friends.

Take the duty we have toward children. Although we may all have a general duty of beneficence toward children—especially given how few there are anymore—I have a special duty to *my* children that you do not have. Assuming that these special obligations do not exist—or that they are simply instances of more general duties—ignores an important feature of our moral lives. Staying with children, the Kantian perspective might even be self-stultifying. For Kant, it seems as if a parent would have a duty to love their children, but a parent ought to be motivated not by love but rather by duty. If a parent really is motivated solely by duty, however, then could they really be loving in the sense the children would require? If not, then would the Kantian parent really be fulfilling their duty?

Some feminist philosophers explain this contrast between care ethics and other ethical theories in terms of differences between how women and men view the moral world and their place within it. Of course, the other ethical theories we have discussed were originally developed by men: Hobbes, Kant, and Bentham/Mill. The fact that these theories were developed by men is no accident, according to this view, but rather reflects a more fundamental moral disposition that men are likely to share. Whereas women tend to find their personal identity bound up with their relationships to other people, men tend to view themselves as autonomous, free, and independent. While women are inclined to view these personal relationships as morally relevant, men often fancy themselves impartial moral judges. The specific circumstances that surround a particular moral decision are more relevant to women than they are to men. Finally, women are likely to view morality as a function of vulnerability and dependence while men view it is as a function of fully-informed individual rationality. Although the male approach dominates the brutally violent present, that may itself be the problem. The survivors that remain are, regardless of gender, more vulnerable and dependent than perhaps they ever have been. If our world is to be knitted together again, it will be through a gradually growing and mutually reinforcing network of caring personal relationships. This network would create the social foundation, furthermore, for the kind of human flourishing discussed in Chapter 2.4.

Care ethics could provide justification for the protagonist's decision not to destroy the turned children. If you felt as the protagonist did, your *emotions* would be telling you not to destroy them. They would provide a normative guide to your action that is based off of the very personal *relationships* that you have developed with the children. Even though the children have undergone a terrible transformation, you still *feel* there is something of them there and that you remain obligated to care for them as well as to provide for their now ravenous needs. Cooper and Karen still have a future, albeit different from the one you originally envisioned for them, and you are committed to securing it for them. Although the other ethical theories would counsel you to destroy the children and hold that you are precluded from providing them with the living flesh they crave, care ethics would hold that *impersonal* appeals to contractual obligations, the inherent rights of persons, or altruism, are secondary to the *personal* relationships of care one has cultivated and the moral feelings that these relationships produce.

As one might suspect, objections have been raised both to the gendered foundation of care ethics and to the theory itself. To begin, one might question it there really are inherent moral differences between genders. Are women and men essentially predisposed to one moral view or another? Even if women and men are predisposed to certain moral views, does this entail that they ought to endorse these views? Just because something *is* the case does not entail that it *ought* to be the case—take the viral outbreak itself for instance.

Turning to the content of care ethics, another worry is that your *feelings* often do not provide a good guide as to what you ought to do. Many forms of discriminatory behavior—sexism, racism, etc.—are predicated on individuals "feeling" a certain way about a group different from themselves. The impartiality that care ethics discounts is exactly what prevents the kinds of prejudice and bias that might otherwise infect your moral judgment. Moral concepts like justice and rights play an important role in constraining you from acting solely in your self-interest, or in the case of care ethics, solely in the interests of those for whom you already care. Also, just because you do not have a personal relationship of care with someone doesn't entail, on its own, that you have no moral obligation to them, for example, the man the hunter captures in Chapter 2.1. Put differently, care ethics appears to restrict the moral community too much since you need not consider individuals you do not know or care about when determining what you ought to do. Finally, care ethics faces the same problem that most other ethical theories face, namely, what do you do when your obligations of care come into conflict with one another? What would the protagonist do, for example, if Karen's needs were incompatible with Cooper's needs as they would be if only one of them had turned?

One way of dealing with the above concerns is to find a way of viewing care ethics as compatible (rather than incompatible) with some of the other ethical theories we have discussed. For example, we might hold that there is a general duty to care which is on par with the other abstract moral principles we have covered. A general principle would have the advantage of extending our duty to care beyond our specific personal relationships. This is a potential weakness for care ethics considered on its own. Even so, we might simultaneously hold that these abstract moral principles serve only as a *general* guide to moral action, but that *particular* moral judgments require taking into account the specific context within which the decision is being made. This approach to moral decision making should remind the reader of Ross's approach discussed in Chapter 5.6. Whereas abstract moral principles would occupy the role of *prima facie* duties in Ross's system, the duty proper is the result of a considered moral judgment that takes into account the specific context of the decision.

A final way of viewing the concept of care is as a *virtue*. This is a concept that we will discuss at much greater length in the next chapter. For present purposes, suffice it to say that care would be a nurturing character trait, arising from daily practice, which is good for an individual to possess. This virtue could be cultivated, for example, by consistently following a general duty to care. Once one has cultivated the appropriate character trait, one would *become* a caring person and would no longer need to consider the general duty. Unlike the protagonist in Chapter 2.1, an individual who has cultivated a caring character would be disinclined to treat others callously—trapping the living to feed zombies—even if doing so helped you to care for the particular undead children you continue to love.

Summary

Neither a cracked up but living loved one nor a moaner who has the same body as your loved one really is your loved one in the sense of being the same *person*. The possibility exists, however, for a talker to be the same person as they were before they turned. At the same time, however, a talker could still fail to be a *moral* person insofar as they fail to possess the will they wish to have. Just because zombies fail to be moral persons, however, does not entail that you have no moral obligations to them whatsoever. Care ethics provides powerful reasons for why you would still have moral obligations to your loved ones after they have turned—assuming they still are your loved ones.

Further study

- Bowman, Cole. "We're Not Free to Save Lee." In *The Ultimate Walking Dead and Philosophy*, edited by Wayne Yuen, 135–150. Chicago: Open Court, 2016.
  - Discusses the theme of free will vs. determinism within the context of *The Walking Dead*.
- Callens, Melissa Vosen. "I Ain't No Hollaback Girl!" In *The Ultimate Walking Dead and Philosophy*, 153–164.
  - Discusses both Kohlberg's and Gilligan's views (mentioned below) through the prism of Carol's killing of Lizzie in *The Walking Dead*.
- *Cargo* (2017), [Film] Dir. Yolanda Ramke, USA: Netflix, 2017.
  - This movie touches on some of the issues raised above in connection with personal identity, moral responsibility, and care ethics. It deals with the lengths that a father goes—both before and after turning—to protect his infant daughter within a post-apocalyptic environment.
- *Colin* (2008), [Film] Dir. Marc Price, UK: Kaleidoscope.
  - This movie is presented entirely from the perspective of its zombie protagonist, who is ravenous but avoids conflict and maintains some latent consciousness from his previous life.
- Frankfurt, Harry. "Alternate Possibilities and Moral Responsibility." *The Journal of Philosophy* 66, no. 23 (1969): 829–839.
  - Argues that moral responsibility does not require that the agent could have done otherwise. The four cases in Chapter 10.3 are adapted from this article. Frankfurt argues that coercion only excuses, from the moral standpoint, when it serves as the *reason* for why the agent acted as they did.
- Frankfurt, Harry. "Freedom of the Will and the Concept of a Person." *The Journal of Philosophy* 68, no. 1 (1971): 5–20.
  - Argues that an addict will only be morally responsible for pursuing the object of their addiction if they wish to have the will they have, that is, if they desire to be an addict.

- Gilligan, Carol. *In a Different Voice*. Cambridge, MA: Harvard University Press, 1982.
  - Defends the idea that men and women have different basic moral viewpoints. She also offers a care ethics response to Kohlberg's hierarchy (mentioned below).
- Greene, Richard. "My Zombie, My Self." In *The Ultimate Walking Dead and Philosophy*, edited by Wayne Yuen, 207–216. Chicago: Open Court, 2016.
  - Examines the question of what it means to be dead as well as how this intersects with questions of personal identity were you to become a zombie.
- Held, Virginia. "Feminist Transformations of Moral Theory." *Philosophy and Phenomenological Research* 50 (1990): 321–344.
  - Presents care ethics as an alternative to ethical theories that rely on appeals to abstract general principles.
- Kenemore, Scott. *Zombie, Ohio*. New York: Skyhorse Publishing, 2011.
  - The story is told from the perspective of a former Philosophy professor—now zombie—who slowly regains his memory while struggling with the moral problems that his new condition creates.
- Kohlberg, Lawrence. *The Philosophy of Moral Disagreement*. New York: Harper and Row, 1981.
  - See pp. 409–412 where he defends a developmental conception of morality. According to his view, an appeal to abstract general principles reflects a more mature moral standpoint than the one prescribed by care ethics.
- Larkin, William. "*Res Corporealis*: Persons, Bodies, and Zombies." In *Zombies, Vampires, and Philosophy: New Life for the Undead*, edited by Richard Greene and K. Silem Mohammad, 15–26. Chicago: Open Court, 2010.
  - Defends the bodily approach to personal identity, when it comes to zombies and their former selves.
- Locke, John. *Essay Concerning Human Understanding*. 1689. Edited with introduction. Indianapolis: Hackett, 1996.
  - See book II, chapter xxvii for Locke's discussion of personal identity. He argues that personal identity consists in sameness of consciousness and rejects the sameness of body as well as the sameness of organism views of personal identity.
- "Locke's Second Reply to the Bishop of Worcester." 1697. In *The Works of John Locke Vol. 3*, 191–498. London: Rivington, 1824.
  - See p. 308 for the passage that inspired the quotation that opens this

chapter. Locke is defending the view that personal identity consists in sameness of consciousness against Bishop Stillingfleet's objections. The Bishop subscribes to the view that personal identity consists in sameness of body and attempts to show that Locke's view is inconsistent with the Christian account of resurrection during final judgment. Locke argues that the Bishop's view is at best incoherent and at worst self-stultifying.

- Miller, Sarah Clark. "The Need for Care: Gender in Moral Theory." In *Ethical Theory: Classical and Contemporary Readings*, edited by Louis Pojman, 172–186. Belmont, CA: Wadsworth, 2011.
  - Defends the idea that care ethics is compatible with general moral principles.

- Noddings, Nel. *Caring: A Feminine Approach to Ethics and Moral Education.* Berkeley: University of California, 2003.
  - Argues that care is a virtue that traditional morality has overlooked.

- Olen, Jeffrey. "Personal Identity and Life after Death." In *Philosophy of Religion: An Anthology*, edited by Louis Pojman and Michael Rea, 345–355. Belmont, CA: Wadsworth, 2003.
  - Connects the continuity of consciousness view of personal identity to the sameness of "brain"—where the latter is understood as a certain functional organization—in order to avoid some of the objections that Reid (see below) poses to Locke.

- Olson, Eric. "An Argument for Animalism." In *Personal Identity*, edited by Raymond Martin and John Barresi, 318–334. Oxford: Wiley-Blackwell, 2002.
  - Defends a version of the sameness of organism view of personal identity that Locke rejects. Also contains arguments against Locke's continuity of consciousness view.

- Reid, Thomas. *Essays on the Intellectual Powers of Man.* 1785. Edited with introduction. Edinburgh: Edinburgh University Press, 2002.
  - See essay III, chapter six, for the objections lodged against Locke's consciousness criterion for personal identity in Chapter 10.2.

- *iZombie* (2015–present), [TV Program] CW.
  - This TV series—previously a comic book series—follows a zombie who can pass for a living person but must periodically consume the brains of others to avoid reverting back into a stereotypical zombie. She inherits the thoughts of others when she consumes their brains. This creates complications for the continuity of consciousness view of personal identity. As mentioned in Chapter 8, a similar conceit is used in *Warm Bodies*.

- Russell, Bertrand. *Why I Am Not a Christian*. London: George Allen & Unwin, 1957.
  - From pp. 88–93, he argues that the person cannot survive the destruction of their brain since one's personality is bound up with the structure of one's brain.
- Thompson, Hamish. "She's Not Your Mother Anymore, She's a Zombie!: Zombies Value, and Personal Identity." In *Zombies, Vampires, and Philosophy*, edited by Richard Greene and K. Silem Mohammad, 27–37. Chicago: Open Court, 2010.
  - Deals with the issues of personal identity, moral considerability, and moral accountability as they relate to the undead.
- *The Walking Dead*, [TV Program].
  - In season 2.7, "Pretty Much Dead Already," the group learns that Hershel has been keeping undead family and friends confined in his barn in an apparent attempt to care for those he considers "sick." In season 3.8, we learn that the Governor has kept his zombie daughter, Penny, chained-up in his house. When Michonne discovers this, the Governor pleads—to no avail—for her not to destroy his daughter. Both examples illustrate the degree to which the living can continue to care about their undead loved ones.
  - Carol's killing of Lizzie in season 4.14 "The Grove," is probably the most interesting episode from the perspective of this chapter. Carol has to weigh obligations of care with other duties she has when she decides to kill Lizzie. Unlike the other survivors, Lizzie does not see a moral difference between the walkers and survivors which puts the survivor community in danger.
- *Wasting Away* (2004), [Film] Dir. Matthew Kohnen, USA: Level 33.
  - This movie presents the viewer with both the zombies' perspective and of the perspective of the living. From the zombies' perspective, they maintain the conscious identity of their living selves and are unaware of being zombies. From the perspective of the living, they see the zombies as they are but are unaware of their inner lives.

11 HOW TO CULTIVATE VIRTUE AMONG THE VICIOUS

One zombie does not make the apocalypse, neither does one vicious day; nor, similarly, does one day, or a brief space of cruelty, make a man cursed and unhappy.

—A FATHER'S LETTER TO HIS YOUNG WARRIOR SON

Until now, this book has focused on what *rules* survivors ought to follow—contractarian, Kantian, or utilitarian—so that their *actions* will be morally right notwithstanding the wanton bloodshed that surrounds them. In other words, the book has focused on what one ought to *do* during the zombie apocalypse rather than the kind of person one ought to *be*. At the end of the last chapter, with care ethics, we started to explore some alternatives to abstract, rule-governed procedures for moral action. This chapter will go even further by focusing exclusively on moral *character* rather than moral *action*. Given the problems with which we began—the specter of psychological breakdown and suicide—questions of character are important. Even if a survivor has refrained from doing what the rules say they ought not to do, if they have not cultivated the right kind of character, specifically a virtuous one, they may not flourish after all.

1. Field exercise: Ambush

I was not always who I have become. A series of *choices*, each of which *I* made, led me down the primrose path away from my better self. Each was a choice intended to insulate me from this wicked world, but together bound me inextricably to it.

I thought survival meant making it across the border. The only news still on the radio was in Spanish and that meant heading south. It was a risk—they would kill you if they caught you—but a chance of safety was better than the certain death that awaited me to the north. Even the system of strongholds had fallen apart. Those that had not been overrun from without had torn themselves apart from within.

We were all dying animals fighting over scraps in the baking sun. That's why I traveled mostly at night, not only to avoid the heat, but more importantly the living who had grown far more dangerous than the undead. All that was left of the strongholds were scattered gangs—bands of thieves and murderers—who preyed on one another to survive. No one stayed in one place for long for fear of being attacked by someone else. That was true for me as well. I stayed on the move.

In some ways traveling at night is a blessing—you don't *see* the horror—but you still *hear* it. What your imagination conjures out of lascivious laughter and piercing screams is always worse for having to envision yourself a part of it. Participant or observer, are we not equally guilty?

I chose to be an observer with the thought that this would save me, both in body and mind. I walked in silence by all manner of torture, pain, and bloodshed. Most assaults I was powerless to stop. Those that I could have stopped I chose not to because of a *cowardice* that I had convinced myself was *temperance*. With only a walking stick to defend me, I persuaded myself that there was little I could do. My sense of morality had atrophied from want of use. Although I didn't harm anyone directly, I still stole what I needed under cover of darkness: food, water, and even a bike I rode until it got a flat. People probably died of hunger, thirst, or a means of escape, but by that point I was not around to see it.

One girl, however, forced me to see it ... or rather *remember*. It was twilight, and I had just started my evening march. She came running toward me out of the approaching darkness and bore a striking resemblance ... a slightly older version of someone now undead.

"Please, help me!" she plead. Panting, she telegraphed an explanation: "Two men are coming ... They killed everyone else ... Saved me for themselves ... You have to stop them!"

"I don't *have* to do anything," I responded without breaking stride.

"My name is *Karen*," she exclaimed as I pushed by her.

I felt a sharp twinge of regret, but buried the feeling quickly under a pile of self-serving rationalizations.

"I only have a stick ... there are *two* of them ... she can't be who she looks like ..." I thought in rapid succession. With her now behind me, I could see two seemingly unarmed men approaching from the path she came down on.

I shouted, "Hey guys! I don't want any trouble ... I don't care what you did or are going to do ... she's yours, just leave me out of it."

"Much obliged!" one of them shouted back.

"Just keep on walkin," drawled the other as I approached. With them still in front of me, I felt my legs go out followed by a sharp pain racing up my back. I did a face-plant in the dirt at their feet.

The girl was standing over me—smiling—holding my walking stick in one hand and a Taser in the other. The two men were kicking me. They paused momentarily to relieve me of my backpack and for her to speak.

FIGURE 19 Two paths diverge in a darkening wood.

"Looks like we caught another one, boys! One look at a zombie and you know what you're gonna get … you cowards are far more dangerous. You know what I say?"

She had asked rhetorically, but clearly wanted me to acknowledge my predicament.

"What?" I croaked.

"When there's no more room in hell, the vicious will walk the earth … We're just cleaning up the Devil's mess."

With that, she smashed me in the skull. I don't know how long I was out, but the next thing I remember I was stumbling toward this church, my arm slung over a man wearing a white robe … Looked like an angel.

* * *

I had been talking for what seemed like an eternity. As I finished, all was silent except for the rhythmic throbbing in my skull.

"Thank you for your confession, my child," the preacher said with a softened expression that suggested empathy though his eyes betrayed a reptilian coolness. "God spared your brain from the heathens for a reason." Looking up at the congregation in the gallery, he smiled broadly and spoke with a rising voice. "You didn't make it to the border, but you'll be saved all the same … Texas has religion!"

"Our *risen* lord is God!" the congregation screamed in unison.

The preacher fed off their energy as he shifted into a lilting cadence. "In *His* temple, we *choose* to leave the vice of *humanity* behind … *We* welcome *you* as the *twelfth*!"

"The twelfth!" the congregation shouted in response. At that point, and to loud applause, my guardian angel strode beaming into the chancel. The preacher turned and welcomed him with a warm embrace. Still smiling, he said to the man, "Join your brothers and sisters in the chancel. Communion is about to begin."

As the man joined the line of those walking toward the altar, the preacher turned back to me and whispered with a voice halfway between entreaty and threat, "Go to the gallery, my child, and witness your salvation."

Leaving the chancel took me close to the blackened nave. Although I could not *see* them, I *heard* the moans emanating from the inky darkness below. Gazing into the void, my imagination conjured its own ghastly image of what "salvation" might be.

2. Aristotle's virtue ethics

For Aristotle, one of the fathers of virtue ethics, human flourishing and human happiness are one and the same. When trying to determine what makes humans happy, Aristotle thinks we need to identify the proper *function* of human beings. If we can figure out what humans are uniquely capable of doing, which the rest of the world is not, then doing that thing *well* is what will constitute human happiness. For example, a good warrior, in these post-apocalyptic times, is someone who destroys the undead quickly and efficiently. That is the proper function of a warrior and doing that grim work well is what it means for a warrior to flourish in this dangerous world. Conversely, a warrior who does this work poorly— soon tiring in battle or merely maiming the undead so they still pose a threat to the living—is a bad warrior.

What is the proper function of a human being? What does it mean to be a good human, one that is happy and flourishing? Well, all humans, at least all those that still survive, are alive. Could this be the proper function of human beings? If it is, then it would have to be *unique* to humans. There are, however, still plants and animals that live in this otherwise desolate world. Living is not unique to us. The same is true of the capacity to feel pleasure and pain. As we saw in Chapter 7, this is something that animals share with us as well as the cracked up but still living. What about the cracked up as well as the undead? Aren't they biologically human? The concern right now, however, is not with what humans *are* as much as what they can uniquely *do*, that is, what is their proper function? If the cracked up and undead are not capable of performing this function, they would fail to be "human" in this particular sense.

Like Kant, Aristotle believes that humans are capable of *reason*, but this is not itself sufficient for human flourishing. Just as there are good and bad warriors, there can be good and bad humans. What makes a human being good, what allows a human being to flourish, is reasoning in a certain way. Specifically, according to Aristotle, the proper function of human beings is rational activity in accordance with **virtue**. A virtue is a character trait that is good for anyone to have. Aristotle offers many examples. Some of these are necessary for us to successfully interact with one another—fairness, honesty, and loyalty—and so attain certain social goods. Other virtues are necessary for us to successfully achieve the goals we set for ourselves—industriousness, perseverance, and temperance— and so attain individual goods.

According to Aristotle, acting virtuously will, in itself, make the virtuous person happy. If you possess the right kind of character, one of complete virtue, then virtuous actions will flow from it. When you are already the person you ought to *be*, then you do not need a rule-governed decision procedure to determine what you ought to *do*. In this way, virtue ethics has a clear practical advantage over rule-governed theories. While a person could be frozen by indecision trying to apply the rules in particular situations—Bentham's act utilitarian decision procedure offers an apt example (mentioned in Chapters 7.1 and 7.3)—the person with a virtuous character need not consult anything other than their own moral dispositions. In addition to this practical advantage, virtue ethics also provides a very powerful reason to survive. Survival is *necessary* for flourishing where flourishing is what constitutes human happiness. Of course, survival is not *sufficient* for flourishing. As we will see below, if one does not cultivate the right kind of character and connections with others, one will be fundamentally unhappy. If someone forecloses the possibility of their own happiness through their actions, furthermore, they reject their own humanity and are arguably worse off than the undead.

One can connect virtue ethics to care ethics through the concept of *friendship*. As noted above, Aristotle thinks that certain virtues are necessary for attaining social goods. Importantly, these social goods are inextricably linked to the good life. For Aristotle, having friends is absolutely vital to human flourishing. As he says, "No one would choose to live without friends even he had all other goods." Friendship means privileging certain relationships over others and being loyal to those that we care about even if this means discounting the interests of other survivors. In this respect, there is a big difference between what care ethics and virtue ethics would counsel as compared to what the Kantian and the Utilitarian would counsel. Both the Kantian and the Utilitarian would say that we need to adopt an *impersonal* standpoint in our consideration of others. For the Utilitarian, we need to weigh the good of others equally with our own good (altruism). It would be wrong to weigh the good of your friend as being more important than the good of a stranger simply because they were your friend. Kant would hold that everyone who is a rational agent is of equal moral value as ends in themselves. Your friend is not more valuable from the moral standpoint simply for being your friend. In contrast, both care ethics and virtue ethics would encourage you to adopt a *personal* standpoint where these friendships generate their own moral value. The friendship itself provides reason for giving greater weight to your friend's good over the good of others. Within the context of the zombie apocalypse, it is important to value the interests of those that are close to you, members of your family that were fortunate enough to survive, or the other members of your group that help keep you alive. In fact, if Aristotle is right, not only are your friends and family necessary for your survival, they are necessary for you to flourish as well.

Aristotle recognizes, however, that a life of virtue is not in itself sufficient for human flourishing. If an individual experiences enough misfortune in their life, as many of us have since the outbreak, then their life will not be one worth living even if they do live a life of virtue. This is where friends and family are important. Without these deep interpersonal relationships, each of us is fundamentally alone. Even if the lonely individual somehow manages to maintain their virtue, they will nonetheless feel cursed and unhappy.

Virtue ethics also recognizes an important obligation that other ethical theories tend to overlook. Not only do we have obligations to *do* certain things, we also have an obligation to *be* a certain kind of person. For someone like Kant, the former kind of obligation is much more important than the latter. In fact, he has special praise for those who are totally disinclined from doing their duty but do it nonetheless. For Kant, this is the surest sign that an individual's action has moral worth since the action would be done *simply* for the sake of duty. The virtue ethicist would find this a strange view since having a virtuous character is the surest guarantee that someone will do what they ought to do, and shouldn't the cultivation of such a character itself have moral worth?

Finally, virtue ethics provides a more plausible account of moral motivations than its rule-governed competitors. According to virtue ethics, the virtuous person does what they ought to do because of the kind of *person* they are. In contrast, Kant's account (mentioned in Chapter 4.6) requires that a person be motivated solely by duty if their action is to have moral worth. This raises the very serious worry—one that Kant himself shared—that no action would have moral worth if all of our actions lacked the appropriate motivation. What if we are always, at some level, motivated by self-interest and never solely by duty? This simply isn't a problem for virtue ethics. As long as an action flows from a virtuous character, it has moral worth.

How do we acquire a virtuous character? Aristotle is very clear that moral virtue must be cultivated over the course of an individual's lifetime. Even if acting virtuously does make the virtuous person happy, a great deal of struggle—and unhappiness—could be involved in becoming the kind of person who feels this way. The process demands experience, reflection, and maturity. Perhaps most important, however, a virtuous character is developed through habitual action. If we wish to be temperate, for example, moderate and self-retrained, then we need to act in these ways consistently over the course of our lives. We have to regularly *choose* to be temperate when faced with situations that call for it. In practice, this is a very hard thing to do. As Aristotle says, "men are bad in countless ways, but good in only one."

3. Hitting the mean

According to Aristotle, virtues always lie at the midway point between two extremes of **vice**. For Aristotle, these character traits exist on a continuum where either an *excess* or a *deficiency* of the character trait are vices. Whereas virtues are character traits that are *good* for a person to have, allowing them to flourish both individually and socially, vices are character traits that are *bad* for a person to have. Take temperance again. This lies at the midway point between the extremes of insensibility (too little of the trait) and self-indulgence (too much of it). If you are consistently self-indulgent and licentious, you will alienate others and fail to achieve anything that requires a modicum of self-control. To see the problem with insensibility, consider yourself in the shoes of the protagonist in the field exercise above. Although you have convinced yourself that you are temperate, given how little you are moved by the suffering of others suggests an insensibility to their pain. The girl is right, you really are a coward, not only morally hollow but alienated and alone.

Another example that Aristotle gives that also shows up in the above story is courage. Courage is a virtue that lies at the midway point between cowardice (too little of the trait) and foolhardiness (too much of it). Someone who is foolhardy will run headlong into danger regardless of the consequences. In these dangerous times, such a person will not last long. Either they will be devoured by a horde that overcomes them or murdered by a gang that outguns them. In contrast, if you were the protagonist, you would be a coward. Even when you could easily do something to save someone else—from the living or the undead—you choose not to do so. You have convinced yourself that this is not cowardice, but rather temperance. As we have seen, however, this purported temperance is really insensibility. The deficiency of this trait is reflected in the deficiency of the other.

What is true of a virtuous character is likewise true of a vicious one. As the opening quote makes clear, it takes *time* to become vicious. Although there are many ways to become vicious, really anything other than hitting the mean, one vicious action does not make one vicious. This requires a long series of vicious choices, habitual actions that cultivate a vicious character. The protagonist has cultivated, over time, just this kind of character. What's most important to notice from Aristotle's viewpoint, however, is just how *unhappy* the protagonist is. Although the vicious path is undoubtedly the easier one to follow in this post-apocalyptic hellscape, it is a path nonetheless guaranteed to leave one cursed and alone.

Even if the protagonist is unhappy, what about members of the wandering gangs the protagonist aims to avoid? Regardless of all of the assaulting, raping, and murdering, couldn't these individuals be happy within their gangs? Aristotle would answer that they can only be happy to the extent that they have cultivated certain virtues, for example, those that are necessary to reap the rewards of social living. If a gang member is not fair, honest, and loyal, they will either be banished or killed by the other gang members. Honor, it would seem, is necessary among thieves. Of course, insofar as they still engage in all manner of vicious conduct, these individuals will fail to possess *complete* virtue and so whatever happiness they experience will be inferior to what the truly virtuous person enjoys.

4. Objections to virtue ethics

One worry with virtue ethics is that it cannot explain why any particular virtue is *good* using only the resources *internal* to the theory. Aristotle says that the virtues are good since they allow us to achieve individual goals or satisfy social needs. These reasons, however, appeal to ethical considerations *external* to virtue ethics. If temperance is good since it allows one to achieve one's individual goals, aren't we really saying that temperance is good since it is to one's own *advantage* to be temperate? Put differently, one ought to be temperate since one ought to do whatever is one's self-interest? This explanation for why temperance is good, however, is appealing not to virtue ethics, but rather to ethical egoism (mentioned in Chapter 2.2). Next, take a moral virtue necessary for sociability, for example, honesty. If we explain the goodness of honesty in terms of what's necessary for us to live together and rely on one another, we are again not explaining the goodness of honesty in terms of virtue ethics, but rather in terms of contractarianism.

Another concern with virtue ethics is how it applies in difficult cases. Assume for the sake of argument that you have cultivated a character of complete virtue. You are both kind and honest. You and your spouse have a mutual friend who you discover, while away on a mission, has been devoured by the undead. When you return home, should you tell your spouse? Your spouse would be heartbroken to discover the truth. Should you be kind and say nothing, or be honest and reveal your mutual friend's violent end? All the virtue ethicist can say is that your virtuous character will lead you to do the right thing. But what is the right thing under these circumstances?

A related problem with virtue ethics is how to resolve ethical dilemmas. There is little guidance as to what one actually ought to do when there are two actions that would seem to follow from a virtuous character but the virtuous agent cannot do both. This is the problem of *application*. Take any moral dilemma we have examined over the course of this book. Should you direct a rampaging horde toward one survivor and away from five others (mentioned in Chapter 6.1)? Should you save the children you care about or the warrior who can defend you (mentioned in Chapter 7.1)? Should you let people into your stronghold who will die without your help or keep them out for the sake of those already within (mentioned in Chapter 9.1)? Again, the best response that virtue ethics can offer is to say that the truly virtuous person would do the right thing in these situations based on their character. It seems plausible though that even a virtuous person might not know what to do. These dilemmas either place virtues at odds with one another, for example, *loyalty* to those within your fortress vs. *fairness* to those outside it, or there are two equally virtuous actions but you cannot perform both, for example, saving the children and the warrior. To be fair, this problem is one faced by most ethical theories. For example, the Kantian has a problem when duties conflict with one another in particular cases and the Rule Utilitarian faces a problem when the rules, chosen using the principle of utility, conflict with one another in specific situations.

A final concern with virtue ethics is that it seems to get the order of moral explanations wrong. We don't explain why saving the defenseless from the undead is right by showing that virtuous people would save those who are defenseless. Rather, we explain why virtuous people would save the defenseless by explaining why saving the defenseless is right. Likewise, we don't explain why rape is wrong by showing that virtuous people would not rape other survivors. Rather, we explain why virtuous people would not rape other survivors by showing why rape is wrong. In either case, the kind of moral explanation we offer would have to appeal to considerations outside of virtue ethics. For example, it is right to save the defenseless from the clutches of the undead because doing so produces the most overall happiness (utilitarian). Alternatively, it is wrong to rape other survivors since doing so treats them merely as a means (Kantian). Explaining the rightness/wrongness of actions simply in terms of what is compatible/incompatible with a virtuous character, furthermore, has much in common with Divine Command Theory (mentioned in Chapter 1.4). Saying that an action is right/ wrong simply because a virtuous person would do/forebear it makes rightness/wrongness just as mysterious as saying that an action is right/ wrong simply because God commands/forbids it. Ultimately, we need to explain the value of virtue in terms of other ethical theories, since we are otherwise left with a picture of virtuous people that makes their choices arbitrary.

That virtue ethics, considered on its own, faces many of the same problems as other ethical theories also suggests a possible solution to these problems. Up to this point, we have considered all of these different ethical theories in isolation from one another. As the objections in this section make clear, however, many of the problems that virtue ethics faces can be avoided if it appeals to moral considerations outside of virtue ethics. Perhaps, the same is true for other ethical theories as well. Instead of considering abstract, rule-based, decision procedures separate from the character of the person using them, maybe the truly happy survivor is the one who is not only armed with the right kind of decision procedure but also the right kind of character so that they are disposed to do the right thing as well. In the Conclusion, I will explore the possibility of integrating these seemingly disparate ethical theories with one another in order to collectively avoid the problems they face individually. This is, I believe, the most promising approach for the survivor who wishes to flourish among both the vicious and the undead.

Summary

The life and (un)death choices we are continually forced to make in this blood-soaked world determine the kind of character we develop. We cultivate either a virtuous or a vicious character through these choices, but the former is much more difficult than the latter. If Aristotle is right, however, cultivating a virtuous character is absolutely necessary if we are to flourish in this apocalyptic wasteland. Even so, a virtuous character is not itself sufficient for flourishing. It must be combined with a community of family and friends as well as other ethical theories that can be action-guiding when virtue itself falls short.

Further study

- Aristotle. *Nicomachean Ethics*. Indianapolis: Hackett, 1985.
  - See 1098a for Aristotle's famous remark that "one swallow does not make a spring." While Aristotle connects this with the cultivation of virtue and human happiness, the opening quotation of this chapter turns it around to consider the cultivation of vice and human unhappiness. Aristotle's book is thought to have been dedicated to his son, Nicomachus, who died in battle while still a youth. For the quote that "men are bad in countless ways, but good in only one," see 1106b. See 1155a for his remark on friendship quoted above in Chapter 11.2.

- Devlin, William and Angel Cooper. "Back from the Dead." In *The Ultimate Walking Dead and Philosophy*, edited by Wayne Yuen, 63–78. Chicago: Open Court, 2016.
  - Discusses various examples from the *Walking Dead* that illustrate ideas from virtue ethics. Some of these are mentioned below.

- Kant, Immanuel. *Groundwork for the Metaphysics of Morals*. 1785. Translated with introduction. Cambridge: Cambridge University Press, 2012.
  - See 4:394 for Kant's discussion of someone who is totally disinclined from doing their duty, has a "stepmotherly nature," but does it nonetheless.

- Kielpinski, Gerald and Brian Gleisberg. *Surviving the Zombie Outbreak: The Official Zombie Survival Field Manual*. Detroit: Aquarius Press, 2011.
  - Spends some time discussing the relative moral status of survivors and zombies, the moral obligations survivors have to one another, as well as the fact that human beings are social creatures that crave interpersonal relationships (p. 32). One can view virtue ethics as providing the moral foundation for such relationships.

- Rard, Elizabeth. "Dead Ends." In *The Walking Dead and Philosophy*, edited by Wayne Yuen, 217–230. Chicago: Open Court, 2012.
  - Discusses Aristotelian virtue ethics within the context of the *Walking Dead* and explains why it needs to be supplemented by another ethical theory.

- *The Walking Dead*, [TV Program].
  - In season 1.3 "Tell it to the Frogs," Rick's compassion compels him to go back to the rooftop to retrieve the violent racist Merle who he had earlier left handcuffed. In the next episode, "Vatos," Rick's generosity compels him to share some of their weapons with a gang that had earlier threatened them when he discovers they are only trying to defend a nursing home. In both cases, Rick is moved to action by his virtuous character.
  - In season three, we witness the aftermath of Rick's decision to kill Shane. He makes a series of choices that further corrupt his character to the point that he is willing to hand Michonne over to the Governor in season 3.13 "Arrow on the Doorpost."
  - Season four follows Rick's efforts to regain his virtue through a series of actions that culminate in his decision, in episode eight "Too Far Gone," to offer the Governor's community sanctuary in his prison stronghold provided they agree to resolve their differences peacefully. The Governor's unfortunate response—decapitating a hostage—is not the one Rick hoped for.

- Wolf, Susan. "Moral Saints." *The Journal of Philosophy* 79, no. 8 (1982): 419–439.
  - Argues against living a life of complete virtue. She believes that those who possessed complete virtue would live barren lives that they would be unable to enjoy. If true, this would undermine Aristotle's claim that a life of complete virtue would be the happiest life.

CONCLUSION: A GUIDE FOR FLOURISHING IN AN UNDEAD WORLD

Suicide can appear right according to one duty and wrong according to another. Whether or not we destroy our infected selves for the sake of the living, our action carries moral risk. We come in the long run, after consideration, to think one duty more pressing than the other, but we do not feel certain that it is so.

—THE RIGHT, THE GOOD, AND THE EVIL UNDEAD

FIGURE 20 Zombie/Survivor.

This book began with the question of suicide, which is also where it will end. Although someone like Kant would argue that suicide is always morally wrong, we have looked at a number of other ethical theories that hold suicide is morally permissible under certain circumstances. More importantly, there seem to be situations, as in Chapter 4, when the absolute duty to preserve your own life comes into conflict with other absolute duties. For Kant, these *perfect* duties do not have exceptions, but if the only way you can keep your promise to a loved one is to kill yourself, then *something* has to give.

This problem of conflicting moral obligations is one that almost all ethical theories face in one guise or another. For the Contractarian, the rules that people agree to abide by for mutual benefit could come into conflict in particular situations (mentioned in Chapter 3.4). For the Rule Utilitarian, the rules that one chooses, using the principle of utility, might end up being incompatible with each other in certain circumstances (mentioned in Chapter 7.4). Finally, the Virtue Ethicist will have difficulty determining which virtue is more important than another when an individual is faced with a case when different virtues dispose you to contradictory actions (mentioned in Chapter 11.4).

At this point, you might be tempted to throw up your hands and return to self-interest as the sole guide for action in these dire times (mentioned in Chapter 2.2). After all, most survivors have made it this far by their wits and looking out exclusively for themselves. Admittedly, in this violent post-apocalyptic nightmare, you will always be tempted to do what seems to expedite your own survival. Even if *survival* is valuable, however, human *flourishing* seems to be of *objective* moral value. Although surviving is necessary for flourishing, it is not sufficient. If what you do to survive undermines your capacity to flourish, for example, by cultivating vice, it is unclear how different you are from the zombies who flourish wholly at your expense.

Put simply, survival at all costs ends up costing each of us so much that surviving loses its value. This is the point at which the specter of suicide reemerges. As this book has argued, flourishing in the land of the undead requires acting morally. This is difficult to do, not only because it is hard to figure out what you *ought* to do, but also because it is hard to muster the will to *do* what you know you ought to do assuming you are fortunate enough to know what that is.

This guidebook has offered several rule-governed procedures for moral action—Contractarian, Kantian, and Utilitarian—that you can use effectively in the field. Even so, as mentioned above, there will be times when these rule-governed procedures fail you because they generate demands that are incompatible with one another. This suggests that **ethical monism**, the view that there is only *one* supreme moral principle from which you can derive all of your moral obligations, is likely false. Neither the categorical imperative (Kant) nor the Greatest Happiness Principle (Mill), to take two examples, can be the source of all your moral obligations.

Philosophers like W.D. Ross offer an alternative, **ethical pluralism**, which holds that there is no single supreme moral principle from which you derive all of your obligations. Instead, for Ross, you should look at all the morally significant relationships you have with other survivors to determine your moral obligations. Although Ross would agree with care ethics (mentioned in Chapter 10.4) that you need to look at your personal relationships—family, in the stronghold, etc.—to determine your moral obligations, he thinks that these obligations are themselves abstract and general rules. They are *prima facie* duties, conditional duties, things that you ought to do as long as they do not conflict with anything else that you ought to do (mentioned in Chapter 5.6). From the perspective of ethical pluralism, these *prima facie* duties can be seen as reflecting both utilitarian (e.g., duty to produce the greatest good) and Kantian (e.g., duty to keep promises) forms of moral obligation.

Again, the problem is that these duties often conflict with one another. If the only way you can keep your promise to a loved one is to commit suicide, then you *must* make a choice between your duty to keep your promises and your duty to preserve your own life. This is the exact choice the husband is faced with in Chapter 5.1 when he must decide whether to commit suicide so as to protect his spouse—something he has promised to do—from the bloodthirsty monster he soon would become. Although the spouse ultimately makes the fatal decision, neither can be certain that the decision was the right one.

For Ross, judgments like this will always be a matter of *considered* opinion. In other words, you need to consider all of the relevant *prima facie* duties, as well as the unique circumstances with which you are faced, when forming your moral opinion. As the quote above makes clear, however, such opinions will always involve moral *risk*. You can never be certain that you are right. The idea that two people could come to considered opinions that are totally opposed to one another might strike you as going against the general tenor of this book. At the outset, I promised to proceed as if moral *realism* were true (mentioned in Chapter 2.4). If our actual duties are ultimately relative to the *opinion* (albeit considered) of the individual survivor, however, am I not ultimately endorsing a form of moral *anti-realism*?

There must be something else you can fall back on in these (all too common) situations besides mere *opinion*. This is where virtue ethics can, I believe, offer a moral backstop to rule-governed decision procedures. When one's duties come into conflict, as they surely will, the individual of complete virtue should rely on the character they have carefully cultivated to decide what to do. The same lesson works in reverse. When a person of complete virtue faces a choice between two courses of action that seem equally vicious, rule-governed procedures—especially when they deliver the same result—can help the person of character to determine what they ought to do in that particular circumstance. Although differing from Ross's view in the details, this solution still maintains the spirit of ethical pluralism he endorses. Even so, there is an objective moral value—human *flourishing*—toward which the entire ethical enterprise is directed.

By consistently striving to live a life of complete virtue, you pursue the best life you can hope for notwithstanding the brutal, violent, post-apocalyptic hellscape you find yourself within. From Aristotle's perspective, happiness is relative to the kind of creature that you are. Whereas the proper function of a zombie may be to consume as much living flesh as possible, the proper function of a human survivor is to reason in accordance with virtue. Doing this *well*, according to Aristotle, is what constitutes true human *happiness*. It allows you to attain both the social and individual goods you need to *flourish* as the kind of creature you are. The vicious may think the virtuous fools, but the vicious are the ones that end up undead, or worse, the suicidal living.

Cultivating a virtuous character in such a wicked world might seem nearly impossible, but if you consistently strive to *do* the right thing, you will *become* the right kind of person. This means deploying your rule-governed procedures whenever possible and then falling back on your virtue whenever these procedures fail you. Ultimately, virtue and rule-governed action are not separate from one another, but mutually supporting from the moral perspective. You need to do the right thing, consistently, to become the right person, but when you don't know what to do, you need to be the right kind of person.

If you follow the prescriptions suggested in this guidebook, not only can you avoid joining the undead, but you will even flourish among them.

The task may be greater, however, than what our wills can provide. The fundamental moral danger of the zombie apocalypse is itself profoundly ironic. Our natural instinct toward survival, if left unchecked by reason, leads us to forfeit what fundamentally makes us human according to Aristotle. In the pursuit of self-interest, too many of us have sacrificed our capacity to reason in accordance with virtue. In so doing, we become worse than the creatures we most fear becoming—zombies—since we are morally responsible for the viciously depraved monsters we have become. Much better it is to be undead than the evil living.

Further study

- Barkman, Adam. "I Don't Think Those Rules Apply Anymore." In *The Walking Dead and Philosophy*, edited by Wayne Yuen, 207–216. Chicago: Open Court, 2012.
  - Defends a version of ethical pluralism within the context of *The Walking Dead*. In addition to having ethical rules, the agent must also possess virtue so that they know how to resolve conflicts between the rules when conflicts unavoidably arise.
- Ross, W. D. *The Right and the Good*. Oxford: Oxford University Press, 1930.
  - See pp. 30–31 for the passage that inspires the quotation that opens the Conclusion.

GLOSSARY

Act/Rule Utilitarianism: Whereas the act utilitarian believes that an act is right just in case no other act the agent could have performed would have produced more overall good, the rule utilitarian holds that an act is right just in case it falls under a relevant moral rule where that rule is chosen because following it tends to produce the most overall good.

Altruism: One ought to weigh one's own good equally with the good of others when determining how one ought to act.

Care Ethics: Rejects the idea that moral decisions ought to be made from an impersonal perspective using abstract principles. It holds instead that our personal relationships and the caring emotion that attaches to these relationships should be the starting point of our moral decision-making.

Categorical Imperative: Whereas the categorical imperative commands absolutely, a hypothetical imperative commands conditionally. While the categorical imperative expresses something that you ought to do regardless of what you desire, the hypothetical imperative expresses something you ought to do if you desire something else. The obligation is cancelled, however, if you lack the desire. For Kant, moral obligations always have categorical form.

Conditional Duties: For W.D. Ross, these are things that you ought to do as long as they do not come into conflict with anything else that you ought to do.

Consequentialism: One ought to produce the most overall good.

Contractarianism: This position holds that morality is a set of rules that individuals agree upon in order to reap the benefits of social living.

Cultural Relativism: Moral values are always relative to the beliefs or opinions of individual cultures. Morality is a matter of opinion and these opinions vary from culture to culture.

Divine Command Theory: Holds that something is morally right (wrong) simply because God command (forbids) it.

Doctrine of Doing and Allowing: Holding all else equal, doing harm is worse than allowing harm to occur. Philippa Foot argues that this doctrine only applies in certain circumstances, namely, when a negative right exists and is not overridden and a positive right either does not exist or is overridden.

Doctrine of Double Effect: Holds that we can draw a moral distinction between (i) the intended consequences of an action and (ii) the consequences that are merely foreseen but not intended under four conditions: (1) Considered independently of its harmful effect, the act is not wrong in itself. (2) The agent intends the good effect and does not intend the harmful effect—either in itself or as a means to the good effect—though this harmful effect can be foreseen. (3) There is no other way of achieving the good effect without causing the harmful effect. (4) The good effect outweighs the harmful effect.

Duty Proper: For W.D. Ross, this is the opinion you form on what you ought to do in a particular situation after considering all of the conditional duties that apply to you in that set of circumstances.

Emotivism: Moral claims are neither true nor false, but are rather just expressions of emotion.

Ends in Themselves: For Kant, these are autonomous beings capable of recognizing what they ought to do and setting their own goals. Rational *persons*.

Ethical/Psychological Egoism: Ethical egoism holds that one *ought* to do whatever is one's individual self-interest while psychological egoism holds that one always *does* in fact act in one's individual self-interest.

Ethical Monism/Pluralism: Whereas ethical monism holds that there is one single principle from which you can derive all of your moral obligations, ethical pluralism holds that there is no such single principle. One must rely on multiple principles to determine one's various moral obligations.

Free-Riders: People who benefit from the terms of the social contract, but do not abide by these terms themselves.

Greatest Happiness Principle: Mill holds that actions are right insofar as they tend to produce happiness and wrong insofar as they tend to produce unhappiness.

Greater Moral Evil Principle: If it is in our power to prevent something bad from happening without thereby sacrificing something of comparable moral significance, we are morally obligated to prevent this bad thing from happening.

Hedonism: Pleasure is the sole intrinsic value.

Higher-Order/Lower-Order Pleasure: Whereas higher-order pleasures are those that require reason to be enjoyed (e.g., aesthetic pleasure), lower-order pleasures are sensuous pleasures that do not require reason to be enjoyed (e.g., being physically satiated).

Hordeology: The zombie equivalent of "trolleyology" or the study of the ethical dilemmas associated with the "trolley problem." In its most basic form, the question is whether an individual driving a runaway trolley should continue down a track where five people will be killed or if the driver should turn the trolley down a side-track where only one person will be killed.

Hypothetical Imperative: See "Categorical/Hypothetical Imperative."

Imperfect/Perfect Duty: An imperfect duty is one you may sometimes ignore in favor of what you want to do while a perfect duty is one you must always perform regardless of what you might want to do.

Lower-Order Pleasure: See "Higher-Order/Lower-Order Pleasure."

Maxim: For Kant, this is a rule for action that you personally endorse.

Mere Means: For Kant, these are objects that lack freedom and are governed wholly by forces outside their control. Non-rational *things*.

Moral Anti-Realism/Moral Realism: Whereas moral anti-realism holds that there are no objective moral values, moral realism holds that there is at least one objective moral value.

Moral Intuitionism: There are objective moral values, but they cannot be defined in terms of natural properties.

Moral Law/Natural Law: Within Kant's theory, the moral law provides a universal and necessary prescription for what a rational being ought to do. In contrast, natural laws provide a universal and necessary description of how things are. The latter should not be confused with Natural Law Theory below.

Moral Naturalism: There are objective moral values that can be defined in terms of natural properties.

Moral Realism: See "Moral Anti-Realism/Moral Realism."

Moral Worth: For Kant, an action must be performed for the sake of duty to be morally praiseworthy.

Natural Law: See "Moral Law/Natural Law."

Natural Law Theory: God has created all natural things with certain purposes and something is good insofar as it serves its purpose well.

Negative/Positive Right: Whereas a negative right corresponds to a duty that others have not to do something to the right holder, e.g., not to kill someone with a right to life, a positive right corresponds to a duty that others have to provide the right holder with a good or service, e.g., to help someone with a right to aid.

Nihilism: All moral claims are false since there are no moral facts that could render them true.

Perfect Duty: See "Imperfect/Perfect Duty."

Philosophical Argument: It has two main components. The *premises* provide reasons for accepting a particular statement. This statement is the *conclusion* which should follow logically from the premises.

Positive Right: See "Negative/Positive Right."

Principle of Alternate Possibilities: You are only responsible for what you have done if you could have done otherwise.

Principle of Utility: This is the prescription to produce the most overall happiness weighing everyone's happiness equally.

Prisoner's Dilemma: A thought experiment where the best individual outcome for each prisoner is to betray the other while the other remains silent. In the situation, the prisoner who does the betraying will be released. If both prisoner's reason this way, however, they will betray one another and be in prison far longer than if they had just cooperated and stayed silent.

Psychological Egoism: See "Ethical/Psychological Egoism."

Rule Utilitarianism: See "Act/Rule Utilitarianism."

Soundness: See Validity/Soundness.

Speciesism: The idea that an individual may have greater moral value simply by virtue of the species—e.g., being biologically human—to which that individual belongs.

State of Nature: People living on their own without the benefit of civil government to make rules and enforce them.

Subjectivism: Moral values are always relative to individual belief or opinion. Morality is a matter of opinion and these opinions vary from individual to individual.

Supererogatory: When your action goes above and beyond what you are obligated to do from the moral standpoint.

Tragedy of the Commons: In a closed system where there are limited resources that everyone shares and requires for their survival, people will take more than their fair share—leading to mutual ruin—without some controls being placed on their consumption of these resources.

Validity/Soundness: A valid argument is one where if its premises are true, then its conclusion must follow from these premises. A sound argument is a valid argument which also has true premises.

Vice: See "Virtue/Vice."

Virtue/Vice: Virtue is a character trait that it is good for anyone to have. It lies at the midpoint between excess and deficiency of that character trait where both of these extremes are vices. For example, courage is a virtue and lies at midpoint between the extremes of deficiency (cowardice) and excess (foolhardiness) where both of these extremes are vices.

ACKNOWLEDGMENTS

There are many people who helped make this book a reality. Above all, I would like to thank Kayla Alarcon who was, at the time, an undergraduate illustration major at St. John's University. She is responsible for all of the fantastic artwork in the book. When it comes to students, I must also thank my fall 2018 honors section of Ethics. We used a draft of this book as the supplementary text for the course, and they provided invaluable feedback over the course of the semester that dramatically improved the quality of the text from a pedagogical perspective. Thanks also to St. John's College of Liberal Arts and Sciences for its support of this project.

A number of colleagues, both inside and outside of Philosophy, helped with the content of the book. This was my first attempt at writing fiction and I am thankful to Tom Philipose and Marty McGovern for applying their expertise in creative writing to improve the quality of the short stories. Thanks also to my wife, Ana Sarbu, for her support and willingness to read draft after draft of the "field exercises." I also appreciate Steve Alvarez and Damian Bravo Zamora for providing their perspectives on the stories dealing with (slightly fictionalized) Mexican-American relations.

I am grateful to Anne Margaret Baxley, Paul Gaffney, Robert Hanna, Walter Ott, and Tait Szabo for offering their valuable feedback on the project in its early stages. Many thanks to Colleen Coalter for her willingness to take a risk on such an unconventional project as well as to the two referees she recruited whose excellent feedback dramatically improved the final product.

INDEX

Lightning Source UK Ltd.
Milton Keynes UK
UKHW020130111221
395450UK00011B/2485